TRIGGER MEN

Also by Hans Halberstadt

Roughneck Nine-One:
The Extraordinary Story of a Special Forces A-team at War
(with Sgt. 1st Class Frank Antenori, US Army [Retired])

TRIGGER MEN

Shadow Team, Spider-Man,

the Magificent Bastards, and

the American Combat Sniper

Hans Halberstadt

ST. MARTIN'S GRIFFIN ≈ NEW YORK

www.stmartins.com

Design by Level C

The Library of Congress has catalogued the hardcover edition as follows:

Halberstadt, Hans.
    Trigger men : shadow team, spider-man, the magnificent bastards, and the American combat sniper / Hans Halberstadt.—1st ed.
        p. cm.
    ISBN-13: 978-0-312-35456-5
    ISBN-10: 0-312-35456-8
    1. Snipers—United States. 2. Sniping (Military science)—History. 3. Iraq War, 2003- —Personal narratives, American. I. Title.
UD330.H35 2008
956.7044'3420922—dc22

                                                        2007047207

ISBN-13: 978-0-312-35472-5 (pbk.)
ISBN-10: 0-312-35472

First St. Martin's

10 9 8 7 6 5 4 3 2 1

For my Ranger buddy Maj. Charles Greene
and
Shadow Team—Staff Sgt. James Gilliland,
Sgt. Harry Martinez, Spc. Aaron Arnold, Spc. Kevin McCaffrey,
Spc. Joseph Bennett, and the rest

CONTENTS

ACKNOWLEDGMENTS

Books like this one are necessarily a team effort, a collection of many voices, insights, and experiences within a single set of covers. Although I have written many books on military communities and military operations, this one is unique in several ways. For example, nearly every man who helped with this story is a veteran of combat; the vast majority of these men have slain other men in mortal combat, and they talked to me about the process in detail.

Maj. Charles Greene, my Ranger buddy, inspired this book with his stories of the jump into Panama and his brilliant sermons on the sniper mission, on the warrior ethos, and on the role of the soldier on the modern battlefield. As always, Rangers lead the way.

Thanks to Capt. Marc Messerschmitt (another Ranger and one of the best), Elsie Jackson at the Public Affairs shop at Fort Benning, Georgia, and the staff of the US Army Sniper School. I was able to follow Class 2006-3 from start to finish as they learned the arts of long-range precision military marksmanship. I am especially grateful to Capt. Ken Crowley, Master Sgt. Frank Valez, Staff Sgt. Larry Davis, Staff Sgt. Stan "Pyro" Crowder, and, from Class 2006-3, Staff

Sgt. Timothy Johns, Sgt. Daniel Porter, and many members of the Omega Group attached to the school.

I am also grateful to Capt. Nick Gottuso of the Hillsborough (California) Police Department, captain of the San Mateo County North-Central Regional SWAT team and also of the sniper section of that team, for his mentorship, help, and hospitality on and off the range.

This book features one US Army sniper section, Shadow Team from 2nd Battalion, 69th Infantry, 3rd Infantry Division (Mechanized), augmented by four men from the Pennsylvania National Guard; this group of about a dozen snipers is perhaps the most successful sniper unit in modern combat operations. Most of the men on Shadow Team helped out with this text; their trust and candor have been a major contribution to the work. I salute Staff Sgt. James Gilliland, Spc. Aaron Arnold, Sgt. Sam "Samuel," Spc. Kevin McCaffrey, Sgt. Seneca Locklear, Spc. Andy Bayette, Sgt. Bryan Pruett, Spc. Ulysses Collett, Sgt. Brad Finney, Spc. Michael Puffer; and also Staff Sgt. Harry Martinez, Spc. Joseph Bennett, Spc. Rick Taylor, and Spc. Jarrod York.

Also, and in no particular order:

Michael Haugen, Remington

Chris Barrett, Barrett Manufacturing

Jon Wiler, Barrett Manufacturing

Staff Sgt. Dillard Johnson

Roy Bryson, Burlingame Police Department/San Mateo County North-Central Regional SWAT Sniper Team Leader

John Matthews, Matthews Armaments

Staff Sgt. St. John, Ranger, Army Marksmanship Unit

US Army 6th Annual International Sniper Competition contestants and coaches

Gene Clark, Army Marksmanship Unit, Fort Benning, Georgia

And all American military snipers owe a great debt to Brian Sain and his support group, American Sniper.Org (www.americansniper.org)

Sgt. Jason Finch, USMC Scout-Sniper

Rob Riedsma, USMC Scout-Sniper (Ret.)

Jeff Chung, former Gunnery Sgt., USMC

Jim Gularte, USMC Scout-Sniper Association

Carl Taylor, USMC Scout-Sniper Association

Staff Sgt. Timothy La Sage, USMC Scout-Sniper

Ryan Cannon, USMC Scout-Sniper

Capt. Craig Roberts, US Army (Ret.)

I also thank Marc Resnick, Sarah Lumnah, Mark A. Fowler, and the editors and designers at St. Martin's Press, including David Stanford Burr, Robert Berkel, Jerry Todd, for their cheerful assistance, considerate dead lines, excellent editing skills, and constant encouragement during the long production of this work. Building a book is a team sport, not an individual effort, and I am blessed to have the help of these marvelous people.

WARNING ORDER

This is a book about the business of hunting people on the modern battlefield and killing them in a calculated, methodical way. It is primarily about the preferred methods of killing people when they are not expecting to be killed, with some detailed accounts of exactly how this is done. This is the story of the ways people are selected and slain, sometimes at long range, sometimes at very close quarters, by soldiers who are, in effect, invisible to their targets. This is the story of the art and science of precision long-range marksmanship and the effect of a bullet on the human body. It is about ambush, battle, mayhem, slaughter, winning, losing, living, dying, and war.

There are many books about wars and warfare, and I have written a lot of them. With very few exceptions—my own previous books included—these accounts dance carefully around the essential part of the story: the details of the deliberate use of violence to resolve an argument and the terminal effects of that violence. You could read most of these books and never think of the pools of blood and shattered bones and pain that are so fundamental to the whole business of military-style conflict resolution, because we authors normally and cowardly omit that distasteful part of our stories.

We write this way because our readers seem to insist upon a kind of sanitized perspective; it is more comfortable for us all. Snipers are brave men (and, occasionally, brave women) and a proper understanding of their art and craft requires brave readers.

Snipers, I think, are perhaps the most honest and most moral men on the battlefield, but they are seldom viewed that way by others. It takes a special kind of moral courage to accept the role of judge, jury, and executioner, to look a man (or a woman, or even, in the most awful circumstances, a child) in the eye, then place the crosshairs of a Leupold Mark 4 scope on that person's chest or head, press the trigger of an M24 or M40 sniper rifle and send a 175-grain bullet slamming precisely into the spot under the crosshairs at tremendous velocity and ending a life. In the clean, tidy, safe world of civil society, doing this to another person is normally a detestable crime; on the battlefield it is the essence of the mission, the goal itself, honorable and commendable.

The sniper's role is unlike that of all other combatants. Snipers, alone on the battlefield, routinely observe the ways that death overcomes their quarry—how a person responds when a bullet hits him in the chest or an extremity, the expression on his face, the way he winces and twitches and falls; or the pink cloud of blood and tissue that results from a good shot to the head. Making that kind of shot requires a special sort of courage, honesty, confidence, and moral integrity that very few people, even warriors, possess. The sniper's mission and the sniper's art are unique on the battlefield, and they see the battle in a unique way, as a personal and an individual relationship with individual enemy combatants.

The sniper community is incredibly tiny; add up all snipers from the Marines, the US Army, the SEALs, and the Rangers who are behind a gun in a combat zone at any one minute, and they will add up to about a few hundred men and no women. Add up all the school-trained Army, Navy, and Marine snipers currently qualified for deployment and in uniform, and the total might be around a thousand. Add up the kills these snipers make and compare them to the results of infantry battalions and brigades and divisions, and you'll find that many of them individually make more kills than entire battalions or brigades operating at the same time in the same area.

You will find few officers mentioned in this story (and they are, with the exception of my exceptional friend Charles Greene, never behind the gun), and no sweeping accounts of battalions and brigades maneuvering against large enemy forces in glorious array. This book is about gunfighters acting in ones and twos, about sergeants, about slaying very human beings in cold blood, warm blood, and the hot blood of close-quarters battle.

"Under any other conditions, what we do would be murder," says Staff Sgt. James Gilliland, a sniper who has done a lot of killing. But under battlefield conditions, it is not murder but part of the organized process to destroy the will to fight of an enemy force. Snipers inflict a kind of terrible psychological warfare on the entire enemy force by hunting and slaying people when they are not expecting to be slain. When snipers are on the battlefield, there is no safety anywhere for the enemy.

This is an uncomfortable topic. Snipers take no prisoners. They win no hearts or minds. Their courage and valor do not make for polite dinner-table conversation. Man for man, bullet for bullet, snipers are the most potent and powerful of all the many killing machines used for conflict resolution on the modern battlefield.

An honest report on their missions, weapons, training, traditions, manners, morals, and especially the "ground truth" of their operations in Iraq and Afghanistan, must have the moral courage to consider the precise application of mayhem and to look at it clearly and without flinching, without regret or remorse.

You have been warned.

FOREWORD

Trigger Men is an important book about modern-day military snipers and the missions they face daily. Long gone are the days of hiding and waiting for targets of opportunity. In intense urban battles the sniper is now a guardian angel for our troops. Nowhere is that more prevalent than in Marine operations. Today's snipers provide protection and guide troops as they move through the urban maze. The one-shot, one-kill mission is replaced by watch-and-cover. Now the sniper can no longer use stealth as his tool. He must expose himself to enemy observation and fire like never before. Today's snipers are at their greatest risk ever. They now shoot from one position for an extended period of time so that they can keep a constant watch on the battlefield. They are the eyes of the unit, seeing through the fog of war. They can kill an enemy fighter hiding in a house, avoiding the use of air or artillery fire. This reduces the loss of innocent lives.

In past wars snipers were looked at as killers, lone gunmen, Murder Incorporated. That's not true in this war. Today's troops appreciate the job they do. A sniper looks into the shadows where the infantry can't see and eliminates the threat. For the sniper, it's still the same effect. He sees the enemy in his scope. He knows when he kills him. There is no guessing for him. This is one of the things that separate him from the grunts on the ground. A soldier may see the fighter go down but not what the bullet has done to the human body. The sniper watches the vapor trail of the bullet's path and sees the impact. He sees the carnage caused by his effort. He may watch his target writhe in pain for long periods until he succumbs to the wounds. He sees the look in the eye of his foe, knowing that this could be him in the next ten minutes.

These images will be with him for life. At best he can only hope to coexist with them. He could be at a ball game and see a hurt player lying on the ground in pain, and his thoughts might go back to a day when he put a man down and watched him bleed out with no trainer to aid his enemy. That is the price he pays for doing his job. The sniper above all is a weapon first and a person second. If he lets a target get by, then he puts his fellow Marines at risk. There are sniper missions going on right now: Special Forces, Navy SEALs, and Marine Force Recon still look to eliminate high-value targets. But in this war, it's the everyday grind of urban warfare that most Marine snipers must face.

—Gunnery Sgt. Jack Coughlin,
USMC (Ret.), author of
Shooter and *Kill Zone*

TRIGGER MEN

RANGERS LEAD THE WAY

This book, like so very many books, began life in a bar. The bar in this particular case was the big oasis deep inside the Officer's Club at Fort Hood, Texas, and unfamiliar territory to me, a very junior enlisted soldier during my years in uniform and now a guest in a somewhat private and somewhat aristocratic club.

Standing next to me at the bar was then Capt. Charles Greene, a mustang officer with ten years as an enlisted soldier before joining the dark side and going to off to Officer Candidate School. Mustang officers are usually interesting guys, and Charles fit the standard—"mustangs" are older and wiser in some fundamental ways, often adored by the troops, often distrusted by other officers, especially the West Point ring-knockers. They know how things are supposed to work according to doctrine and the manuals, but they also know how things work at the bottom of the food chain. Mustang officers have strong opinions and loud voices and tend to retire as majors instead of colonels, if they get to retire at all. I knew a little about Captain Greene when we met at the bar and a lot more about him and about the new kind of American warrior when we left.

I met Charles during 2002 while I was a long-term guest of his unit, 2nd Battalion, 8th Infantry Regiment, 4th Infantry Division (Mechanized) as it prepared for war. Charles was the S3, or operations officer, for the battalion at the time, and our paths didn't cross much during the duty day; I was out with the soldiers in the 110-degree heat rehearsing how to clear trench lines while he was working on the training schedule in air-conditioned comfort.

Two-Eight (as the battalion is informally called by its inmates and associates) was loaded with Rangers at the time, and nearly all the officers and sergeants wore Ranger tabs on their left sleeves. This little bit of embroidered cloth would not mean much to a civilian, but it has great significance within the Army, where it identifies a man who has endured an ordeal that tests him physically, mentally, and emotionally in extraordinary ways. Ranger students are challenged to endure conditions of extreme physical distress and still be effective leaders and followers. Students typically lose twenty or more pounds during the sixty-one days of the course and are rated by both instructors and their peers. Over the past twenty years or so the Army has been developing a sort of secret weapon, a new kind of American warrior. These Rangers have been leading the way toward a redesigned institution, a place that values people far above weapons, with a particular kind of virtue taught only in Ranger school and in Marine Corps boot camp.

While Ranger tabs have become a sort of ticket punch for career-minded officers and are common enough in any infantry battalion now, Charles and a few others in Two-Eight wore a bigger and more important bit of embroidered fabric on their right shoulders where your so-called combat patch is displayed. Charles, along with the battalion commander, Lt. Col. Rick Riera, wore the scroll of the 75th Ranger Regiment on the right; they had both parachuted into Panama with the regiment and fought during Operation Just Cause. Both had "mustard smears" (as the small gold stars signifying a combat jump are sometimes called) on their jump wings, and both wore the Combat Infantryman Badge (C.I.B.) as well. Both insignia were rare enough in 2002 because so few soldiers at that time had made combat jumps or had spent enough time in combat for the C.I.B.

There are two kinds of Rangers, the kind who made it through the sixty-one-day Ranger Course, and the other kind who served in the Ranger Regiment where the hardest of the Army's hard-core serve. Capt. Greene was one of these legendary few from the regiment.

I was down at Fort Hood trying to understand how the Army had evolved since the first Gulf War of 1991 and where it was headed as an institution preparing for war. Some people in my business like to focus on the hardware and the technology of warfare; others study the generals and what goes on at what soldiers call the "god level" of the Pentagon.

I focus on what happens on the ground when bullets fly and blood flows—the guys and gals in the enlisted ranks who pull triggers and kick down doors and do whatever bleeding may be required. They are America's unsung heroes, and I love them.

I knew in 2002 that the business of war and warriors had been changing for about twenty years and that a different kind of warfighter was about to fight a different kind of war. The role of the Rangers was clearly a major factor in the evolution of the Army as a modern institution, something that was new and different and that the general public hadn't noticed.

"You ought to talk to Chuck," Lt. Col. Riera told me, so I did . . . or, rather, I listened to him. The O-Club bar on a noisy Friday evening was the perfect place for Ranger Greene to bring me up to speed on the new Army as it prepared for another round of festivities in the Persian Gulf.

Old combat soldiers and Marines are notorious for telling war stories and I have been listening to them for many years. War stories are different from dull, dry, formal history in all sorts of ways. They are told typically by men who tend to be ignored by formal historians. Perhaps because I served as a young, low-ranking enlisted soldier in combat, I listen carefully when guys like Charles Greene, a Ranger sergeant with a regimental scroll on his shoulder and a mustard smear on his jump wings, start to tell a war story.

"Tell me about your sniping in Panama," I asked over the first beer.

He described how he and the rest of the 3rd Battalion of the 75th Ranger Regiment had been alerted, received its warning order, and prepared for combat in the first days of December 1989. Operation Just Cause would be an early test for this newly reconstituted Ranger Regiment. Greene talked at length about how he and the other Rangers prepared for combat, how terribly overloaded they all were, and how the jump from five hundred feet barely allowed their parachutes to open.

This real-world mission was more complicated than training. Almost immediately after landing, Greene used his night-sight-equipped M16 rifle to kill a civilian truck driver. The truck was seconds away from running over Rangers getting out of their chutes on the drop zone. Greene described how he noticed the sound of the truck's airbrakes engaging every time he put a bullet into the driver until the truck rolled to a stop. Then he turned around and began shooting Panamanian Defense Force soldiers off the top of the control tower several hundred meters away. Charles Greene's story about his role in Just Cause is included later in this book, along with his stories about countersniper missions in Iraq and his report on how he, himself, was shot by a sniper.

His Iraqi adventures, however, were still in the future. In 2002, standing at the bar, we were both looking into the proverbial crystal ball that might predict how American war fighters would do battle in the future. Captain Greene saw something different than most

Americans did at the time, from a Ranger's perspective. To him, only one weapon was really effective at dealing with a situation like the one in Panama: a Ranger or a Marine and his rifle. He very forcefully made the point that the Ranger Regiment in general and Ranger snipers in particular dominated that battlefield in a way that was not much different from the way American infantrymen had dominated battlefields in years past.

Until that time, my interest and attention had been fixed largely on the M1A3 Abrams tanks, M2 Bradley armored fighting vehicles, AH-64 Apache helicopters, M109 Paladin self-propelled artillery systems, and all the other complicated, expensive, and precious machines of war. The common foot soldier—we call them "Eleven Bravos" in the Army—were going to be along for the ride when America went to war again, useful to tidy up the battlefield after the complicated technology of the armor, artillery, and aviation had finished pulverizing the next enemy . . . or so most of us thought.

Ranger Greene's war story was intended as a cautionary tale, and I got the message. His crystal ball showed a different vision of a different kind of battlefield, a place where the expensive technology was parked at the side of the road and where the Eleven Bravos with their M16s and sniper rifles would be the only way to win a fight.

"Pay attention to the Eleven Bravos," Greene told me, "and keep an eye on the snipers in particular. They're the guys who will do the killing and who will win the fights. The tanks and Apaches are just support for the rifleman, not the other way around."

Back in 2002, snipers were the loneliest guys in any battalion, invisible in all sorts of ways. While the rest of the soldiers and Marine infantrymen were busy throwing grenades and riding around in amphibious assault vehicles (AAVs) and Bradleys, you could find the snipers—if you could find them at all—under a bush somewhere, roasting in the sun and fighting a losing battle with chiggers and ticks.

At the time, they served as scouts, watching over objectives that

would later be assaulted by somebody else. The Abrams tanks and
the Bradley AFVs would destroy the enemy out in the open desert,
and the Eleven Bravos would round up the survivors when they
surrendered. The snipers could help pull guard duty and maybe
would help with security while everybody else was busy winning
the war.

At 0534 hours, local time, 20 March 2003, combat operations
against Iraq began. For the first days and weeks, they looked a lot like
the rehearsals at Fort Hood and at the National Training Center in
California's vast Mojave Desert. The Abrams tanks and Apache helicopters went forth and generally ripped the Iraqi army into little
bloody chunks exactly as advertised. The Eleven Bravos popped out
of the troop compartments of the Bradleys right on cue and policed
the surviving and surrendering enemy soldiers. The snipers occasionally had a chance to help with the reconnaissance and security
missions, but—just as in training—they were along for the ride.

Then the battlefield changed and the battle changed with it, just
as my friend Ranger Greene predicted it would. Pushed back into the
cities, the remaining enemy forces tried their best to use built-up
areas and civilians for cover and concealment, with limited success.
Platoon and company commanders faced their worst nightmare—
dismounted infantry combat in urban terrain—and began coming
under fire from little bands of enemy soldiers popping out of the
side streets and urban warrens of Basra and Baghdad. "Snipers up!"
they called over their battalion net, and at last the Marine and Army
snipers had work to do.

Craig Roberts and Charles Sasser describe how things got interesting for two Marine snipers from the Surveillance and Target Acquisition (STA) platoon of 3rd Battalion, 7th Marines, just outside
Baghdad at Al Rashid airbase.* The Marines were Sgt. Josh Hamblin

---

* Craig Roberts and Charles W. Sasser, *Crosshairs on the Kill Zone* (Simon & Schuster, 2004).

and Cpl. Owen Mulder, both with M40 rifles, one with a PVS-10 day/night scope, the other with a Unertl 10-power day optical sight. They were sent up on a rooftop to watch for Iraqi soldiers attempting to assault the Marine position. They didn't have long to wait.

The first attack came that night under what the enemy soldiers must have assumed was the cover of darkness. Through their night observation devices (NODs), both Marines saw a truck pull up about four hundred meters from their perimeter, then watched a squad-sized group of men dismount, all with weapons. Hamblin shot the driver first while Mulder killed one of the soldiers. While the Marines reloaded and prepared to reengage, the enemy soldiers tried to pick up their dying comrades and get them back in the truck, a fatal error for most of them. Mulder and Hamblin methodically engaged the survivors, splitting the group down the middle, one Marine working the left side and the other taking the right, dropping one enemy soldier after another until a couple of lucky ones managed to get into the truck and drive away.

At first light the next morning, another enemy soldier appeared, this time on foot and alone. Sgt. Mulder killed him with one shot at 450 meters.

Then two troop trucks rolled into view, stopped, and another squad of Iraqi infantry dismounted with their weapons, apparently ready to make a probe of the Marine position. They never got a chance—the two snipers, again methodically splitting the group, cut them down one at a time. With no place to hide, and no visible enemy at which to return fire, the enemy soldiers milled about in panic as one after another was struck and killed. One man survived long enough to pull the dead driver from one truck, start it up, and drive off . . . but not quite fast enough. Both Marines fired at the fleeing vehicle, and, in a scene right out of the movies, one bullet apparently hit the fuel tank, causing a spark—and the truck exploded in flames. With sixteen cartridges expended and sixteen enemy soldiers dead in front of their position, the two Marines were living up to the old sniper motto, "One shot, one kill."

Enemy soldiers continued to attempt attacks on the Marines for three days. The pair of Marine snipers stayed up on the roof and behind their rifles the whole time, killing Iraqi soldiers one after another with their precise, discriminating rifle fire. At the end, the two had used up a couple boxes of M118LR ammunition that cost the US government about $40—and that had cost thirty-two enemy soldiers their lives.

This was exactly the sort of battlefield success story that Ranger Greene had been sermonizing about. Here were a couple of Marines with their old-fashioned rifles utterly dominating the battlefield, and doing it with a trivial expenditure in ammunition.

American Marines and conventional-unit soldiers had never done much training for this sort of war. They had trained a bit at MOUT sites. "MOUT" stands for "military operations in urban terrain." There is a MOUT site on most military installations, each designed to replicate the layout of a village. But MOUT training had previously been designed to prepare warfighters to deal with uniformed enemy forces in built-up areas, not insurgents in civilian clothes using noncombatants for cover and concealment.

The Army and Marine Corps have adapted to this new battlefield and new kind of enemy pretty much just as Ranger Greene suggested they should, by emphasizing the sorts of infantry skills that have always been the foundation of the Ranger Regiment's bag of tricks—excellent close-quarters-combat skills, superb infiltration and extraction SOPs (standard operating procedures), plus room- and building-clearing techniques that had been elevated to an art form. Today's Army and Marine infantry battalions are working like five hundred-man SWAT teams on steroids, swarming through the worst neighborhoods in the combat zone, grabbing bad guys by the scruffs of their necks and hauling them off to jail.

Instead of the 120mm main gun of the Abrams tank, these American combatants are using M16 rifles, M9 pistols, M249 Squad Automatic Weapons (SAWs) in a very selective and discriminating way, somewhat like police officers do when deadly force is required during their operations. In fact, current urban military operations bear a very close resemblance to American law-enforcement special-operations missions in every respect—training, planning, team organization, weapons, techniques, rules of engagement (ROE)—and all of them look a bit like the way Rangers and Marines conduct business.

Captain Greene and Two-Eight went off to war in Iraq in 2004, and Charles and my other friends in the box (or "sandbox," as the combat zone is currently called) provided occasional sitreps* from downrange where their missions were not at all like their training at Fort Hood.

His reports on the role of snipers and sniping were entertaining and evangelical and were converting me to a believer in the importance of precision long-range fire and accurate observation. When one of his men was shot (in the penis), Greene was able to immediately determine where the shot had come from. He quickly identified the building where the shot had been fired, grabbed an FN-FAL rifle (a Belgian battle rifle used by many NATO units) from one of his soldiers, and when the insurgent sniper revealed himself Greene killed him with his first shot.

Charles was shot himself a few weeks later. The enemy sniper—a very young man, as it turned out, who hadn't long to live—was a pretty good shot, but not quite good enough to kill my Ranger buddy. He made a head shot on Greene, but the bullet struck Greene on the left side of the face, traveled along the jaw, and most of the fragments of the projectile exited behind the left ear. Fortunately, the round had been fired at long range and some of its energy had dissipated by the time it hit him. It was a very close call for

---

* Situation reports.

my friend; he tells the whole story in his own words later in this book, in chapter 3.

AARS AND LESSONS LEARNED

Soldiers and Marines have a great way to learn from their operations—the successful ones and the disasters both—through something called an after-action review, or AAR, and I am using it in this report. Charles and I conducted an informal AAR when he returned from Iraq and could talk again. He had a lot to say and I recorded it all. This AAR formed the foundation for this book and encouraged me to investigate more about the role of snipers on this new battlefield. Then I was permitted to follow a class of soldiers through their entire training at Fort Benning, Georgia, to see who were becoming Army snipers, why, and how they were being prepared for their role in combat. Following that, in October and November 2006 I attended the Sixth Annual US Army International Sniper Competition, where I had the opportunity to meet and watch snipers from Israel, Canada, Britain, the US Air Force, and the US Marine Corps, as well as from about a dozen US Army units shoot it out for the first-place trophy. Many offered their experiences and insights for this book.

There are really two parts to the after-action-review process. The first part looks at what was supposed to happen, then what actually happened—the "war stories" from the event. The second part, the brilliant part, asks the participants, from the lowest-ranking Eleven Bravo to the most senior commander, what lessons were learned from the experience, what to think about the next time a similar mission is planned. The Army takes these lessons very seriously and publishes and promotes them through the Center for Army Lessons Learned (CALL).

But these AARs and lessons-learned are really for internal consumption, not for the public. This is unfortunate because, although

America's war fighters are probably the best—as individuals and as combat teams—in history, these great men and women are also the least known, least understood, and least appreciated by the general public.

Snipers are interesting people, as individuals, as teams, and as part of a larger fight. There are really very few of them, around four hundred total at any one moment. They have a complex and challenging mission, and the responsibility to look people in the eye and decide if those people will live or die. As my Ranger friend Charles Greene has so eloquently said, it is not a job for everybody; it is, actually, a job for a very unusual person. Some of those rare people have shared their experiences and observations with me. Here are their stories.

CHAPTER ONE

SNIPER MISSION BASICS

At 0300 hours on a cool, quiet morning, Staff Sgt. Harry Martinez and three snipers slip out of the gate of Camp Corregidor on the eastern side of Ramadi, Iraq, and begin to carefully insinuate themselves into the dark and dangerous streets. The little team is officially designated Shadow Four, and they are on the first solo mission of their deployment.

Ramadi is, as one Marine sniper observed, a gunfighter's paradise for both insurgents and coalition war fighters, a place where killing and dying are part of the daily routine, where the sound of bullets and bombs surprise no one. When you are a sniper in Ramadi, there is no safe time or route to go to work, but three in the morning tends to be a little safer than broad daylight, when the streets are full.

Martinez and his little band of merry men are heading by an indirect route to a house on the northern side of the city, up near No Name Road and Entry Point Five. This particular little neighborhood hasn't been hunted by the snipers for a while and the word from the S2 (intel) shop is that the local bad guys are getting confident and bold enough to operate openly in daylight. That should mean good hunting for Martinez and his team if they can get into their hide site undetected.

The distance from the compound to the hide site is a half mile or so and would be only a ten-minute stroll in any American city. Here, though, the route Shadow Four takes is indirect, in the shadows, in order to keep their movements unpredictable to the enemy. They sneak through town like deer hunters in the woods, as quietly and unobtrusively as they can. They slip into dark alleys and change course often, always checking to see if they are hunters being hunted—followed on the street, perhaps, or observed from windows or doorways.

All four men are members of the National Guard; the active-duty soldiers call them "weekend warriors," and that is not a compliment. The part-timers are seldom admired or trusted by the regulars, who consider them ill-trained and equipped, old and out of shape. Martinez, however, is a cop and an FBI-trained SWAT sniper back home in New Jersey. He's forty—that's elderly in the active-duty Army—but he is not out of shape, ill trained, or ill equipped.

When Harry Martinez and his unit arrived in Iraq, his parent unit really didn't know what to do with their snipers—a very common problem for Guard units called up for deployment—and so he and his men were told to go find something useful to occupy themselves and to stay out of the way.

Sgt. Martinez wandered over to where 2nd Battalion, 69th Infantry Regiment, 3rd Infantry Division's recon platoon was based, on the other side of Camp Corregidor, and introduced himself to Sgt. Sam "Samuel,"* one of the snipers on Two-Six-nine's ten-man Shadow Team. Samuel quickly started bringing Martinez up to speed on local operations, on urban sniper ops, on local rules of engagement, on all the big and little topics of interest that a soldier with experience can pass along to a new arrival.

---

* A pseudonym, at his request.

As every soldier and Marine knows, personnel and mission assignments are only done with stacks of paperwork, lots of signatures, all the right initials, proper SOPs, and all the other details carefully observed. That may be the way it is supposed to work during peacetime training, but sometimes during war, and often in places like Ramadi, things are a bit more casual. "Say, Harry," Sgt. Samuel asked, "we're going out on an operation tonight—would you and your guys like to go along?"

"Sure!" Martinez said immediately, not believing what he was hearing.

"Have your sniper rifles arrived yet?" Samuel asked.

"No, not yet," Martinez answered, expecting the M24s to be a requirement for the mission.

"Well, how about your M16s? Do you have your secondary weapons? If you do, that's good enough—you can provide us some security and learn something at the same time."

With Martinez's positive response, Samuel called up the section leader, Staff Sgt. James Gilliland. "Hey, Sgt. G, I have four new snipers from the Guard unit here and they'd like to go along with us tonight. They don't have their M24s but do have their M16s. What do you think, over?"

"Sweet!" Staff Sgt. Gilliland radioed back, "Tell them to get their gear together and where to show up!"

Very suddenly, less than two days after arriving in Iraq, Martinez and his little team were very busy cleaning their weapons, collecting their gear, and getting ready for a combat operation in deepest, darkest Ramadi and marveling at the casual, confident attitude of Samuel and Gilliland. Welcome to the war, sniper-style!

The Guardsmen showed up on time, took their positions in the order of march (travel sequence), followed directions, and soaked up the lessons of the real world like four sponges. Shortly after sunrise, as if to help with the lesson plan, the insurgents showed up with a car full of bad guys and a trunk full of improvised explosive devices (IEDs).

When the shooting stopped, Martinez had killed three with his M16 and another member of his team had killed two more; the entire enemy team had been killed. The weekend warriors demonstrated that however old or badly trained or ill equipped, they showed excellent discipline under fire and could put steel on target. Although they were officially assigned to another unit, the Guardsmen happily found themselves chopped, or temporarily assigned, to Gilliland's section, where they became Shadow Four. For the next few weeks, Martinez and company tagged along with the Two-Six-nine snipers, learning their trade and becoming journeymen combat soldiers. Then, at last, the training wheels were off and they had a mission to execute all by themselves.

As before, they prepared by studying maps, talking to the Intel section, and reading reports from previous patrols. They selected a hide site in advance, planned the route, and executed the infiltration in the early hours when Ramadi was under curfew and asleep.

Shadow Four approaches their objective about 0400, an hour after leaving the gate. The door to the building is chained shut; they cut the chain, slip inside, and lock it again with a lock of their own. Other snipers have used this place before, but not recently. After a careful check of the building for booby traps or waiting enemies, they set up their weapons, spotting scopes, radios, and packs as daylight comes to Iraq and the city begins to wake up. Their observation post (OP) is now ready. Martinez checks in with his unit's tactical operations center (TOC) and reports that they are in position and beginning to execute their sniper mission.

Around daybreak, Martinez, who had been on the gun for a while, trades off with his spotter, Spc. Jarrod York. Before going off for a nap, Martinez says, "Listen, York, about seven or eight, they are going to come out and hit this place with an IED, so be extra alert!"

York tucks himself behind the M24 and begins to scan the streets and rooftops of the gritty neighborhood through a small hole in the wall, virtually invisible from the road below. Around 0700, just as the city is coming to life, York notices a man ride into his sector on a bicycle. Many men ride bicycles in Iraq, and many men carry backpacks, but this man seems nervous and uncertain, and that gets the sniper's attention. York watches as the man looks around, apparently scouting the location. You can't shoot a guy for looking at the side of the road, but you can keep an eye on him.

Beside the road is a pile of dirt about five feet high, and the man on the bike seems to take particular interest in this dirt. He rides off, turns around, comes back, and gets off his bike. Jarrod watches him extract from his backpack a mortar round fused and prepared as a remote-controlled bomb, an IED. The man begins burying the device in the dirt. You *can* shoot a man for planting an IED, and that is exactly what York intends to do. But rather than make a snap shot, he wants to make sure the insurgent won't escape. York calls to Rick Taylor, another sniper nearby, "Taylor, get in here! There's a guy planting an IED in the road—let's do a volley fire on him!"

By the time the two make their plan, the man has finished placing the IED and is getting back on his bike. York fires, hitting the man in the chest. The man falls to the road, his legs still around the bike, and is still.

Martinez runs up the steps and uses the spotting scope to study the man on the ground. Not much blood is visible; he appears to be dead. There is a quick discussion of what to do next—pull out or stick around? Martinez decides to stick around, use the man on the bike as bait, and see if there is anything else to catch.

Snipers are among the most patient war fighters on the battlefield, and Shadow Four waits quietly in its hide to see if any of the insurgent's buddies will come along to check up on him. It takes an hour for somebody to get the word back to Bad Guy Headquarters, but at last two vehicles arrive—the local insurgent's casualty evacuation team, ready to recover their comrade and to get the IED back, too, if they can.

The first vehicle is a taxi. It makes a careful approach from the south, slowing as it passes the fallen man, then makes a quick U-turn. "That taxi is coming back!" Taylor yells.

At the same time, another vehicle approaches the fallen man, but Sgt. Martinez's attention is fixed on the taxi and he doesn't even hear Taylor's report. A man gets out and tries to pick up the fallen insurgent, who is still somehow alive. He and the man from the taxi have a quick conversation, and the man points to the south, apparently the direction from which he thought he was shot. Martinez now recognizes that both are part of the IED emplacement team, and they are attempting to evacuate their casualty and locate the American sniper team. The second vehicle pulls up from the opposite direction and stops alongside the first car. The vehicles mask the fallen man, protecting both insurgents from direct fire.

"Engage!" Martinez commands. "Select targets and engage!"

Martinez grabs his secondary weapon, an M16A4, and runs to a window. As the shooting starts, the insurgents in the cars fire their weapons from inside the vehicles. Not knowing where the fire is coming from, they cut loose in all directions, a final and futile gesture. The second vehicle zooms off, leaving its passenger—the man who had gotten out to collect the casualty—stranded in the street. Martinez selects this man standing in the road and methodically pumps bullets into him. The wounded insurgent is hit in the leg but manages to hobble to the far side of the road. He takes cover behind a wall but pops up his head every few seconds to look around.

Rick Taylor and Joey Bennett, the fourth sniper, use their M16s to put suppressive fire on the surviving vehicle, and it spins out of control before rolling right toward the front of the building where Shadow Four is hiding.

Martinez realizes that the excitement and adrenalin of the mo-

ment are overcoming him. Trained for such situations at the FBI
sniper academy, he takes a few seconds to breathe deeply and get his
heart rate under control. Then he yells to his spotter, "York, that guy
is going to pop up again—when he does, we're going to shoot him!"
Seconds later, the head pops up again. Martinez has the red dot of
his sight on the spot, where he expects him to appear, and the man
unknowingly places his head in perfect alignment with the weapon.
Martinez and York fire simultaneously, and the man's head snaps
back as he squeals and drops out of sight.

By now the second car has managed to get under cover only a few
feet from the room where the snipers are shooting. A solid concrete
wall and metal gate protect the vehicle and its occupants from
Shadow Four's rifles. Now the insurgents are almost on top of the
team and can, if they decide to, breach the wall protecting Shadow.
Bennett calls, "Harry, can I throw the hand grenades?"

"Throw them! Throw them, damn it!" Martinez yells.

Bennett quickly lobs two M67 frags (fragmentation grenades) over
the wall, one landing on the far side of the street and the other on the
median, but both close to the vehicle, which is now just inches from
the front gate of the hide site and still protected by its cover. Martinez
sees the passenger dismount about the time Bennett's second
grenade lands on the street. The insurgents below still don't know
who is shooting at them or from where. They are shocked and confused. As the second grenade detonates, the man in the street is hit by
its fragments and the snipers hear him scream, as Martinez later describes it, like a little girl.

Martinez, realizing that the surviving insurgents are still a threat
and anticipating an attack by the pair, takes one of his own grenades,
pulls the pin, and throws it high in the air, hoping to have it land
just beyond the wall where the pair has taken cover. Instead, it lands
on the wrong side of the wall and explodes, adding a bit more adrenaline and excitement to the moment.

"We're in heavy contact!" Martinez reports by radio to his TOC. He makes a quick spot report while the other snipers continue to deliver accurate, disciplined fire on the enemy, now only twenty meters away. Then he runs down to the ground floor and gives the team's security element (other soldiers, not snipers, who are along to guard the team) a quick briefing while the other three keep shooting.

"There are still two insurgents out there on the other side of the wall," Martinez tells the security team leader, a sergeant.

"Okay, we're going to go out there and kill them!" the sergeant answers.

"All right," Martinez says. "We will support you from the roof while you make your approach." The sergeant and one of his riflemen move to the gate. The rifleman makes several deliberate shots through an opening between the gate and the courtyard wall, then hoses the vehicle and finally sends another M67 over the wall. The grenade kills the remaining two members of the IED team.

With the fight apparently over, it is time to leave. Martinez expects the quick reaction force (QRF) and their Bradleys to roll up any moment, ready to give the snipers and security team a ride home in armored comfort. They all pick up their gear and move downstairs to the courtyard, anxious to catch the bus back to camp.

The team pops smoke to cover their withdrawal and Martinez opens the gate to the street, leading the way out. But the quick reaction force has not reacted yet—there are no Bradleys in sight! Another sniper team has been overwatching them and their leader calls up, "Get back in the house! There are still guys on the street trying to kill you!" The teams move back inside the house, take up fighting positions, and wait.

After thirty tense minutes, the Bradleys and the QRF can be heard rolling into the area, but the commander of the QRF doesn't want to bring his vehicles into the immediate battle area and they stop about two hundred meters away. The snipers and security team will have to make a run for them.

Again Martinez opens the gate and leads the way into the street. Not far away, between them and the Bradleys, is the man who placed the IED. Martinez approaches the body, moving quickly but alert for hostile action. It comes from an unexpected place—the man on the bike, who had placed the IED, sits up as the sergeant approaches.

He reaches under his shirt for something, looks Martinez in the eye, and calls out, "Mister!"

Thinking that he is about to trigger the IED or pull out a weapon, Martinez pumps several quick shots into his chest from a range of three feet. The man on the bike falls back to the street as Martinez runs past.

As Shadow Four scrambles toward safety, it is their turn to be engaged. Heavy machine-gun fire from an unseen insurgent weapon begins to pepper the street. Two of the security team find a target, part of the IED emplacement team providing support, and they pause long enough to engage the enemy with their weapons and quickly win their part of the fight. The Bradleys open up with their machine guns in response while the Americans dash across the street and up the open ramps of the armored vehicles to safety.

This is one sniper mission by one team in one place at one time. A very few rounds of ammunition have been expended, one insurgent IED emplacement team has been slain, one message has been delivered to the enemy in Ramadi. It is a little victory that will never be reported on CNN or in *The New York Times,* by warriors who are almost invisible and almost anonymous even within their battalion and brigade. But little missions like Shadow Four's are, with variations, being repeated all over what war fighters today call their battle space, and the cumulative effect is profound.

Sniper operations, weapons, and missions have become a critical part of modern combat. The chapters that follow are a report on current doctrine, training, weapons, and execution of real-world sniper missions, often in the voice of real-world snipers. At a time when a very tiny percentage of military personnel ever actually see an enemy combatant, the snipers whose voices are presented in this book have (with one exception) methodically slain dozens of enemy personnel. Their weapons and tactics are not new, but they are perhaps the most feared and respected by enemy soldiers.

INTRODUCTION AND BASICS

The sniper is a new kind of warrior in the ranks of tactical units today. Although sharpshooters and marksmen have been part of American ground forces since the Revolution, there is a quiet revolution going on today in the way combat operations are conducted on the ground. This revolution is about twenty years old and has seen a shift in emphasis within the armed forces from preparation for fights between heavy conventional units to small-unit counterinsurgency actions and the silent knife fights of special operations units.

Snipers—sniper teams, really—are a rapidly growing component within the Marine Corps, the Army, and many of the military forces around the world. The Russians have a long tradition of precision military shooting at long range. The Israelis have many snipers in the field. A Canadian team recently made a rifle shot that killed an enemy soldier at a range of well over a mile.

The Army and Marine Corps are generating snipers as fast as they can push candidates into the training pipeline and sending them off to war. When they get to war, these snipers make contributions far out of proportion to their numbers.

SNIPER WAR

As Shadow Four's engagement with the man on the bike and the IED emplacement team demonstrates, there is a new kind of fight and a new kind of fighter on the battlefield. The new fighter is the modern sniper, and he is reshaping the battlefield in ways never imagined until very recently. The old notion that snipers quietly and methodically engaged targets at long range, making one shot to make one kill, is obsolete. Snipers today still make their kills at long ranges, but as Staff Sgt. Martinez's fight with the man on the bicycle illustrates, they make their kills at close quarters, too, sometimes with grenades and occasionally with their bare hands.

Snipers are by nature and by training quiet and reclusive. Their mission is hard to explain to wives and girlfriends or anybody else outside the community. Their photo albums tend to have some messy portraits of people they have slain, people with the backs of their heads blown off and people lying in vast puddles of fresh blood. It is difficult to explain to people who are not snipers why doing such things is a good idea, so snipers tend to be evasive about what they do and how they do it.

According to media reports, Americans generally seem to think that such killing of other human beings would traumatize a man for life. Certainly there are many soldiers who are reluctant, when the time comes, to pull the trigger on another person. Such people do not belong in the sniper's trade.

This book is based on the observations of about thirty military snipers with combat experience, and nearly all of them have multiple kills. There is a surprising consensus among them about the act of killing: without exception, these men have no remorse or regret about the people they killed. They all say that they pulled the trigger only on people whose behavior demonstrated hostile intent and that endangered others, and that the people they killed had made the fatal decision themselves by their conduct.

We've all heard about the legendary snipers who can recall the faces and expressions of each person they have slain, but none of the men I spoke with had such memories. We have heard of soldiers and

Marines traumatized by the deaths they have inflicted, but to my surprise and perhaps yours as well, all the snipers I interviewed seemed content and well adjusted. As one of the best US Army snipers, a man with about thirty kills, told me, "Maybe I will have problems with my kills ten years from now, and if I do, I will work on those problems then. Right now, I have no regrets."

The role of snipers on the modern battlefield has been a surprise to almost everybody, even to the snipers themselves. There have never been very many of them, only a few hundred actually performing the mission at any one time. They are all enlisted soldiers, Marines, Army Special Forces and Rangers, Navy SEALs, and occasionally people from nameless, so-called black organizations. They are usually young and hold ranks of staff sergeant (E-6) and below. While billions of dollars have been spent on new technology for fighter aircraft and attack helicopters and stealth bombers, for Abrams tanks and Bradley fighting vehicles, for missiles and radars and all the other battery-powered billion-dollar programs, today's Marine or Army sniper uses a weapon that hasn't really changed in seventy years and that is so simple to use that you can buy one yourself at many sporting-goods stores around the country.

While most American, British, and NATO ground-combat units won't go across the street in groups smaller than a platoon, and with a few tanks or other armored-gun systems along for protection, snipers ooze off into the night in little groups of three or four, move silently through the shadows, and slip into places to hide. These little groups will hole up for a few hours, or a day or two. Invisible, they watch and wait for something to show up, like duck hunters waiting for prey.

When the conventional infantry patrols, with their noisy vehicles and predictable routes, blunder through the mean streets of Basra, Mosul, Baghdad, Ramadi, and Fallujah, insurgents have plenty of warning and plenty of time to set up their own ambushes and attacks in this lethal game of hide-and-seek. The insurgents offer battle only on their own terms, on their own choice of ground, and with their own rules of engagement. When these conventional patrols are ambushed or engaged, the enemy almost always has the initiative. Reacting to such contact, American infantry pours a large volume of fire into homes, businesses, cars, schools, and anything else in the line of fire. Sometimes a few insurgents are even injured or killed in these engagements, but bystanders (innocent or not) are more likely to be hurt. Conventional military operations in urban terrain, against unconventional forces employing unconventional techniques, give the insurgents a rich selection of targets, and the insurgents have become very good at engaging them. Traditional infantry tactics, techniques, and procedures, when used alone against urban insurgents, is a bit like using a club to kill a mosquito—a clumsy business involving more work than it should and damaging a lot more than the intended target.

American war-fighting doctrine and tactical methods began to change in the 1980s and are changing still, adapting to new threats in new ways. Snipers have been part of the whole grand plan for many years, but the part they have been asked to play has suddenly changed, and without a lot of attention outside the tiny community of military snipers. As long as American and allied forces were fighting a uniformed conventional enemy, as during the brief first Gulf War in 1991 or the equally brief Operation Iraqi Freedom in 2003, conventional ground-warfare doctrine was brilliantly successful. Snipers had a very marginal role. A few snipers killed a few enemy soldiers, knocked out a few vehicles, and made a small contribution to the overall battle.

But when the conventional battle ended and the unconventional fight began, those big mechanized infantry battalions and brigades were—and still are—essentially useless against an enemy that operates the way these insurgents do today.

The reason that a few hundred snipers are so important now is that they, almost alone on the unconventional battlefield of today, are effective at killing enemy personnel in meaningful numbers. As one US Navy SEAL officer told me recently, American snipers in the battle of Fallujah (from the SEALs, Marines, Army Special Forces, Deltas, Rangers, and other units) comprised less than 1 percent of the total number of friendly personnel on the battlefield but accounted for roughly 50 percent of enemy kills during the siege. These little sniper teams, with their simple weapons and simple tactics, are slaying the enemy in huge numbers.

In this book I have featured one small sniper section, Shadow Team from 2nd Battalion, 69th Infantry Regiment, 3rd Infantry Division. This team included about fourteen men at any one time. These men, in six months' time, made confirmed kills on approximately 267 enemy insurgents, plus hundreds of additional probable kills that could not be confirmed. These 267 kills were careful, deliberate, surgical, and precise engagements that removed enemy combatants with minimal collateral damage. Shadow Team was just a tiny little part of its vast parental battalion, but these few men probably did most of the killing for the whole unit.

In previous American wars, large and small, the role of snipers and their close relatives, the sharpshooters, was interesting but, considering the big tactical picture, trivial. In combat operations today, the sniper teams are doing the bulk of the killing, and they are killing the right people at the right places and the right time. They make their kills at long range, intermediate range, and—as described before—at point-blank range.

When the enemy took off his uniform and changed into civilian clothes, then began moving his combat units from the barracks to civilian neighborhoods, he adapted to our methods of combat and, to an extent, defeated them. During World War II, the Korean War, and even during the war in Vietnam, our enemies—despite their numerous bad habits and character flaws—had the good battlefield manners to wear uniforms that identified them as playing for the opposing team. Today's enemy does not do that.

The Iraqi insurgent is perfectly happy to use women or children to help execute his missions. His uniform is anything that helps him blend into the crowd. He will use a crowd to provide cover for his IED placement operations. When women aren't available to help, he will sometimes dress up like a woman because he knows Americans are very reluctant to shoot females. If the insurgent can goad American units to inadvertently kill innocents, he will use these deaths for political purposes; such casualties are actually an advantage to the insurgent and are part of his battle plan.

Under these circumstances, snipers are among the most useful tools a commander has available to fight and destroy insurgent units. Snipers are able to identify an insurgent with a rocket-propelled grenade (RPG) in a crowd on the street and drop him in his tracks without touching the women or children nearby. Snipers routinely identify and destroy entire insurgent teams, killing them all without injuring others. When an insurgent starts digging a hole at the side of the road, he really can't be sure anymore that—day or night—a set of crosshairs have being aligned on his chest and that a bullet fired from some invisible place nearby will strike him dead on the spot.

So many insurgents have been struck dead on the very spot of their labors that in places like Ramadi's Badlands neighborhood all the residents of the city know that there is no safe place to plant a bomb or to peek around a corner and get off a few bursts at an American patrol with an AK-47.

American units have learned to use their sniper teams in creative ways that adapt to the insurgent's own adaptations. Infantry patrols go out to goad insurgents to give battle, and the insurgents often oblige by peeking around corners to deliver harassing fire. They are more careful about these engagements now, however, because sniper teams have learned to set traps and ambush the people who are trying to ambush the patrol.

MORAL ASPECTS OF THE MISSION

The business of sniping is full of odd moral issues and contradictions. As warriors, their job is to close with and destroy the enemy, and they do this with all the violence they can bring to bear. Modern war uses artillery, rockets, missiles, bombs (some dumb, some smart), 120mm cannon fire from main battle tanks, cluster munitions, and machine-gun fire in many calibers. The effects of these many weapons arrive unannounced, as a literal and proverbial bolt from the blue, slaying people in theatrical ways. We seldom object when an AH-64 delivers a Hellfire missile into a residential structure that enemy personnel are known to inhabit; they may be asleep in bed, or having dinner, or watching television with the kids when the Hellfire arrives, and if the wife and kids are slain along with Mullah Fred or whoever, well, too bad. As long as the primary target met the rules of engagement, tough luck for the noncombatants.

When that Apache gunner makes the shot, few people question his morals or motives in making the shot. Nobody challenges the weapon systems operator on an F/A-18 Hornet crew when they put an Mk 82 five hundred-pound bomb on a platoon of enemy infantry and shreds them all and anybody else within three hundred meters, combatant or not.

But there is something about the sniper mission that just seems to bother many people in and out of the armed forces. Virtually every military sniper interviewed has described incidents where their personal integrity has been questioned because of their role on the battlefield. You'd expect a certain level of such criticism from civilians, especially the ones who haven't studied the moral aspects of war and who object to any and all forms of violence. That sort of criticism has some moral integrity.

The bulk of the criticism, amazingly, comes not from civilians but from other warriors. "You guys are out of control," one officer remarked to a sniper team after they had executed a successful engagement, even though they had observed the rules of engagement carefully. Snipers are commonly accused of being cowboys—another expression for wild, undisciplined behavior—by members of their own units and chain of command. But civilians are critical, too. When Canadian snipers killed Taliban fighters at 2,500 meters, a new record for such engagements, the accomplishment made the papers and resulted in hostile letters and negative comments instead of praise.

Snipers are often called murderers, assassins, and worse. No other combatant in our armed forces is as careful and discriminatory about the use of violence as the sniper, and more thoughtful or cautious about the act of killing, but that somehow seems to make the sniper's tactics and missions even more uncomfortable for some observers, civilian and military. No wonder snipers tend to keep to themselves.

So much of the sniper's mission is psychological warfare. If you are an insurgent on the mean streets of Ramadi these days, or a member of an IED emplacement team in Baghdad, Mosul, Basra, or dozens of other places in the country that soldiers and Marines call the sandbox, you are scared. Death and martyrdom are not far away. Even when the streets and highways are empty of American soldiers, they are probably not far away, and they might be watching.

If you are an insurgent in Iraq, or Afghanistan, or the West Bank, or Chechnya, you know that the snipers are out there, waiting, hunting. In places like Ramadi alone, hundreds of your comrades have been suddenly surprised to discover that a bullet has slammed into their chest and that they will shortly die. These bullets seem like a kind of divine vengeance—they come from nowhere, with no warning, no hint of danger. If you are an insurgent in Iraq, Afghanistan, or anywhere else today, the risk of sudden death is real, the threat is large, and it is something to think about.

American snipers' weapons are of very simple and elderly design; the bolt-action rifles used by Marines and soldiers fire their rounds slowly and have capacity for only five cartridges. But when used by a trained rifleman, those rifles are extremely accurate. Pretty much every shot out to six hundred meters will kill a stationary man, and—as described later—they can kill to twice that distance when the fates and fortunes of war are smiling.

Snipers have been piling up insurgents by the hundreds, leaving their bloated bodies on the street as object lessons to their friends.

Precision long-range rifle fire has been a component of American military doctrine since well before the United States was founded, and the legend of the Kentucky and Pennsylvania backwoods riflemen picking off British officers and men firing from concealed positions at long range during the Revolutionary War is well known by American schoolchildren.

But, then and now, snipers don't fit neatly into military or law-enforcement organizations. True snipers normally operate somewhat independently, and that conflicts badly with the way commanders want to control the battle. The problems of sniper employment on the battlefield will be discussed later. The basic conflict between snipers and their commanders is based on the sniper's need to be static and independent, and a tactical commander's need is to keep his units mobile and under constant control. This conflict has been a problem since the American Civil War and is as much of an issue today as it was 140 years ago.

As a result, snipers during the World Wars, Korea, and Vietnam tended to be used as sharpshooters on a short leash rather than as true snipers. Occasionally during Vietnam trusted snipers like the legendary Carlos Hathcock were permitted to design and execute their own operations, but the tendency was to keep them within infantry squads and to use them, if at all, only as sharpshooters who operated in platoon- or company-sized units on patrols. Such employment wastes a sniper's skills at covert battlefield surveillance and his ability to ambush enemy forces at long range and from concealment.

The role of snipers in military and law enforcement units has grown steadily since the 1970s as the result of a succession of hostage incidents, a change in the doctrine of land warfare among NATO and other nations, the development of police SWAT teams, and battlefield experience in places like Chechnya, Bosnia, Grenada, Panama, the Falklands, Afghanistan, Iraq, Lebanon, Israel, and elsewhere. The most instructive of these lessons have been the disasters—situations where sniper skills were needed and not available, or where available doctrine, training, and tools were not up to the needs of the moment. The botched, attempted rescue of Israeli athletes at the 1972 Munich Olympics was one wake-up call for tactical unit commanders that better sniper employment procedures were needed. A hostage situation at the Sacramento, California, Good Guys electronics store in 1991 was another. Argentine snipers' ability to stall an attack by British soldiers in the Falklands in 1982 was another. During major conflicts, the need for sniper skills are recognized and developed, then allowed to decay at the end of hostilities.

The 1972 Munich Olympics hostage incident was a typical disaster of the time and one whose lessons helped shape the development of modern counterterrorist units like the US Army's Delta, Germany's GSG 9, and other specialized tactical units. The incident began when members of the Palestinian Black September organization infiltrated the quarters of the Israeli Olympic team, killing two and taking another nine hostage. The terrorists made a series of impossible demands, and the whole drama was broadcast live on television. The situation caught the German security forces off guard and entirely unprepared for an effective response. An ad-hoc rescue was planned with five snipers playing a key role. The problem was that Germany had no snipers, only competitive rifle shooters, and five of these were selected for the mission. None had any tactical experience. When the order to fire finally came, the result was total chaos. All the hostages were killed by the terrorists, five of the terrorists and one German police officer were also killed, and three of the Black September group survived and were captured. All three were later released by Germany. This catastrophe, along with others, inspired the development of counterterrorist units and effective, qualified, professional sniper teams. Each of these many units trains, equips, and employs snipers in somewhat different ways, but common to each is the ability to deliver long-range precision fire from concealed positions on designated targets.

The mission that has evolved varies a bit from one unit to another, but common to all is the ability to make first-shot kills with a rifle on selected enemy personnel targets at ranges well beyond the capabilities of a rifleman. "Shooting is only ten percent of the mission," snipers like to say, and that is true—but without that 10 percent, the rest doesn't make much sense. Student military snipers are taught to become invisible in rural and urban terrain, to move long distances to their final firing position without being detected, to build and occupy hide sites that blend perfectly with their surroundings, and to remain hidden for hours or days. They learn to identify targets that are only partially exposed, to estimate ranges with great precision with and without laser range finders, and to observe and report activity in their field of view. But nobody gets out of any of the military or law-enforcement sniper training programs without being able to shoot well, with the ability to hit a stationary man from at least eight hundred meters or a moving man from six hundred meters.

THE MILITARY SNIPER MISSION

The classic sniper mission generally uses snipers to support larger units when they conduct operations. The sniper team finds a hide site where it can hole up and wait for targets while the larger infantry platoons, companies, or battalions conduct patrols or assaults. When these larger units flush out enemy soldiers, the snipers report them by radio and then take their shots. Sniper priority targets are enemy commanders, officers, sergeants, radio operators, crew-served weapons personnel, tank commanders when standing exposed in their turret hatches, and, when possible, enemy equipment like fuel tankers, aircraft, and missiles. The priority target for all sniper teams is an enemy sniper, and such countersniper engagements are surprisingly common on today's battlefield. Sniper teams often are tasked with surveillance missions that don't involve rifle fire at all; these teams make their kills with calls for artillery fire or close air support from aircraft.

THE LAW-ENFORCEMENT SNIPER MISSION

Modern SWAT teams and other civil law-enforcement units have their own snipers and their own set of missions, and are properly part of this story. While the military sniper is primarily tasked with making shots at ranges beyond five hundred meters, the police sniper knows that his shot, if he ever makes one, is likely to be at a target no more than one hundred meters away, and that the average for SWAT snipers is about half that distance.

When the police sniper does take a shot, it normally must be delivered with even more precision than that expected of the war fighter. That is because police, FBI, DEA, Secret Service, and similar police snipers deal with hostage situations and incidents that require killing in a way that instantly incapacitates the target. There is only one spot in the body where a bullet will drop a human being without a twitch—the small area at the base of the skull containing the brain stem. A hit in this small area will produce instant and complete muscle relaxation. Hit a man anywhere else, even the heart, and he can keep fighting for at least ten seconds, long enough to kill his hostage and some police officers, too.

Police snipers are, more than anything, an incident commander's eyes on the scene. They can move undetected into an observation position and stay hidden for many hours, reporting back what they see.

Fitting somewhere between the military mission and the law-enforcement mission is the role of US Coast Guard snipers. Now a component of the Homeland Security Department, Coasties deal with maritime terrorists, drug runners, pirates, and smugglers. They have their own sniper teams, and these teams are very adept at using their .50cal Barrett rifles to disable fleeing small craft by firing into their engines.

A SHORT HISTORY

The end of the Cold War changed many things, one of which was the role of heavy armor and artillery to win wars. About the same time, in the late 1980s and early 1990s, American forces were tasked with the first of a series of smaller, less conventional actions that had no role for Abrams tanks or 155mm Paladin self-propelled artillery. Grenada, Panama, Somalia, and Lebanon each involved the use of light conventional and unconventional forces against light enemy forces, and in every case the friendly forces ran into problems that the old training and old weapons couldn't solve.

Previously among American commanders, there had long been a

presumption that complex and expensive systems—F15E Strike Eagle aircraft, for example, or M1 Abrams tanks—would be decisive in combat; the common foot soldier with his rifle would follow along to clean up whatever little messes were left after the bombs and tank rounds had done their work. That presumption was challenged in these little fights, and commanders began to anticipate a new kind of battlefield: one that had no room for heavy armored vehicles or time to get them in the fight; conflicts where innocent civilians were mixed in with enemy combatants; and battles where the adversary didn't wear a uniform or fight in a predictable or traditional way.

Beginning with the assault on Grenada, American forces began a dependence on light forces—the 75th Ranger Regiment, the 82nd Airborne, the light infantry divisions, and the Marine expeditionary units. These are fundamentally traditional infantry units that show up on the enemy's doorstep uninvited and unexpected, then use boots and rifles to take control.

The rifle has been and still is the ultimate American weapon of war. A skilled rifleman dominates the terrain around him to at least three hundred meters. A rifle is capable of precision engagements in ways that not the smartest of smart bombs can come close to duplicating. Only skilled rifleman can take out an enemy soldier with an RPG while sparing noncombatants nearby; no bomb, no rocket, no machine gun can be so discriminating.

THE MARINE CORPS FOUNDATION

The US Marines have never forgotten the power of the rifle and the rifleman. All Marines are riflemen first and always. While Army basic trainees learn to shoot to three hundred meters, Marines qualify out to five hundred and are expected to be able to kill at that distance with their M16s and iron sights. In this age of expensive technology, the rifle and the rifleman are still essential elements of ground-combat operations.

American forces have used sharpshooters and expert marksmen from Colonial times and the Revolution. They were especially important during the Civil War when both the Union and Confederate forces used specially trained and equipped soldiers, often operating independently, to selectively engage high-value targets like enemy commanders and cannon crews. Confederate sharpshooters with Whitworth rifles were particularly feared for their ability to make kills at ranges up to one thousand yards.

The modern era of sniping really began during the war in Southeast Asia. While both the US Army and the Marine Corps employed snipers in the 1960s and early 1970s, their training was informal, unstandardized, and minimal by today's standards.

American sniping today is based on the Marine Corps experience and the accomplishments of one man, Gunnery Sgt. Carlos Hathcock, during the war in Vietnam. Hathcock had been on the Marine Corps rifle team and had won many championships, including the Wimbledon Cup, prior to deployment to the combat zone. He and a few others invented modern American sniping there. Hathcock combined the field-craft skills of a hunter with the marksmanship skills of a competitive long-range shooter and put them to work on the battlefield. He had ninety-three confirmed kills and many more probables, the longest at a reported 2,500 yards. Hathcock was a killing machine in Vietnam and his legendary exploits have been described in many books.

The Marine Corps doesn't forget its history or its lessons learned. Although several attempts had been made previously to formalize sniper training, starting in World War II and again during Vietnam, it wasn't until 1977 that the first official school was established at Quantico, Virginia, and began training Marines to be certified snipers. Based very much on Carlos Hathcock's accomplishments and teachings, this school continues today to set the standard for American snipers. Marine snipers are trained at three schools, each using the same basic program of instruction, at Quantico, Camp Pendleton, California, and Camp Lejeune, North Carolina.

In 1987 Col. Barry McCaffrey tasked Staff Sgt. Bill Knox with establishing a similar school for the Army as part of the School of Infantry at Fort Benning, Georgia. Knox contacted the Marine school at Quantico and was offered eight student slots in a class. The eight graduates became the first cadre at the Army Sniper School. This generous offer of support got the Army school off to a fast start.

Among the many changes in American armed forces and law-enforcement tactical units over the past several decades, one of the most important developments is a rising emphasis on the role of the sniper. They are used by the Army in conventional and special operations units, by the Navy SEALs, by the Marines very extensively, by the Secret Service, the FBI, the ATF, Homeland Security, the Coast Guard, and nearly every police department in the country big enough for a SWAT team.

DEFINITION OF A SNIPER

Although qualifications vary a bit from one organization to another, snipers today are expected to be able to move and occupy firing positions undetected, to operate independently as very small units of only one or two people, to be able to stay in position for hours or days without being compromised, to select and engage specific targets, and to make first-shot incapacitating hits on man-sized targets out to eight hundred meters.

Snipers do more than just shoot at people far away; a large part of the job involves surveillance and reporting. A sniper-and-observer team can call in artillery or air strikes instead of using their own weapons.

Marines vary this a bit by calling their version of the role "scout-snipers," and emphasizing the intelligence-gathering potential of two guys hidden out on the battlefield with a radio and trained eyes. While Army snipers might have the same radio and the same well-trained eyes, they are probably a bit more likely to use their own M24 rifles than to call for an air strike or an artillery fire mission.

THE ART OF THE ONE-SHOT KILL

There is some of the quality of art to the sniper's business. It is a killing job that probably involves more deliberate calculation and intellectual effort than any other form of applied force. When a sniper elects to fire, he makes a careful and specific decision to kill someone in a kind of surgical way. He is able to kill one person while intentionally sparing the person standing next to him, or even the child in his arms.

Unique among war fighters, the sniper knows his adversary on a kind of personal level. The weapon systems officer of a fighter-bomber overhead sees spots moving around his targeting display, and he has no tool to slay the insurgents while sparing the innocents nearby. The sniper sees the beard stubble on his target's face, perhaps a wedding ring on his finger, or that the target is twelve years old—or that the target is a girl carrying a bag of RPG rounds for use by enemy combatants.

Given enough ammunition and time, anybody can hit a stationary enemy soldier 835 meters away. But the sniper's art assumes that time is fleeting, that the target is not stationary, and that the first shot must be the killing shot. In order to make the first-shot kill at 835 meters, the sniper has to know precisely what the range really is, what the angle to the target is, how hot or cold the propellant in the cartridge is, and where his particular rifle throws a projectile from a cold bore. He needs to know the air density, wind speed and direction, the humidity, and how to incorporate all this information into a ballistic solution for this particular tactical engagement.

Snipers understand that they don't point the rifle at targets 835 meters away. Instead they point it at an invisible spot about fifteen feet above the target, knowing that the bullet will be dropping at a steep angle as it bears down on its unsuspecting victim. The common Eleven Bravo infantryman doesn't need to give any thought to the rainbowlike trajectory of bullets at longer ranges, so he doesn't think much about precise range estimation; but the sniper's success depends first and foremost on knowing how much adjustment is needed to direct the trajectory of the bullet so it strikes the center of the target. Likewise, wind is not a factor in normal infantry engagements, but the sniper's bullet may be pushed left or right twenty inches in a brisk breeze, and it must be measured and sight corrections made if that first bullet is to strike its target. The sniper's art is cerebral and calculating in many ways.

Snipers have never been in such demand nor so highly trained as they are today.

THE SQUAD-DESIGNATED MARKSMAN

Any discussion of long-range-precision battlefield marksmanship these days always includes mention of war fighters who would in the Civil War have been called "marksmen" for their superior shooting skills at long range. Today's marksmen are not snipers, but they fill the gap in capability between the Eleven Bravo infantry rifleman and the Bravo Four [B-4, military skills identifier for a sniper] sniper. They are known as the squad-designated marksmen (SDM). Until American forces began operating in wide-open desert terrain, few people in the Army worried much about the ability of a soldier to effectively engage enemy targets beyond three hundred meters or so. The Marines, as usual, had different ideas and trained to a five-hundred-meter standard, even though the standard-issue M16 rifle and its tiny, light projectile loses much of its energy and incapacitating ability at that distance.

Common doctrine held that riflemen would engage enemy targets out to three hundred or five hundred meters, and anything past that distance was a chore for mortars, artillery, or crew-served weapons like the Mk19 grenade launcher or the .50cal heavy machine gun. The Marines demonstrated that riflemen could be effective to at least five hundred meters, even with the 5.56mm round, a distance at which snipers are expected to make one-shot kills.

So the Army has once again used the Marine model to upgrade the training of soldiers to this higher standard. The program takes soldiers who are proficient at the three-hundred-meter and closer ranges and teaches them to make consistent hits under combat conditions out to five hundred meters. The course is three weeks long and is conducted at many sites.

These squad-designated marksmen have been getting excellent reviews from units that have used them in combat. Previously, enemy combatants knew to keep three hundred meters between themselves and American forces when possible; anything closer was dangerous, anything further away provided some safety. Now that stand-off distance is extended another two hundred meters to over a quarter mile, and that makes their own fire even more ineffective.

"The squad-designated marksman is not a sniper," all the snipers say, because SDMs are not trained in covert-movement techniques, how to select, construct, and occupy a hide site, or how to employ the specialized rifles required for engagements against personnel at eight hundred meters and beyond.

Standard-issue M16s and M4s with iron sights are used for most of the training, although SDM-qualified soldiers are often issued weapons that have been upgraded by the gunsmiths at the Army Marksmanship Unit with heavier barrels, better double-stage triggers, and ACOG optical sights. These weapons are prepared by the same craftsmen who build the rifles used in shooting competitions, and they are built to a very high standard. Soldiers who have used them in combat are very enthusiastic about their performance.

CHAPTER TWO

STAFF SGT. JAMES GULARTE, USMC SNIPER

Staff Sgt. James Gularte enlisted in the Marine Corps in 1967 and attended the USMC Scout-Sniper School at Camp Pendleton, California, before deployment to Vietnam in February 1968. He operated in the I Corps area (the far north) of the Republic of South Vietnam while assigned to units of the 1st Marine Division and 7th Marine Regiment. He received the Bronze Star with V (for valor) device, four Purple Heart decorations for combat wounds, two Vietnamese Cross of Gallantry awards, and several additional decorations. After a year of rehab following his fourth combat injury, Gularte became a police officer. His career in law enforcement included two years as a federal air marshal. He currently is an ambassador for the Marine Corps Scout-Sniper Association and remains active in the training of new Marine scout-snipers at the Camp Pendleton, California, school. The 1st Marine Division Scout-Sniper School established the Staff Sgt. James H. Gularte trophy in his name and awards it to the honor graduate of each class for achieving the status of being the top scout-sniper in his class.

I deployed to Vietnam early in 1968 and was attached to the 26th Marine Regiment right after they arrived at Da Nang and had moved to the remote outpost at Khe Sanh. The siege of that place by the NVA [North Vietnamese Army] had begun about that time and anybody with an 8541 MOS* was almost automatically sent out there.

Not long after arriving, I was outside the wire at a listening post when our position was somehow compromised and we were hit by mortar rounds. One Marine was killed when the round detonated almost on top of him, but I was far enough away to just get spattered with shrapnel and get a concussion and some internal injuries. After a brief period in the hospital at Da Nang, I was able to get sent to Hue City right at the end of the Tet Offensive and saw a little action while assisting the 5th Marines before that excitement ended.

Then I was fortunate enough to work with some very experienced Marine snipers around Hill 55. Some of these guys had been in country for two or three years and had a huge amount of experience and wisdom in the trade. The command group of 7th Marines, too, had a commander and a sergeant major who were both very supportive of the sniper mission. It was a very good time and place to be a young sniper learning the business.

Marine Corps sniping had not been an official part of the program very long, just a couple of years at this point, and the book was being written—everybody was getting on-the-job-training with a lot of help from the VC [Viet Cong] and NVA. I started out as a spotter for one of the more experienced guys, a Marine corporal who had been in Vietnam for eight or nine months at this point and who had plenty of kills. He explained to me that we'd be working as a two-man team and that he'd take me out and show me the ropes. He started out by teaching me about booby traps, about monitoring enemy movement, about hand-and-arm signals, and all the

---

* "8541" is the Marine Corps military occupational specialty (MOS) for scout-sniper.

rest—things that had been taught in the basic scout-sniper course but the corporal's instruction covered at a much higher level of intensity.

My first mission with my team leader involved monitoring a village on the banks of one of the rivers in the area to see if there was any enemy movement or activity—dropping off supplies or using the village as a staging area. We had one of the early Starlight scopes and late one night were able to observe a lot of NVA movement in the village. Those early night-vision devices weren't nearly as good as they are today, but we could see plenty of activity only about two hundred meters from our position. We both figured that around first light we ought to have some targets.

Sure enough, around dawn I saw a boy walking along a paddy dike carrying a backpack, and clearly visible in the pack were RPG and mortar rounds. The boy was moving briskly toward a distant tree line and I expected the corporal to make the shot. Instead, he said, "This is a good time for you to get your feet wet and make your first kill," and handed me the Remington 700 sniper rifle. I was dumbfounded—the kid looked like he was not much more than ten years old. My team leader understood what was going on in my mind and he said, "The enemy has no age, no gender—if we don't take care of those mortar rounds now, they are something Marines are going to have to eat later today or sometime soon."

It was an easy kill. The kid was well within five hundred meters—I put him in the scope, figured that the point of aim was the point of impact. He was a moving target, but not a very fast one. I went through the whole schoolhouse drill, settled down, and made the shot. The kid dropped and didn't move.

The team leader took the sniper rifle back and returned my M14 as we wondered what would happen next. We watched the body for a while, hoping that somebody else would come looking for him, but nobody came. He was almost to the far tree line and far enough from the village that nobody noticed the shot or the missing kid. But we had plenty of other targets later that day.

As NVA targets began to appear here and there in front of us, in the village and on the river, we began to take them out one at a time. For example, we would see a soldier with an AK walking out of the cluster of buildings and kill him. We killed eight or nine that way, then began taking return fire. It wasn't aimed or effective, but the NVA had a rough idea of where we might be, and they began shooting in our general direction. We had no radios at all, no way to call in an air strike. "Time to go," the corporal said, and we went. We crawled back into the jungle, out of sight of the village, and headed back to our unit. I had made my first kills, the boy and another three—the latter were head shots with the M14; the team leader was a strong advocate of head shots. This was my first real introduction to practical sniping and I had four kills out of it, learned a lot of practical lessons, and found that it was something I was comfortable doing.

Some of these lessons could not be taught in school. For example, how long can you stay in position after making a shot before the enemy is likely to start dropping mortars on you or otherwise engage you effectively? The school solution is to make one shot and move to a new location. Movement has its own risks, and maybe you give up additional kills that could be made at low risk—the risk factor is dependent on the situation, and you can't balance the hazards with the opportunities without real-world experience and the judgment that comes with it. I was getting that experience from my team leader, and it really paid off later.

There were certainly lots of targets in range on that day, but one of the lessons I learned and try to pass along to new Marine scout-snipers today is: Do what you have to, inflict the damage that you can at reasonable risk, then get out of there—you can come back tomorrow, if you have to.

My team leader and I were out for a week, just the two of us, sneaking and peeking, with me learning a whole new set of scout-sniper skills. Although it seems strange today, at the time there were no hard-and-fast rules about what you could or couldn't do on an operation, and two guys going off in the bush for a week without a radio was not considered anything special. I liked that—we were responsible for our own missions instead of having somebody else telling us where to go, how to go there, and who to shoot when we arrived. It made for lots of kills.

At other times we had to go out with larger patrols, and that was always a bit frustrating. Those Marines were great warriors, but they carried a lot of stuff, made a lot of noise, and the NVA always knew exactly where one of these patrols was. They could make or break contact on their own terms, and when we got into a firefight on one of these patrols, you could expect that it would be a nasty one. When two or four of us went out by ourselves we were invisible to the enemy, and we started the shooting on our terms.

Although we had a lot of freedom, we didn't just go out of the wire and wander around. My corporal would begin his mission planning by going to the S2 Intel shop (a part of Tactical Units that provides research services) and find out where the enemy was operating in the area, if they were NVA or VC, and what kind of information the command wanted to get back. Sometimes that was to find out what sort of weapons we could see in use—did they have heavy mortars, for example, or crew-served antiaircraft weapons? How many passed a certain point in a certain time, and in what direction? How effective were recent air strikes, they would want to know, and my team leader and I would go out and examine bodies. Were the enemy soldiers in good condition or malnourished? What sort of condition were their weapons in? How much ammunition did they have? All these factors provided clues about the successes and failures of both sides, and it was the scout-snipers' job to collect those clues and bring them back for evaluation. Making kills on these missions could be completely counterproductive and we would pass up easy shots to avoid being detected.

Coordinating with the other Marine units patrolling in the area was essential and something I had to learn right away, and the more experienced men coached me on what to do and what to expect. First, before we could go out on a mission, we had to let everybody know where we intended to be. This was accomplished by meeting patrol leaders face-to-face or through the S2, where we tried to make sure that their maps had our intended route of march on it. Despite these precautions, if you bumped into a friendly unit, you could expect them to fire on you on first contact. Since we didn't have radios, we had to develop ways to communicate with these units and with aircraft overhead, so I had to become adept with things like signal mirrors and signal panels and smoke grenades. The more experienced snipers explained how to do all these things, to make contact with patrols, and to avoid coming under friendly fire.

The experience was very stressful and nerve-racking. For a young nineteen-year-old not long out of sniper school, I had to make a lot of decisions and think on my feet. There were a lot of ways to die out there if you were careless or casual. It was not a job where you could afford distractions. You had to have a lot of skills beyond using the rifle—you had to know how to use a compass, how to use a signal mirror, and to live in the jungle for extended periods without support. You had to know how to kill people before they could kill you.

TWO MARINES AGAINST TWELVE NVA

Within a few months, my mentor was gone and I was now the veteran sniper training a new spotter, passing along the lessons I had just learned myself. My spotter was, as I had been, fresh out of school. He knew the things you can learn in school, but not the things that I had been taught about real-world operations.

The two of us went out on our first mission as a team, and this time I had the Remington 700 and he was the one with the M14. We found a good hide site on an elevated position alongside one of the many well-worn NVA trails in the area and settled in to wait.

We didn't have to wait long before an enemy patrol appeared, and it was clear by the way they operated that they were real professionals. They moved silently, and stopped often to watch and listen. There were a dozen of them, all NVA, and they were out looking for information about us just as carefully as a good Marine patrol went looking for them.

My spotter and I were both very impressed with the professionalism of these enemy soldiers, but that didn't keep me from killing them all. I turned to the spotter and said, "Let's take them on."

He looked at me as if I had lost my mind, and whispered something like, "But there are twelve of them and two of us . . . and your rifle only holds five rounds! How are you going to make this work?"

"Here's how we're going to make this work," I told him. "We are going to start out by figuring out who the patrol leader is, and kill him first. Then we will see who 'goes to guns' on us most quickly and kill them next. After that, you and I will split up the rest of them and work on them from the ends of the patrol toward the center—you take the right and I will start from the left. I will shoot my five men first, as fast as I can, and then you take over with your M14 while I reload. But first we need to figure out who the leader is and take him out."

We observed the enemy patrol a bit more as they moved slowly down the trail. One man about fourth from the point seemed to be in control. That would be the normal location for the patrol leader; I decided to engage him first, then see what happened next. But first we had to make sure we were ready.

"Get your spare magazines out and ready to reload," I told the spotter. "Get them out of the pouch and with each oriented so you can get it in the rifle immediately.

My spotter had been in country for only a couple of months, and all this was a new experience for him. The look in his eyes seemed to say, *Oh my God, we are going to die!* But he got out his spare mags and set them right by the gun, ready to go.

When we had our game plan all sorted out, I lined up on the soldier I thought was the patrol leader and killed him with a shot to the head, and he dropped. Predictably, several of the survivors reacted timidly—these were the point man and the two following him, and they seemed startled and uncertain what to do next. One tried to take cover, and all were trying to figure out where the shot had come from. Several NVA behind the leader, though, began to put out suppressive fire to the flanks with their AKs in a nice, professional way, so I killed them next. As luck would have it, I hit each one without a miss—point of aim, point of impact! Five down, seven to go.

During this part of the engagement, I didn't hear any firing from my spotter and wondered if he had frozen on the gun, but I was too busy to look at him. As I bolted in the fifth round, I called, "Last round going out!" Then, as I frantically began to stuff five more cartridges in the Remington 700, I said, "It's on you now!"

Now he took over and started putting serious fire downrange, and he was hitting with a lot of them. About the time I got the fifth round in the gun and got back in the fight, I heard him fumbling with his weapon but didn't have time to pay much attention to what he was doing.

He had killed three or four of them with his twenty rounds and now there were just a few left alive and confused—and we were not done until they were. I killed each of them. After waiting a few moments to make sure they were all done, I looked over at my spotter; he had not reloaded but was looking at the carnage in a state of shock. We had killed all twelve NVA in the space of a minute or two.

"God, that was good!" he said. "Let's do it again!"

"Not before you learn to reload," I told him.

We watched the bodies for a while to see if any other NVA would come looking for these guys and we could maybe kill some of them, too, but none showed up. I had placed booby traps on our flanks when we moved into the position as a precaution and none of them went off, so I figured we were pretty safe for the moment—we just stayed put and waited.

Finally, we moved up to check out the bodies and see what we had done and to collect any papers or other intel that might be useful to the S2. I was particularly curious to see if my partner had put multiple rounds into any of the NVA and to see where we made our hits. We had both done well. My apprentice sniper had shot well and not entirely lost his focus during the engagement, even if he neglected to put a fresh magazine in when it was all over.

This was an interesting time. We were all writing the book on sniper operations, both for ourselves and for our parent units. We had the problems of figuring out how to conduct our own operations and also to help figure out where we fit in the larger scheme of things. There weren't a lot of us (and there still aren't), and when a company commander or a battalion S3 [Operations officer] was told, "You now have a platoon of scout-snipers," the reaction was predictably, "What am I supposed to do with them?"

Recon, at that time, was better established and was considered to have adult leadership and a role in the battalion. Snipers were a company asset for a grunt unit, somewhat like the heavy machine-gun and mortar sections, but we were an entirely new resource that many of these leaders did not know how to use. So besides learning how to run missions, we had to learn how to teach our leaders how to lead us. I was a lance corporal at the time, and attempting to explain what we could do to captains, majors, sergeants major, and others at the top of the Marine Corps food chain sometimes was not successful. These men didn't expect to take the guidance of young, low-ranking, enlisted Marines for anything. Some of these leaders wanted to use their snipers only for guard duty, fire watch, and very petty, menial details. When that happened, there sometimes were verbal confrontations and arguments about how scout-sniper Marines should be employed.

On the other hand, when I had a chance to visit with Marine snipers from other units—the 5th, 7th, and 9th Marine regiments, for example—they would sometimes tell me how welcome they were in their units, how much approval and support they got from some commanders and some senior NCOs. These companies were elated to have snipers available and turned them loose on the enemy. It was a learning experience for everybody.

Some of those lessons were lost after Vietnam, in the years between 1975 and 1991, when we really didn't have much real-world combat experience except for a few engagements in Lebanon. When Marines went off to combat again in 2003, we ran right back into some of the same conflicts and attitudes that snipers had to deal with forty years previously.

BETTER THAN SEX

There is a sort of mystique about what a sniper does and about killing an enemy in this very calculated and deliberate way. So—what's it like? It's a rush, an unbelievable rush that will stay with you for the rest of your life. It is an adrenaline high more intense than anything you have ever experienced!

Snipers are sometimes accused of making godlike decisions. We do—and a good sniper enjoys making those decisions. I can look at an enemy soldier through my scope and tell you when he is going to die, how he is going to be killed, how far he will fall, and what body part will explode and what it will look like—and then I can make it happen. There are no other MOSs in the Marine Corps where you you have so much control over another's death.

The F/A-18 pilot dropping bombs, the artillery crews, and mortar teams all send weapons downrange that may or may not kill people—but they never see what they have done, never see the expression on the faces of those they slay. Those of us in the scout-sniper community, however, can tell you if the target needed a haircut or wore glasses, among other intimate details, before our bullets hit him or the bombs we've called down from overhead impact on his position.

On the other hand, these kills will stay with a sniper for much longer than, say, with an artillery crew or a close-air-support pilot; both are insulated from their kills. I love killing enemy soldiers. I love putting the hurt on the enemy—every guy we kill means one less threat to our Marines or other Americans. But making these kills is a much more intense experience for a sniper than for somebody who does their killing from a distance, somebody who never sees the impact of the round.

If you ask any good sniper, he will tell you that making the kill is better than sex. If you offer this sniper an opportunity to shoot twelve enemy soldiers or to hop in bed with a Playboy playmate, the sniper will choose the chance to make the kills first—then he will want the girl, too!

CHAPTER THREE

BRAVO FOURS AND 8541s: SNIPER SELECTION AND TRAINING

So much for the formal and informal roles for snipers within their units. Clearly, these soldiers and Marines are the odd ducks of the battalion in almost every way. But what sort of person is selected and trained to be part of this tiny, tight, and aristocratic brotherhood of professional killers, and how does the process work?

The process begins with a decision by the individual to apply for this sort of training, and the application can be submitted only by people who are already part of a fairly small talent pool. Standards change slightly but generally require that an applicant be male, enlisted, be an excellent shot, be in good physical and emotional condition, have no significant discipline problems, and have at least a year left on his enlistment contract. The US Air Force has similar standards but allows women to apply because they serve in security units resembling police departments rather than offensive tactical units as in the Marines and Army.

There are five major military sniper schools operated by the US Army and the Marine Corps, and both operate several part-time, occasional programs. Each has similar standards, and they are remarkably high. For the formal sniper schools, all are men (although some women are being trained in the Squad Designated Marksman program and its variants). These men all come out of the combat-arms skill specialties—the infantry, artillery, armor, Rangers, Special Forces, and a few other communities. They have very extensive experience, usually with the M16 rifle, and they have consistently shot very well with it during annual qualifications.

Most students are on their second or third enlistment. Many have been in uniform for ten years and wear the three chevrons and single rocker of an E-6 staff sergeant. These men have already had successful military careers, are experienced leaders, know where they fit in the military food chain, and are not shy about taking the initiative and making decisions without a note from mommy. They've been doing a lot of physical training (PT) for years and are, with few exceptions, in very good physical condition with excellent upper-body strength and endurance. Maturity, initiative, sound judgment, strength, and endurance are all requirements for a good sniper and a good sniper student.

Like so many other roles in the war-fighting business, there are two sets of criteria: the formal ones carved in doctrine and published in documents like Field Manual 7-10, FM 7-92, and especially the bible for snipers, FM 23-10, *Sniper Training*, as well as the informal criteria that are part of the legend and lore of the business. As in any business, there are qualifications for the job, and then there is the interview. Many candidates meet the qualifications but don't get the job because of the unwritten and subjective value judgments made by the interviewer. The formal job requirements are laid out in FM 23-10.

First, he needs to be an expert marksman—that he routinely qualifies as Expert with the M16. He should be in superior physical condition, better than the average infantry soldier and a guy who can normally max the annual PT test. His vision needs to be 20/20, with or without glasses, and he should not use tobacco in any form. When candidates are screened by their commanders for the job, their intelligence and emotional condition are major considerations. As the manual advises:

> The commander must determine if the candidate will pull the trigger at the right time and place. Some traits to look for are reliability, initiative, loyalty, discipline, and emotional stability. A psychological evaluation of the candidate can aid the commander in the selection process. . . .
>
> The sniper must be able to calmly and deliberately kill targets that may not pose an immediate threat to him. It is much easier to kill in self-defense or in the defense of others than it is to kill without apparent provocation. The sniper must not be susceptible to emotions such as anxiety or remorse. Candidates whose motivation toward sniper training rests mainly in the desire for prestige may not be capable of the cold rationality that the sniper's job requires.*

The Army Sniper School is the primary training facility for soldiers in the conventional forces—those from the 82nd Airborne, the 3rd, 4th, and 25th infantry divisions, the 101st Airborne (Air Assault), 10th Mountain, and similar units. These organizations select candidates who meet the standards for attendance and send them off for five weeks of intense instruction. Each class normally begins with about forty students and ends with about thirty-five. The Army also operates a second school, the Special Operations Target Interdiction Course (SOTIC). Besides these, the Army Sniper School sends mobile training teams (MTTs) to units around the world to present marksmanship training at the home stations of

---

* Department of the Army, *Sniper Training*, Field Manual 23-10 (Washington, DC, 1994), section 1-3.

units who need the instruction but don't have the time or budget to send people to the Benning course. While the Army turns out around 13,000 qualified paratroopers every year, the number of graduates of the sniper school is only about 250, each of whom gets a B-4 [Bravo Four] identifier tacked on to his military skill designation.

USMC SCOUT-SNIPER SELECTION AND TRAINING

The Marines operate three major full-time scout-sniper schools: the big one at Quantico, Virginia; one at Camp Lejeune, North Carolina; and a third at Camp Pendleton, California. In addition, several classes each year are offered at Marine Corps Base Hawaii, part of Kaneohe Bay's Regimental Schools. The Marine program lasts ten weeks instead of five, includes a lot more training on scouting techniques—surveillance, calling for artillery fire, and related military arts apart from shooting. The Marines also do considerably more shooting, too.

Although somewhat similar to the Army selection process, the Marines have their own ideas of how to select and train their snipers, and they have their own ideas of the mission as well, and that shapes the selection and training system.

The scout-sniper role in the Marine Corps is highly respected and acceptance to the school is a major accomplishment for any Marine. There is a great deal of competition for slots at the school, and a very challenging process has been designed to identify the most qualified prospects long before they can attend any of the three schools. It is an excellent system, and here's how it works:

Each Marine Corps infantry battalion has a Surveillance and Target Acquisition (STA) platoon that is similar in form and function to the Army battalion's recon platoon. The platoon has four teams of operators, each with four Marines, plus a headquarters team composed of the platoon commander, the platoon sergeant, a corps-man, and a driver. Almost all of these, excepting the driver and the corpsman, are fully qualified scout-snipers with an 8541 military occupational specialty (MOS). Each four-man Marine STA team has a team leader, an assistant team leader, a radio operator, and a point man. A typical STA platoon will have a lieutenant, a gunnery sergeant, and as many as a dozen or more NCOs in grade E-5 [sergeant] or E-6 [staff sergeant], which is a far higher proportion of NCOs than will be found in a normal infantry platoon.

For all these and other reasons, the STA platoon is one of the most elite and prestigious units in the battalion, and many hard-charging Marines aspire to join it. There are only about twenty slots in the platoon, and vacancies typically occur only a few times each year. So when a member of the platoon decides he is going to leave the service or move off to a different job, the platoon prepares to fill that vacancy.

Since the STA platoon is such an important and prestigious unit, and since it can pick and choose who may join, the battalion holds try-outs for the platoon each year, and anybody can participate. This tryout program is called Indoc (for "indoctrination") and lasts two challenging weeks. About fifty Marines will normally sign up for Indoc and all of them know in advance that only a few—perhaps a dozen—will successfully complete the program and qualify to attend scout-sniper school.

The first week combines lots of PT with lots of class work, both designed to smoke all but the most qualified Marines. The classes cover the fundamentals of the job with a heavy emphasis on observation and surveillance, stalking, building hide sites, land navigation, mission planning, reporting, and making calls for fire support.

"I was very interested in trying out for the STA platoon," Sgt. Jason Finch says. "It was considered the best platoon in the battalion, and as a young Marine you are always attracted to the places with the highest standards. Anybody can try out, and the only person who can tell you that you can't is the battalion commander, something that he almost never does—scout-snipers are the eyes and ears of the battalion and the commander's trigger finger, so of course he wants the best."

Indoc begins with a PT test about 0400 on the morning of Day One (Monday) and is followed immediately with a run through the obstacle course. That is followed by a few hours of introductory classes on the overall mission, and then everybody goes out and does more PT. The whole week cycles between classroom work and PT, both at an exhausting pace.

Over the first weekend, the cadre issues a warning order for missions to be performed during the following week. There is no rest for the survivors of this first week, because they now must work on a detailed operations order that incorporates the lessons of the classroom in field problems and exercises. This is what Marines call a "smoke check," a calculated ordeal that filters out anybody who is not very seriously committed to becoming part of the STA platoon.

The surviving candidates are split up into four-man teams. Early on Monday morning, each team is inserted and begins patrolling toward their objective. This insertion phase takes about six hours and requires the Marines to move over very difficult terrain. Once at the objective they begin surveillance, using the procedures they've been taught during the previous week.

More than a test of academics, Week Two is a test of physical and mental toughness. Once the patrol is safely tucked into its hide site and each of the four Marines get comfortable, the cadre call up on the radio with a fragmentary order (FRAGO) that sends them right back eight or nine miles to a location they passed earlier in the day.

To keep things interesting, the STA platoon cadre tries to intercept and ambush the Indoc candidates. "They mess with your head for most of the week," Sgt. Finch says, "but leave you alone on the last day. That's when your team makes a stalk to a final firing position where you can see a group of guys role-playing the enemy. You get a call on the radio describing a specific person to look for, and when he shows up, you call back and report that you've got eyes on the guy. Then they give everybody a countdown over the radio so that all the teams can fire at exactly the same moment. That makes it impossible to tell where any of the shots are coming from. Indoc is tough and is meant to be tough. Seventy-five Marines tried out with me. Eighteen made it through the full two weeks of Indoc, and of those, thirteen were accepted as qualified to attend scout-sniper school."

For those thirteen who are accepted, the process of qualifying for the 8541 MOS has only begun. Each battalion will likely have only three slots for a class, and since classes are conducted only four times each year, it can be a long wait for some of those who have succeeded in getting through the Indoc phase. While they are waiting, they all become part of the STA platoon, where they are treated as apprentice scouts and snipers with a lot to learn. They will be trained on all the skills covered in the course and will be pushed to attain a very high level of physical fitness. When each finally goes off to the ten-week school, he will already have a lot of experience on the M40 rifle and will have learned a lot about each of the skills covered in the course.

For Sgt. Finch the wait was eighteen months, and during that time the platoon was training him to be trained. There is a very strong tradition in the Marines and Army that the honor of the unit is represented by the quality of the men it sends off for training, so when a soldier or Marine quits or fails a course like scout-sniper school, both he and his parent unit are dishonored. Such failures are often career-ending events, so everybody concerned is extremely careful about who is selected for scout-sniper training and how each man is prepared when his name finally gets on the course schedule.

A typical Marine Corps scout-sniper school class will have about fifteen or twenty students and will be taught by at least five or six instructors. The classes conducted at Quantico, Lejune, and Kaneohe Bay are each ten weeks long, while students at Camp Pendleton get two more.

"You come out of the school extremely proficient at making the call for fire, reporting and observation, stalking, and land navigation. All our final exercises were in the remote, rugged training area, and that place was hell on earth! It was full of ravines, saw grass, and miserable terrain, and was hot and humid," Finch says.

ARMY SNIPER SCHOOL CLASS 2006-3

The Army Sniper School is a tiny facility tucked away in a remote corner of Fort Benning's Harmony Church area, not far from another legendary school, the Ranger Training Brigade. It is enclosed by a high fence and gate. Early on an April morning, forty-three students from all around the Army are in their PT shorts and shirts, ready for the first test of the program, the run.

Each student is a volunteer, and nearly all are Eleven Bravos. Of the forty-three, quite a few have seen combat in Iraq or Afghanistan, and some of these have on-the-job training as snipers. Several of these, including Staff Sgt. Timothy Johns, come from the Ranger Regiment, one of the most prestigious organizations in the Army; Johns has already served as a sniper in combat. Of the forty-three students, about ten have received the Purple Heart for combat wounds, and a vast majority wears the Combat Infantryman Badge over their nametapes and a combat-unit patch on their right shoulders. These are serious, mature, experienced war fighters without illusions.

Several students have at least some experience with the sniper mission, either in combat or in stateside training. The Army and

Marine Corps believe in training everybody in a team to be able to do the job of every other member of the team if and when somebody takes a bullet or is otherwise unavailable. So ordinary Eleven Bravos in a scout section are likely to get hauled off to the range with the sniper team to get some time on the M24 or M40, and many of these guys find the sniper mission fascinating and desirable. But until each successfully completes the five-week program, he will not be fully qualified for the sniper mission or the B4 identifier that is attached to his 11B MOS.

At 0530, each prospective student runs a two-mile loop on roads around the school. Passing times are based on the student's age. Since most are in the twenty-two- to twenty-six-year-old category, these men must have times of sixteen minutes thirty-six seconds or better to pass. After a few minutes to recover, each soldier or Marine is tested for push-ups (forty minimum) and then for sit-ups (fifty minimum).

Class 2006-3 has three students who fail one of the tests. These three will be allowed to stay with the rest of the group until the following day when they are retested. One passes; the other two fail and are immediately sent back to their parent unit.

The routine for the students is intense and demanding. PT every morning from 0600 to 0700, chow and shower till 0745, then ready for class by 0800. The first few days will include introductory classes on the several aspects of the course but gets right into practical information. The M24 rifle class comes on the first day, and all the students will be proficient at disassembling it and putting it back together by Monday afternoon.

The instructors make it plain right away that students are expected to operate under "big boy" rules—there are not a lot of formations or inspections; everyone is responsible for his own PT; no alcohol may be consumed within twenty-four hours of scheduled weapons firing. This latter provision means that the only time any of them can have a beer is on Friday or Saturday night. Any DUIs or similar problems with the MPs or local law enforcement will result in immediate dismissal from the school. This is no gentleman's course but five weeks of very long days, intense instruction, high standards, frequent tests, and little tolerance for any sort of failure. Unlike many other Army schools, the day begins at 0800 and often lasts until eight or ten at night.

The first week includes some classroom lectures and Power Point presentations, but there is a lot of time for hands-on field work, and all of them get into it on Tuesday.

Every day for the next week will begin with the same ritual—all the students line up at the arms room door and draw their M24 rifle and spotting scope. Most have combat experience and wear their personal battle rattle: either the old-style load-bearing H or Y harness and pistol belt design or one of the many newer assault vests. All will have a rucksack of some sort, large or small, and all will have a couple of quarts of water either in canteens or in CamelBak hydration systems built into their packs. By 0800 they are either jammed into a small classroom or jammed into the back of a truck and on their way to one of the range complexes tucked away in the forests of Fort Benning.

The instructors dive right in and demand that the students keep up, first with the classroom lectures and demonstrations, then with the practical field exercises. A day may begin with a class in target detection at Burroughs Range, then move on to range estimation at Maertens Range, a few minutes to gulp down a meal ready to eat (MRE) for lunch, then an afternoon putting some of the pieces of the puzzle together by shooting at targets all afternoon, a brief break for dinner, some time for discussion with one of the mentors, then two classroom presentations, one on cover and concealment, the other on sniper tactics and employment. These classes end at 8:00 P.M., and the students are expected to spend the rest of the evening working on their ghillie suits [environmental camoflage] and cleaning and maintaining their rifles.

Although each man is supposed to be very proficient with the M16 rifle, they will have to demonstrate their individual shooting skills again during the first week, this time with the M24 Sniper Weapon System. After the classroom familiarization, it is off to Maertens Range to zero their rifles and get familiar with the Leupold Mark 3 sight and its Mil-Dot reticle.

Week One is a very busy getting-to-know-you time, US Army–style. A huge amount of information is thrown at the students, and they have to absorb it all and put it to use immediately. There is a great deal of note taking in the little green memo books carried by most soldiers and lots of study of the military sniper's bible, FM 23-10. This manual may be the best textbook ever issued to military personnel, loaded with good information that has been logically organized, illustrated with excellent tables and illustrations, and written in a remarkably clear style.* By the end of the five-week course, each student's copy will be dog-eared and battered from frequent reference.

They all have a lot to learn: how to determine the range to the target, how to select targets and assign priorities to each, the many ways to develop a hide site, and how to move undetected to a final firing position. They will shoot hundreds of rounds of M118 ammunition and become intimately familiar with the ballistics of this cartridge and its potential for killing people at long distances—that the ballistic coefficient for a Mk211 Mod 0 .50cal explosive projectile, for example, is .647, and the M118LR's is .505—and, by the way, the ballistics test will be Monday morning.

---

* FM 23-10 is currently a public document and is not classified. Anybody can obtain a copy by downloading it on the Internet at no cost. The manual is currently undergoing revision and the new version may not be available to the public.

Each student sniper will get to know the maddening effects of wind on a bullet and on the adjustments that must be made when firing uphill or down. He'll also learn the effect of temperature changes, barometric pressure, atmospheric drag, gravity, and altitude on the point of impact, and that for every twenty degrees the temperature rises, the point of impact will rise at the rate of one minute of angle, or about one inch for every one hundred yards, and that of all these factors, wind will make the largest difference in point of impact.

They will become highly familiar with the anatomy of their weapons and ammunition, learn more than they want to know about ballistic coefficients, barrel harmonics, muzzle- and mid-range velocities, lines of departure and of sight, spin drift, and how to crank all these considerations into a Leupold Mk3A sight before making a shot.

They learn about minutes of angle and milliradians. They also learn that snipers are the only infantrymen on the battlefield who need calculators and Palm Pilots to make their kills.

Each learns that the only way to reliably and immediately incapacitate a human target is with a shot to the small part of the head called the brain stem, that the point of aim for such a shot is the tip of the nose, and to avoid such shots beyond 300 meters.

This week introduces the M24 rifle, the mission, some fundamental skills, and a group of mentors. The staff of the school is about half active-duty military personnel and half civilian contractors with military experience from a company called Omega Group. Together they provide both formal and informal instruction in marksmanship, observation, stealth, hide-site construction; the recon mission, the proper and improper ways snipers are used on the battlefield, and many other topics.

THE ART OF OBSERVATION

A huge portion of the sniper's job and the school's instruction deals with the art of observation, analysis, and reporting. Most of the first two weeks are devoted to training students to methodically observe terrain with the unaided eye and with binoculars and the M149 spotting scope, to draw terrain sketches and maps to a military standard, to estimate ranges to distant objects, and record these details in logs. Although sniper teams conducting combat operations will normally have laser range finders, students learn to make accurate estimates by eye alone and with the calibrated reticle inside the rifle scope.

The process starts with a Power Point presentation in the classroom that covers the fundamentals, then it is onto the trucks and off to Burroughs Range for some practical experience. The first exercises are not easy. Prior to their arrival, instructors have placed a half-dozen familiar military objects in front of the class, some partially hidden, others in plain sight. Plain sight in the observation class, however, doesn't make the process of detection automatic because of the angle of exposure, the distance from the observer, or the color. All of the new students have been told how to observe—with the unaided eye first, scanning in sweeps covering about ten-meter bands beginning at their immediate front and working outwards. Sgt. Aaron Welch from the 10th Mountain Division picks up several of the objects right away, a radio battery near the corner of a building and a 20mm cartridge case tucked into the supports of a bleacher. Most of the others see these as well, and, using a form supplied by the instructors, methodically list and identify the objects.

When they are done with the preliminary search, they each get out their M22 binoculars. These are 20-power optics that allow Welch and the others to closely inspect suspicious areas, and they begin to pick up more hidden objects. Some of these will be partly hidden for this early exercise, but the exercises will become progressively more challenging during the next several weeks.

THE KIMS GAME

Snipers have a mission that demands a tremendous amount of thoughtful analysis, careful observation, disciplined behavior, and some very surprising skills. One of these is a trained memory that can remember in detail things observed during an operation, a skill developed at sniper school with a technique first popularized by the nineteenth-century author Rudyard Kipling in the novel *Kim*. The game involves observing a series of objects for a short period of time, committing them to memory, then recalling each accurately at a later time.

At the school, this is taught by placing objects where the students will pass by, perhaps on the way to the range or chow—for example, a plastic ammunition drum for an M249 machine gun, a barrel assembly for a rifle, a canteen, a battery for a radio, and perhaps another half-dozen military items will be left by the side of the road just outside the school compound. The students will pass the objects during the day and are expected to notice them and to later recall each in detail and in sequence as they were arranged on the ground.

STEALTH AND CONCEALMENT

The Army has an instruction philosophy summarized by the phrase "crawl, walk, run," and that is exactly how covert movement is taught. Late one afternoon during week two, the students line up on the smooth grass of an athletic field and are taught how to crawl. They begin with the sniper low crawl, the most covert movement technique of all, completely flattened against the ground. Hands and feet move with painful slowness and the students take ten minutes to move a few yards. The medium- and high-crawl techniques are taught, always with the emphasis on using movement methods suitable for terrain and threat level.

GHILLIE SUITS: THE CLOAK OF INVISIBILITY

A traditional item of camouflage equipment for all snipers, military and law enforcement alike, is the ghillie suit. Although seldom used in Afghanistan or Iraq, all aspiring snipers are usually required to own one. The design and construction of these suits are part of the education of both Marine and Army snipers.

The ghillie suit originated in Scotland during the eighteenth and nineteenth centuries by gamekeepers attempting to catch poachers on private estates. They used natural vegetation for camouflage and concealment by attaching this material to an overgarment, and this made them nearly invisible. When some of these ghillies went to war in 1914 and served as snipers in the British army, they constructed suits for use against the Germans. These suits were very effective at breaking up the outline of the human form and at providing color and texture that matched the sniper's natural surroundings.

Although ghillie suits may be designed for use in jungle, grassland, snow, desert, or urban terrain, sniper-school students manufacture a custom outfit of their own for the dense forest surrounding the school. Starting in the first week, students build their own ghillie suits for use in the class, and each will be graded on the result. It is a laborious process that will require many hours, a lot of trips to local craft stores for supplies, plus an old uniform shirt and pants to use as a foundation and a floppy jungle hat for a head cover.

Strips of burlap and other material and netting are firmly attached to the shirts and pants to hold fresh vegetation. Strips of raffia from the craft store are both tied and glued on. Spray paint in browns, grays, and greens are artfully applied. Holes are cut in the back of the shirt to provide ventilation. Since the snipers anticipate using these suits primarily from the prone position, all this material is added to the back of the shirt and pants as well. Some of the instructors supervise the process, offering critiques and suggestions as everybody cuts and sews their custom fashion creations.

The hat in particular gets special attention. Many attach some form of netting to the brim to help break up the shine and recognizable form of the human face. The front of the pants and elbows of the shirt are reinforced with canvas glued on with a heavy, flexible silicon adhesive to help protect against damage from abrasion during stalking crawls. Camouflage is also added to rucksacks and the nylon container (or "drag bag") for each man's rifle.

When it is time to try these suits on, everybody looks a bit like King Kong with a bad haircut—canvas strips stick out in all directions and the whole effect is momentarily comic. It is even more comic when the whole class suits up and moves down the road for an introductory lesson on stalking while wearing the camouflage.

During the second week these suits are inspected and graded. The exercise is not entirely academic because each student will soon need his ghillie suit for the stalking exercises that begin in Week Three.

But the process of making a ghillie suit isn't complete until it has been washed, and it has to be washed in a very special way—in the legendary Ghillie Washer. The Ghillie Washer is no ordinary washing machine but a twenty-yard portion of the small creek across the road from the school compound. Here the instructors have added many features to help insure that the new suits are properly broken in and that all the starch and smell of the new material is carefully removed. These features include log barriers, deep holes, lots of mud, and plenty of very cold water. One at a time, each student climbs down into the creek and low-crawls along past each obstacle, sometimes covered in mud, sometimes completely under the muddy water.

STALKING EXERCISES

Another essential skill these student snipers must learn is the ability to move undetected to a final firing position within range of a planned target, a process called stalking. The emphasis in the school is on learning to make stalks in a rural environment, but the terrain of Fort Benning is nothing like that of rural Iraq or Afghanistan. The basic principles are taught in a classroom session, and then it is off to one of the wooded training areas nearby for what the cadre* call a stalk-ex, or stalking exercise.

A stalk-ex is a game with deadly implications. On one team are Staff Sgt. Campbell and Staff Sgt. Stan Crowder, both with radios, M22 binoculars, and lots of experience at detecting students attempting to move unseen through the brush.

On the other team are the individual students, now attired in their new ghillie suits. They veg up by adding fresh foliage to the netting on their shirts and hats, cammie up with camouflage face paint, then move out through the brush to try to sneak up on the watching instructors. About six hundred meters from their target, the students prepare by checking their packs for the tools of the trade—pruning shears, saw, binoculars, 550 cord, compass, knife, combination tool, blank ammunition, and full canteens or Camel-Baks. All will wear gloves regardless of the temperature to camouflage their hands. By the time they've prepared for the stalk, each looks like a fugitive from a flower shop in their shaggy ghillie suits adorned with grass and leaves. Each loads up with two blank cartridges, makes sure his weapon is on SAFE, and moves off into the woods.

The only way students can win is to move undetected all the way within range, fire the two blanks without being spotted, and then

---

* "Cadre" are all school personnel, military and civilian, instructors and administration staff.

withdraw, all without being observed by the staff sergeants. Roaming the area near the students are several other instructors called "walkers," also with radios. If Campbell or Crowder spots something out of place, he calls up one of the walkers and directs him to the spot. If there is a student at that spot, he fails the exercise.

Early stalk-ex terrain is heavily wooded, with plenty of low spots for crawling. The instructors like to tell stories about previous stalking demonstrations by snipers in bright clown outfits and Ronald McDonald costumes who have managed to get in range and get their two shots off without being spotted, but the new sniper students have enough trouble with the exercise despite the advantages of their new ghillie suits. Sometimes they will be betrayed by movement of a bush or grass, other times by an unnatural variation in the pattern or color of their camouflage. Campbell calls one of the walkers, says, "Face left and move ten meters." Davis moves to the spot where a sergeant has bumped a small bush, causing it to move unnaturally. "You're busted, Sergeant" he says; the sergeant stands up—he's failed the exercise. Each subsequent stalk exercise will be in progressively more challenging terrain, the last very open and requiring a great deal of very slow and very low crawling.

Students are tested in two major ways: in written examinations and in practical demonstrations. Passing scores on both are required to complete the course. Every Friday afternoon the cadre provides a review of material covered during the previous week, with suggestions for study over the weekend. Monday of each week begins with a written examination.

Out on the range and in the woods, students have to pass practical examinations on range estimation, target detection, and shooting at stationary targets at known and then at unknown distances. They will have to be able to hit movers—cardboard targets moving at a walking pace—and they will have only a few seconds to successfully make the shot. Each student will have to demonstrate proficiency at shooting a target representing a hostage taker without hitting the hostage. They will be scored on their ability to shoot when they are under stress, after running and while their heartbeat and respiration are elevated.

By the beginning of Week Four, all the fundamentals have been thoroughly covered and the classes start to cover the more exotic aspects of the mission—alternate firing positions, urban operations, countersniper missions, escape and evasion, survival, tracking, angle firing, and stalking.

On Monday of the last week they all get to spend some time firing the M107 Barrett .50cal rifle at targets out to a mile downrange. The ammunition for this training is high-explosive incendiary; each hit produces a satisfying flash when it smacks the derelict tanks and artillery used for targets on Coolidge Left Range.

There are more classes on the exotic aspects of the mission, the final graded tests of marksmanship, and a last review of the academic portion of the class that runs late into Tuesday night. On Thursday morning at 0600, instead of PT, the students take their final examination in the classroom and it is almost over. Much of the rest of the day will be spent on an ungraded competition, a final ordeal like a compressed "Best Ranger" competition that has them all running from one location to another, burdened with M107 Barretts, shooting under stress, and getting smoked for the last time.

Friday morning Class 2006-3 cleans up its billets, packs its gear, puts on its cleanest uniforms, and at 1100 forms up in the compound for graduation. Staff Sgt. Tim Johns has been selected as the Honor Graduate, a great accomplishment. Thirty-seven of the original forty-three students have successfully passed the course; each will have "B-4" added to their MOSs. Each gets a certificate and a handshake, and soon they are off to catch planes or make the long drive back to their parent units. Of these thirty-seven graduates, many will deploy within weeks to Iraq or Afghanistan. The cadre at the school take a long weekend off, then get ready for Class 2006-4 and another five weeks of shooting, stalking, range estimation, and all the rest of the skills needed by an Army sniper on the battlefield.

There is a desperate need for these snipers and a lot of pressure on the school to churn out as many as possible. One of the people waiting for them is Maj. Charles Greene, recovering from his insurgent-sniper-inflicted wound at Fort Richardson, Alaska. "The sniping community is scrambling to catch up with the demand for trained snipers on the battlefield. In peacetime we tend to overlook and side-line the sniper; his job is too distasteful to many people," Major Greene says. "A sniper is a kind of assassin, no matter how you want to slice it. He is trying to kill somebody who doesn't even know he's around. We neglected this training before 2001 and are trying to make up for it now—all the sniper training programs—the Marine schools at Quantico, Pendleton, and Lejeune, the Army school at Fort Benning, and the Special Operations Target Interdiction Course [SOTIC] at Fort Bragg—are all surging as many students as they can manage."

The need for snipers, school-trained and B-4 designated or not, is so great that anybody in an Army recon platoon with an interest in the job and a history of shooting well will probably get a look from the sniper section NCO. Staff Sgt. Tim Wilson, a Special Forces tabbed (or qualified) soldier, describes how this conflict between the school graduates and the volunteers worked in his unit in Iraq in 2006:

> The sniper section leader is the senior NCO, the guy with the most time on the gun. At the beginning of our train-up, when we just had the M24s, I had three four-man teams in the section, each with a shooter, a spotter, and two security guys. The security guys were stolen from the scout squads, guys who already had a lot of the skills of a sniper but without the school

training and experience on the rifles. Later, when my section got three additional rifles, the .50cal M107s, we needed more people.

Of course these new guys got cross-trained on every piece of gear we had, especially the weapons. You had to assume that someday one of us was going to catch a round, and when that happened, the guy closest to the gun needed to be able to get behind it and put precision fire downrange.

There is some sensitivity about mixing school-trained, B-4–rated guys on a sniper team with guys from the scout squads who haven't been to school. Some of the B-4 guys have objected to me about putting one of these guys on the gun as a shooter, objected to somebody else using the rifle that these B-4 guys had been issued. I told them, "Listen, that isn't your gun, it belongs to the US Army. Your job is to train this guy in the skills you learned at sniper school. Don't worry if the gun goes off while you are asleep; you're part of a successful kill."

So the recon guys were really excited to come over and start learning to be snipers. The recon squad leaders were not excited at all to be losing their best guys, so here was another political issue that we had to sort out within the "family."

CHAPTER FOUR

MAJ. CHARLES GREENE, US ARMY RANGER

*C*harles Greene is a veteran soldier, long-time Ranger sniper, and combat veteran of both the Panama invasion (Operation Just Cause), and two tours in Iraq. Captain Greene was shot by an enemy sniper while leading a patrol of Iraqi Special Forces soldiers in Mosul.

RED ROMEO ON THE DROP ZONE

Late in 1989, tensions due to several disputes between the US and Panama over corruption and drug smuggling escalated to the boiling point, and American special operations forces from the Army, Navy, and Air Force were tasked with missions intended to neutralize Panamanian units and to capture the country's president, Manuel Noriega.

The 75th Ranger Regiment (Task Force Red) was assigned two initial missions—the seizure of Tocumen/Torrijos Airport and the neutralization of a company of Panamanian infantry, and the seizure of another airport at Rio Hato where another two enemy infantry units were based.

Charles Greene was a sergeant in Alpha Company, 3rd Battalion, 75th Rangers, at the time. Along with elements of the regiment's 2nd Battalion, these units became Task Force Red Romeo and jumped into combat at 0100 hours on 20 December 1989.

When the time came to jump, my M24 sniper rifle was strapped to a Ranger Support Operations Vehicle, (RSOV) that would be air-landed several hours after the initial airborne assault. Although I was a sniper, the SOP at the time was that I would fight initially on the drop zone with an M16A2 and then later get the sniper rifle. The rationale behind this was that the rifles cost over $5,000 each, and because they were aluminum pillar bedded, they were not certified to be jumped. Although my rifle was a conventional M16A2, it had a Litton night sight that became very useful when we landed.

We came in at about 450 feet above the ground. I was carrying so much gear that I could barely move, but once I got out of the harness and got my rifle out of the weapon container, I could see a huge tractor-trailer driving right toward us on the drop zone. My orders were to kill anything that wasn't a Ranger. The truck driver was not a Ranger, and he was about to run over a lot of Rangers with his truck.

In the night sight, the driver looked like he was right on top of me, but the range was actually more like seventy-five yards. The driver filled the scope. I shot him about six times—each time, he must have stepped on the brake because I could hear the air brake engage and release. About the time I finished killing the guy, he eased off to the side of the road and the truck stopped with him slumped over the wheel. Only then did two machine guns open up on the truck; the machine gunners had night observation devices (NODs) and must have seen me kill the man, but they waited till he was dead to shoot. The willingness to kill is not in every soldier, even in the Ranger Regiment, and I think these two gunners were reluctant to do the killing.

I turned around. The control tower for the airfield was only about two hundred meters away. From the catwalk at the top, Panamanian soldiers were firing down on Rangers as they landed. I started picking them off one at a time, and as I hit them, each fell to the ground below. This allowed the 2nd Ranger Battalion guys to make their way up inside the tower; they quickly eliminated any remaining resistance and took control of the position.

The funniest thing for me about the whole initial assault was a pickup truck. It was barreling down a side road adjacent to the drop zone with its headlights on! In the back of it were about six Panamanian defenders attempting to spray down the drop zone while fleeing. I took up the lead and began picking them off. The driver quickly realized his error and turned his lights off!

About this time a Panamanian armored car rolled onto the drop zone. This was a VP-150, a wheeled vehicle of Russian manufacture that mounted a heavy machine gun, which the Panamanians used to hose down the drop zone. Although I couldn't defeat the VP-150, I started firing at the vehicle's vision blocks to distract the driver and gunner long enough for somebody with more firepower to come along and take him out. That was done by the ever-present AC-130H Spectre gunship overhead. Just prior to my engaging him, the gunship had fired once and missed, probably because it was going so fast. Then I was able to get the driver to stop for a moment and the Spectre gunship nailed him. I killed the survivors as they ran out of the burning vehicle. Then I fired up a motorcycle attempting to get off the drop zone before our H-hour mission was complete.

OUTSMARTING THE ENEMY

There are many ways to kill the enemy, and they often require you to be smarter than he is. For example, when I was assigned as an advisor to the Iraqi special forces, my unit began to come under harassing fire by an enemy mortar every day, and it was frustrating because my Iraqis were taking casualties. The enemy mortar team had a good routine—they had their tube in a small truck, hidden with hay, and would roll into a firing position. Then they would quickly set up the weapon, fire three or four rounds at us, and drive away before an Apache gunship could find them. Our counterartillery radar could calculate where the rounds were fired from, but by the time the data was processed the truck and its enemy team were long gone.

I called up our supporting American unit, 2nd Battalion, 325th Parachute Infantry Regiment, 82nd Airborne, and told Lieutenant Colonel Gibson, the commander, "You've got to help me, sir—my Iraqis are getting hammered; they are afraid to go out on patrol." Lieutenant Colonel Gibson offered a sniper team and asked, "Where should we put them?"

I told him that based on the fire detection radar information and other intel, the enemy team might be operating out of a building, which I showed him on the map. There was nothing sure about it, just a suspicion. But there was also a good overwatch position from a four-story building a few hundred meters away. A squad was infiltrated into the overwatch position—a sniper/spotter team and a security element to protect them, and they settled in to wait.

Sure enough, the team didn't have long to wait. I heard them firing, one deliberate shot at a time. The sniper team watched the enemy crew drive up, position the baseplate, and begin to set up a 60mm mortar. The enemy gunner was almost ready to shoot when his ammo handler ran up with four prepared rounds. A good mortar crew could have all four in the air and be back on the road before the first landed, but not this time. The snipers took out the first guy, then the second, before they really understood what was happening. When a platoon moved forward to investigate, both of the enemy were dead. Nearby, in a small building that we had searched many times before, ninety mortar rounds were found.

That is one way you can use a sniper team to take out an enemy mortar team, but it was done with a certain amount of risk. If that squad had been compromised by an enemy platoon, they could have quickly been rolled up and killed.

SNIPER EMPLOYMENT ISSUES

One of the things that has been driving all of us in the sniper community nuts is the problems conventional-force commanders have understanding two things about snipers—how to employ the ones the commander "owns," and how to deal with the enemy's snipers.

For example, not long after the incident with the enemy mortar team, our compound came under mortar fire again—six rounds this time, killing one of my men, wounding two others—this time from an 82mm weapon, and it was causing serious problems. I called the 82nd Airborne again because we had no suitable weapons of our own to deal with this threat. They handed me off to a company commander.

"Okay, Chuck," the company commander said, "we'll do some crater analysis and figure out where they are that way."

"No, don't do that," I answered. "Your guys are going to get shot by one of the enemy snipers!"

"I'll send a rifle squad along with the crater analysis guys to protect them," he said.

"I would not recommend that! We are taking sniper fire here every day, right in that area!" I told him. (I would ultimately be shot by a sniper myself, right in this same neighborhood.) But he wasn't convinced and insisted on doing it his way. Pretty soon I saw his squad of infantry walking over from their combat outpost nearby. Two fire teams took up positions, one on each side of the road, and the crater analysis team was out in the street looking at the hole. I had my binos out and was behind good cover, looking for the sniper that I was sure would find such easy targets irresistible. Sure enough, I heard the first shot and turned to see one of the 82nd guys drop like a sack of rocks.

About this time a local man drove by in his little Toyota car. I knew he had nothing to do with the shot, but the infantry guys concluded otherwise and opened up on him from fifty yards away. Iraqi civilians have their own immediate action drill for such situations, and the driver executed it perfectly—he ducked down as far as he could with just his eyes peeking out over the steering wheel as he hit the gas and made his escape while all these weapons were lighting up his little car. Despite numerous hits on the car, he drove away and disappeared around a corner. The infantryman was evacuated and all I could think was: How foolish!

SHOT BY A SNIPER AT THE CIRCLE OF DEATH

I arrived in Mosul on 12 January 2004 and was assigned as an advisor to an Iraqi special forces battalion in the area. From the day I arrived and started conducting operations in our sector, we were taking harassing fire from an enemy sniper. This sniper probably wasn't school trained, but he could have been—some of the insurgents had been to schools operated by the Fedeyeen and others; we will never know where he learned to shoot. But he had an SVD, a Russian-made sniper rifle, and he was taking shots at my guys from six hundred to one thousand yards away. I know the distances because I had enough experience in this business to use the interval between the impact of the bullet to the sound of the shot to estimate the shooter's range. I was shot at and missed by this guy numerous times, and ultimately my luck ran out. While he was not up to American standards, he was learning his business, and his misses were closer and closer day by day.

We'd typically go out and conduct combat patrols three or four times every day. Although we'd change our operational patterns, the enemy's pattern never changed. Every day we'd take a few mortar rounds, then this guy would get in a few shots at us. Several times I had one of my Iraqi soldiers wounded or killed by this guy. He made some good shots. On a cold and snowy day, typical of Mosul in January, one of my Iraqi machine gunners was killed while mounting a PKC [Russian machine gun] on the rear of one of our Nissan pickups. He took a round through the patch on his left shoulder. The bullet ranged into his upper chest cavity; he died instantly in the arms of one of my Marine advisors. That's not a bad shot from four hundred-plus yards.

As painful as it was, I often had to intentionally use our Iraqi force to draw fire from the hidden insurgent snipers. Knowing how the insurgents operated, one of my Marine Corps scout-snipers or I would sit in an overwatch hide scanning rooflines and the terrain as our patrols came and went. This strategy proved fruitful on more than a few occasions. This cat-and-mouse game went on for about a week, with one or two of my guys being hit every day or so. At this stage of the war it was frustrating because you can't engage an enemy until he has demonstrated hostile intent. Consequently, in most engagements the enemy gets the first shot.

True to form, one of my patrolling Iraqi soldiers was shot—he was hit in the penis. While the other guys were attending to him, I was able to triangulate the path of the bullet that indicated his general firing position. The sniper's bullet went through the cab of the pickup truck in which the Iraqi soldier was riding and made two holes—one in the windshield, the other in the rear window—before hitting my soldier. Since the truck was stopped at the time of the shot, lining up the holes easily showed where the bullet came from, an apartment building a couple of blocks away. However, from my position this information alone did not make him a sure thing. Then he made a Sniper 101 mistake: he took another shot directly at me—and missed! His muzzle flash betrayed the terrorist's concealed position. I could easily see his hide from about four hundred yards away—I had an FN-FAL [Belgian-made NATO rifle] and killed him instantly.

To my amazement we continued to get hit by another sniper. On 10 January, one of my fellow advisors, a Marine Corps gunny sergeant, got hit in the neck. Luckily, it was a flesh wound. Our routine was a four-kilometer foot patrol through the slum areas of the city. As was typical of these dismounted patrols, the insurgents would shadow us, waiting until we were almost done for the day, then just as we were pulling into our safe area, they'd hit us.

Two days later, we were conducting a cordon-and-search with two companies of Iraqis. As we reached a place all US forces fondly nicknamed the Circle of Death, on Main Supply Route (MSR) Tampa, an enemy unit heavily engaged my unit. My assistant team leader, USMC Captain Derrick Szopa, took a bullet to the front of his Kevlar helmet, destroying the night-vision-goggle mounting bracket. The impact knocked him out for about thirty seconds. Alongside him, one of the Iraqis was hit and killed instantly. Two more were wounded.

As I was assessing the situation, we started receiving RPG rounds. The Iraqis were finally returning effective fire when I got hit. The bullet impacted on the left side of my jaw entering at about a forty-five-degree angle, traveling through my ear canal, finally resting in the base of my skull. This knocked me to my knees. Then I got up, continued to fight and assess the situation for a few moments before dropping to my knees again and losing consciousness temporarily.

I was lucky. The guy was at about six hundred yards or so, which allowed the bullet to bleed off some of its kinetic energy. Anything closer and it would have blown my head off. My Iraqi Special Forces soldiers were extremely loyal. When I got hit, there had to be some retribution. Up to that point, they'd been solid soldiers, but not particularly aggressive; afterward, I heard that they started kicking ass.

While I was being medevacked, my remaining two American advisors and our Iraqis got the fight under control—they killed a couple of the enemy, captured a bunch, and ran off the rest. Later one of the captured terrorists bragged to my Iraqi soldiers that he knew about an insurgent team that was killing Americans, and from him they got enough information to conduct a raid on a nearby enemy safe house. During the ensuing fight, one insurgent came out fighting and was instantly shot down at the door. Inside, my guys captured two more and killed a third—a sniper with an SVD. We think this was the guy that shot me. Since 13 February, it has been much quieter in our sector.

STAY-BEHIND MISSIONS

One standard method for inserting a sniper team is to attach them to an infantry unit conducting a cordon-and-search mission. While the infantry are kicking in doors and moving through the neighborhood, the sniper team dismounts from a Stryker wheeled armored vehicle and quietly moves into a building where they occupy a hide site—in other words, they go to ground and stay hidden. The Stryker unit finishes its mission and goes away, leaving the snipers in position. Two days later the Strykers come back, conduct a raid, and the sniper team hops back on the vehicle.

As an example, my Iraqi commando battalion found a large cache of RPG rounds in an abandoned school. There were hundreds of these rounds, and we reported the find. I was ordered to get everybody out of the building, and we moved to another nearby location were we could still see the school.

About 1400 hours the next day, a van pulled up and several Americans got out. They wore sterile uniforms and had long hair and beards—they could have been from any of several units: Navy SEALs, Blackwater contractors, Delta, or the Ranger long-hair teams. They took their gear into a four-story building overlooking the school. This looked interesting and I was anxious to get into any fight that might develop, so I walked over and introduced myself. They were setting up a .50cal sniper rifle.

"Hi, I'm Captain Greene, and I'm the advisor to the Iraqi commando battalion that found the cache of RPG rounds," I told them. We chatted for a while, caught up on the war without getting too specific about our roles. They invited me to hang out with them for a while, but without mentioning who they were or what unit they came from.

"So, what the fuck are you guys doing and what's your objective? You're in my AOR [area of responsibility]," I said, "and I would like to know what's going on."

"There's an RPG cache down the road," the mystery sniper said, "and we're going to overwatch it for a while and see who shows up."

"I know about the rounds—we found them," I said. "What do you think is going to happen?"

"Well, somebody will usually come by to take some of the rounds and when they do, we'll shoot them."

We sat there for about three hours. I was watching through binos when a little guy appeared on the otherwise empty street. He behaved suspiciously, looking nervous, checking left and right. Then he headed for the RPG cache. I was still watching through the binos when the .50cal rifle fired, and I was not prepared for the noise and the blast.

The range to the guy was only about 350 or 400 meters. When I recovered from the shot and looked through the binos again, I could see the man thrashing on the road. Another little guy appeared and went to the guy on the ground. *BOOM!* The sniper fired again, killing this guy also.

When I looked around at the team, they were already busy packing up their gear and getting ready to go. "You can take the cache down now," one of them said, and they climbed back in their van and drove away. I still have no idea who they worked for. We picked up the bodies, cleaned out the RPG rounds, and went back to our patrols.

THE SQUAD-DESIGNATED MARKSMAN PROGRAM

The idea behind the Army Squad-Designated Marksman (SDM) Program we are teaching here at Fort Richardson, Alaska, is that we take a guy or gal who is a proficient shooter at 300 meters and teach them how to get to the next level, to be effective at 300 to 600 meters. That has been a neglected zone until recently, with the rifleman able to engage up to 300 meters and the sniper working on targets at 600 meters and beyond. We don't have enough snipers, so somebody has to be able to engage a terrorist at 400 or 500 meters, and that is what we are teaching these people to do. It was my experience in Iraq that the insurgents tried to take us on from these ranges where they felt comparatively secure.

The guys and gals who apply for the SDM training have the same motivations as a regular sniper candidate: they want to do something more than just ride around in a patrol; they want to engage the enemy at long range, to make a contribution to the fight. But training snipers is expensive, and there are very few school slots available for most conventional force units.

I came from a Ranger battalion where we had lots of money for ammunition and training, and I was able to attend the SOTIC sniper training program, but for years I was the only school-trained sniper in Alpha Company, 3rd Battalion, 75th Rangers. There were only a half-dozen or so snipers in the whole battalion during the late 1980s and early 1990s.

That changed with our experience in Somalia and increases in funding for special operations forces in the early 1990s. I wrote the memorandum of instruction (MOI) for sniper employment in the Ranger regiment in 1993.

I've been around snipers for about twenty years, and there are two kinds of people who get into this business—target shooters and killers. A guy can go to sniper school and graduate with honors, but you don't know if he'll actually pull the trigger until the time comes to execute the killing shot. And unless you are right there watching the guy, you won't know what he actually did when the time comes to make a kill. Many people can hit a paper target at a thousand yards, but not so many people can hit a man at the same distance. The difference has to do with the act of killing a human being.

For those of us who train snipers, we see three kinds of students. The first kind of guy will make one kill but then becomes remorseful; his conscience will prevent him from ever making another kill. This man will find an excuse to avoid killing next time, either by failing to fire or by intentionally missing, or he will get out of the assignment and do something else.

The second type of guy will not shoot at all; he will report that he didn't have a target.

The third kind of guy will make a kill, then break for lunch and come back to make another kill. He has the kind of stuff we're looking for in a shooter within DEVGROUP or Delta, or for any of the special operations units that employ snipers.

We tend to be introverted people who don't need a lot of attention or approval from others. We can operate independently in support of the larger mission.

One part of the business is the science of delivering a bullet to a very small target at very long range. Today, anybody can use modern rifles and scopes to shoot with reasonable precision to 1,000 yards. A competent military sniper today needs to be able to hit a man-sized target at 1,400 yards or beyond; the rifles, ammunition, and sighting systems available to us permit engagements against individual enemy soldiers out to 2,000 yards—over a mile. I personally enjoy using a much-modified Remington 700 rifle chambered in .300 Winchester Magnum for medium-range work: 1,000–1,400 yards.

Sniping in the Army and the Marine Corps has become tremendously important during my career. The Iraq war is a boots-on-the-ground long-range war. Consequently, the schools are turning out snipers in large numbers, and the graduates are going off to war to do great things. The war in Iraq is a thousand-yard war—many of our engagements have been against enemy targets at extremely long range, even in urban combat.

Our rules of engagement vary somewhat from unit to unit, and even region to region, but at the beginning of the fight, if we saw a guy on the street with a weapon, he died on the spot. It didn't matter what sort of weapon—AK, RPG, anything—a sniper would take him out. These guys fresh out of the training program were consistently making excellent shots at eight hundred to a thousand yards.

When you shoot somebody, you try to pull back and wait to see if anybody comes to help the wounded or collect a dead body. The local good people won't touch the body of a slain insurgent; anyone touching the body will be another insurgent, and you shoot them. His buddies will come to get his weapon, his documents, and if he is still alive they will try to get him to medical attention. Nobody else will touch him.

CHAPTER FIVE

STAFF SGT. JAMES GILLILAND, SECTION LEADER

Staff Sgt. James Gilliland's Shadow Team provided sniper services to 2nd Battalion, 69th Infantry Regiment, 3rd Infantry Division for a twelve-month period during 2005 and 2006.

There were only ten of us in the Two-Six-Nine sniper unit and technically that made us just a squad, but we operated as a sniper section, a unit that is normally twice as large. I was the section leader and found myself doing jobs normally assigned to lieutenants—planning operations, doing coordination with friendly units, and related tactical decisions—then doing a platoon sergeant's work later in the day: assigning guard duty, requesting rations, and related administrative duties. It worked out well for us, though.

There are a lot of ways for a sniper element to conduct business, but the way that worked for us was to plan our own operations and execute them in our own way. Sometimes other units thought we were nuts, and here is one example why: instead of going in by vehicle, as most infantry patrols always did, we insisted on going in on foot. Other sniper elements traditionally have tagged along with a larger, platoon-sized patrol and will drop off from that patrol when it passes the place where the snipers want to set up a hide. Later, perhaps a day later, another patrol will come along and the snipers will join up for their extraction. We tried that a few times and had some problems with the technique, so we did things differently.

Shadow Team's missions began with a visit to the local line infantry companies to chat with the platoon leaders and platoon sergeants about what they were seeing and what they had to say about what we could do for them. Then we went over to the Intel section and looked at the maps—where the IEDs were going off, where groups of suspected insurgents were seen congregating, we listened to the humint (human intelligence) reports on what was happening, the sigint (signals intelligence) reports about what was being picked up from cell phone conversations, telephone surveillance, and the rumor mill. We built our missions on real-world information, then coordinated the missions just the same way all the other tactical units did, by communicating with the line companies and the other local players.

Most of the time, "dictated" missions—ones tasked by somebody outside our little loop—were useless and unproductive. When somebody told us, "Go to this location and see what you can do from here," we didn't see much or do much.

What always worked best—but that was hard for some commanders to do—was when our senior officers trusted us to design and execute our missions by ourselves. This is not something squad-sized units frequently do. There is always the concern, especially at first that the snipers will want to be cowboys, that they will look different from the rest of the soldiers, operate without proper coordination, and get everybody into trouble . . . because that sort of thing has happened in the past. But we were lucky to have the trust of our commander, and that made all the difference for us.

A week or two before launching a mission, we'd announce that we planned to insert ourselves into a general area of the city at a specific day and time, just to give the other units a heads-up for their own planning. We informed them that we'd give them a call later in the planning sequence and tell them what we intended in more detail.

Our area of responsibility in Ramadi was fairly small, and there were a million ways to get from our outpost to our intended hide sites.

While some guys on the ground carried huge numbers of magazines for their M4s and M16s, we didn't do that. There are two ways to fight—"spray and pray" and single, well-aimed shots. The insurgents and a lot of Americans both use the first technique and put a lot of lead downrange without hitting anything. I learned in the Ranger Regiment to select key points on the battlefield where an enemy soldier is likely to be—at the base of a tree, for example, or at the edge of an open doorway, around building corners, or behind windows. Instead of just shooting in the direction where you think the enemy fire is coming from, you put two well-aimed rounds at the base of each tree, two into each window and each corner, and two into each doorway. This is a proven technique that uses less ammunition and hits more bad guys.

I had to train one of the guys in this technique when we were on a mission at the sports stadium in Ramadi and came under fire from insurgents who were also in the stadium. Shots were hitting a wall right in front of us, some just inches from our guys, and one of my guys took his M4, held it over the top of the wall, and cut loose without aiming. "What are you doing?" I asked him.

"Putting down suppressive fire!" he answered.

"But you aren't hitting anything," I told him. Instead, I showed him the Ranger technique—I stood up, fired three shots into each of a couple of likely windows, then dropped back under cover. Then

I moved to a new location, popped up again, and did the same thing for a few more, methodically placing accurate fire on likely locations for enemy positions.

"Well, when do you know to get up and shoot? Are you waiting for a lull in the firing?"

"This is a firefight," I told him. "There is no guarantee that you're not going to get shot, but if you don't get up and return fire and kill him, the enemy is going to keep shooting till he gets you. The chances of one of those guys getting me, the way they shoot, is a lot less than my chances of getting them by putting accurate fire on the places they are likely to be using for their positions. We are trained to shoot, to move, and to communicate. You come up, engage your selected targets, go back down, move left or right, and do it again. At the same time, you're telling me and the other guys what you are doing. Sooner or later you will either get him this way or you will see his muzzle flash and know where to shoot."

SHADOW TEAM'S LONGEST SHOT

Now, people can believe this story or not—and some do and some don't, but it is pretty well documented. We made a confirmed kill on an insurgent at 1,250 meters, an extreme long-range shot that currently seems to be the record for such engagements with .308cal rifles.

We were in OP Hotel (a.k.a. the Ramadi Inn) and I was sitting near a window facing toward the north. To our immediate front was an industrial area of small shops with roll-up metal doors. There was a lot of trash and debris on the street, lots of abandoned cars, all covering our immediate front and for a distance of around four hundred meters. Beyond this industrial area was a zone of residential development, and beyond that the Ramadi hospital.

Our Alpha Company was conducting a large patrol in this same area at the same time. Although we were not really part of their operation, we naturally took interest in what they were doing and tried to give them a little extra protection. This involved watching for any suspicious activity that might be related to the patrol—people sneaking around behind buildings out of sight of the patrol, for example.

I was on the spotting scope, a Leupold Gold Ring 45-to-60-power, and checked frequently on the progress of the patrol. They stopped in sight of our position and sent a security element up to the roof of an adjacent building. We never did that because when you "skyline" yourself you make it easy for an enemy to see and engage you.

One of the guys was recognizable even at this distance as a friend of mine, Staff Sgt. Jason Benford, who had always been a little casual about exposing himself to possible enemy fire. He would ride around in his Bradley with the hatch open and his upper body exposed. When I tried to counsel him to be more careful, he just said, "I always feel much safer when you guys have my back."

"We can't see everything," I told him, "and you need to use cover better—take a knee, get behind a wall if you can."

"Everything will be all right," Jason said.

I could easily see him moving around on the rooftop, oblivious to the risk of insurgent snipers. The other guys were easy to see, too. I got on the radio and called them up. "You guys need to get behind some cover! If you have to stay on the roof, at least take a knee—that will protect you from fire from the buildings and alleyways closest to you."

I used the scope to inspect the area for threats but turned it back on the guys on the roof from time to time, and they were still way too exposed and visible. I picked up the handset for the radio and was about to press the transmit button when we heard the shot.

All hell broke loose. There was a lot of radio traffic and a report of one man down. There was more shooting, but then the company commander got on the radio with the call: "Tell the snipers that we are getting shot at from the hospital!"

When I heard that, I turned the spotting scope toward the hospital, and there I saw a man in the window of one of the top floors, looking toward the rooftop where the security team still was and holding a rifle in his hand.

Sgt. Bryan Pruett was nearby. "Bryan," I told him, "I'm going to take a shot at a guy in the hospital—I need to have you spot for me!"

My M24 was in reach. It was the only sniper rifle that hadn't been painted and still had its black finish. We all consequently called it the Black Gun, and I claimed it for my own. I cranked the bullet-drop-compensator up as far as it would go, to 1,000 meters, and we knew from previous measurements with our laser range finder that the hospital was 1,250 meters from our current position. I had to do a quick calculation for the ballistic correction for the extra 250 meters and came up with an additional nine-foot drop. The Mil-Dot reticle* in the scope allowed me a reasonably good way to measure hold-off.

My intention was to get a round into the window to at least suppress this guy. Making a killing shot under the circumstances was not a realistic expectation. The range was way beyond what the cartridge was designed to do, and the ballistics at that distance were awful—the projectile is falling out of the sky at a steep angle. But the guy was still there with his rifle and I had to engage him even so.

Bryan quickly moved over and got behind the spotting scope. "Are you on him?" I asked, but it took Bryan a few moments to get oriented. I made a quick evaluation of the wind, held three mils high and two mils to the left, and fired.

As I recovered from the recoil, I saw the man in the window suddenly grimace, his shoulders hunched in an unnatural way, and collapse out of sight. I turned to Bryan and asked, "Did you see that? I hit that fucking guy!"

---

* A calibration feature of the rifle scope that permits accurate visual adjustments by shifting, or "holding off," from the intended point of impact.

"No, all I saw was the back of your head," Bryan said. I had fired before he'd gotten lined up on the target.

Sergeant Thompson, one of the squad leaders from the Alpha Company platoon under fire, showed up about this time to help us coordinate our fire on the insurgents in the hospital. He looked at me with the M24 and asked, "Why are you shooting *that*? Why aren't you shooting the Barrett?"

Well, I used the M24 because it was the first sniper rifle I could grab, but Sergeant Thompson was right. The M107 Barrett's .50cal round was much more appropriate for the range and the nature of the targets. We set the Barrett up, supporting it on a windowsill, and I started methodically putting rounds into the windows at the top of the building.

Capt. Jerry Coburn, the Alpha Company commander, called on the radio about this time, and he said, "We're still taking fire from the hospital—engage!" Captain Coburn started spotting our hits for us, almost like a forward observer does for an artillery battery. I put rounds into each of the windows that faced the roof, working my way along that side of the building, shooting into any place that could hide enemy threats. I fired thirty-five or forty rounds from the Barrett before two Apache helicopters showed up with their cannon. The squad from Alpha Company popped smoke to cover their movement and began to pull back from the engagement.

It seemed like a very long time but probably only took a few minutes. The other snipers in the room and I were all worried about who had been hurt and how badly. We continued to scan the area for threats while we speculated on what had happened . . . and to whom. I had a hunch Jason had been shot because he was such a big target and because he was so casual about using cover. But we continued to monitor the area because the insurgents often moved in after firefights to collect and record anything of propaganda value; they would videotape blood on the ground, for example, and then broadcast it with a story about how many Americans had been killed. We were looking for the guys with the cameras and anybody else that looked suspicious while Alpha withdrew.

One of the guys on Shadow Team, Sgt. Samuel, had been especially close with Jason and their wives were also best friends. The news that Jason had been killed made for an especially somber evening.

Nothing much was said at the time about the shot that killed the insurgent who probably had killed Jason. We all knew it was an extreme shot, and a lucky one, but our thoughts were more on the loss of Staff Sergeant Benford than anything else. A British reporter showed up, Toby Harnden from the London *Telegraph,* and he was the one who got excited about the 1,250-meter shot. A newspaper article that we thought would be about Shadow Team ended up being about that one shot, and it brought me more attention than I wanted.

We heard later that the kill had been confirmed—somebody went up to the hospital building and to the room where I engaged the man with the rifle and found an insurgent dead on the floor with a single bullet wound to the chest.

TERMINAL BALLISTICS

The effect of a hit on a human target varies tremendously. Part of the effect has to do with what the target is doing at the time of impact. A hit on an enemy during a firefight, when he is running hard and his blood is heavily oxygenated and loaded with adrenaline, will be much less immediately incapacitating than an identical hit on the same guy who is placing an IED or walking down the street. In the first case, the guy can take a shot and not even feel it; he can keep fighting for a considerable length of time before he bleeds out, loses consciousness, and is finally incapacitated. Unless you hit this second guy in the brain stem or a bone that prevents mechanical movement, he may have a fatal wound but he has seconds or even minutes to keep fighting, and he can still kill you or other people during that time.

WHAT-IFS

Even before Shadow Team and Two-Six-nine deployed, we spent a lot of time discussing how we would deal with different scenarios, war-gaming all the likely and unlikely possibilities we could face in combat. This paid off on our second major engagement: "What do we do if we engage an insurgent, and then the local bad guys decide to use the occasion to come out in force and take us on? If you suddenly have several targets instead of one, what will you do?"

We decided that in a large firefight, when you are outnumbered, putting the enemy down immediately is more important than killing them immediately. That means that our policy under such conditions was to aim at the center of mass, even at the risk of not making an instantaneously incapacitating hit, rather than take the extra time required to make a head shot that would be instantly incapacitating. The head shot takes much more time to execute; if you miss, you have an alert enemy target that will take cover and be even harder to get. You have wasted time that permitted the enemy to maneuver or engage you. Our policy was to get good hits on as many bad guys as possible, as fast as possible.

I gave one of the guys a bad time about such a shot. He made a head shot on an insurgent and killed him. But I told him afterward, "It does no good to miss a head shot when you can make a body shot! If you hit a guy in the chest, he is going to be out of the fight pretty soon, and he isn't going to get away. If you miss a head shot, you have real problems when other guys are maneuvering on you. If you can hit five guys in the chest in the same amount of time it takes to immediately kill two, you'll be much better off than if you have two dead guys on the ground and three healthy guys putting fire on your position. If you put all five down wounded, once things slow down a bit and you have more time, then that is the time to shoot them again and kill them." And we ran into such situations later and this war-gaming paid off.

Here's another scenario we considered: A car pulls up with an IED team of insurgents. Two guys get out of the back of the car; the driver stays where he is. We have two shooters who can engage—which target do you shoot first? Most people would say that you should shoot the IED team, but that's not how we planned it. Our SOP was to shoot the guy with the IED who was closest to cover and you shoot the driver. You save the second guy on the IED team until the guys who are most likely to escape are killed. The driver has the best chance of escape, and he dies immediately. The other two guys are on foot, exposed, and don't have many options for escape except to run. Even if you miss the third guy, you will still have a good chance of getting him on a follow-up shot.

War-gaming was the best thing we did to prepare for combat. The guys would come to me and ask, "What do we do if this happens, or that happens?" or, "In this situation, what would you do?" Rather than tell them what I would do, I got them to talk through the scenario and ask them what they thought made the most sense. This helped prepare each one of the team to make his own decisions without depending on me to come up with the right answer every time. I knew that there would be plenty of times when the other guys would be in a hide when I was not present and targets would appear. If they had to wait for approval from me or anybody else, the target would be gone; they had to understand when and how they should engage or not engage.

I was very fortunate to lead Shadow Team. I had some of the very best soldiers and snipers anybody could ask for. The personalities all meshed really well—it was like working with a dozen brothers, like being part of a family. During our time in Ramadi we all lived in the same room; we all cooked and ate together, and did everything as a family and a team. Of course some of us would go off on missions at times while others on the team had different assignments for the day or the week. The guys usually called me Sergeant G, but otherwise we were on a first-name or nickname basis. My attitude was that in a combat environment where the level of danger was very high and where we needed to depend on each other for our safety and to accomplish our missions, a leader has to treat each member of the team like an adult, not like a child who has to be told what to do and when to do it. That means having guys you can trust to solve problems by themselves when necessary.

KILLING

Nobody knows how they will respond emotionally to making a sniper kill until they do it the first time. Every one of us reacts somewhat differently. I have been told that I am an emotionless assassin, that normal people don't and can't talk about this kind of killing as if it were just any sort of common daily chore.

A sniper's work is not like any daily chore. On one occasion I had to shoot a little boy who was probably about eight years old, and here's why: The insurgents routinely used children as part of their operations, sometimes as shields, sometimes to act as lookouts, sometimes to signal when a convoy was about to pass an IED. We had a house in our area where this was being done repeatedly. We saw this kid making what seemed to be signals previously and tried to scare him off with a shot into the ground. Then a convoy approached and he started signaling again; an IED detonated next to a Bradley and it stopped. While the crew escaped the vehicle, some of them on fire, one of the other Bradleys moved up to provide security, and another IED blew up near it. When we looked back where the kid had been, we could see him on the roof of the home, directing a group of insurgents who were moving up to attack the convoy now that it was stopped and vulnerable. I got on the radio and discussed the situation with our command and we both agreed that there was hostile intent. An adult behaving this way would have already been shot, but when a child is involved, the situation is different. We made the decision to shoot him.

One of my soldiers Spc. Aaron Arnold, was covering that area and normally it would have been his shot, but not this time. It was not something that you tell somebody else to do—I took it myself. I will not have one of my subordinates have emotional problems some-time in the future over a decision that was mine; if anybody is going to have emotional problems about such a shot, it ought to be me. I lined up on the kid and took the shot—and haven't really thought too much about it since then.

I don't know if I suppress the emotions that other people think I am supposed to feel, or if I have built such a strong moral case for each shot I have taken that I am emotionally protected. I have seen Americans being shot; I have personally witnessed insurgents plac-ing IEDs that have, in one case, killed seven Americans in a single detonation, seen the videos of the beheadings, seen how they treat each other. I have built a moral case for myself that justified the kind of shots I took. When I have not been sure of the circumstances, I have avoided taking a shot—and in one case I let a man walk that I ought to have killed. He turned out to have been the number four man on the Ramadi Most Wanted list; I had him in my sights but let him go because I wasn't sure.

ALL YOU FEEL IS THE RECOIL

"All you feel is the recoil" is an old stock answer for the question war-riors sometimes get from people who never have to kill anything at all. For those of us who are professional war fighters, that has to be essentially true. It takes a certain kind of emotional approach to be able to look at somebody through the scope and make the decision to kill them, and then to put the scope on somebody else and kill them, too, and then go off for dinner or a nap. It may be that I will have psychological problems with these kills some time in the future, and if I do, I will deal with them at that time. For now, my conscience is clear.

You can train to be an infantryman for a whole career, but you will never know for sure how you're going to react in combat until somebody finally decides to shoot at you with the intention of killing you. Snipers train for years by shooting at all kinds of targets that are supposed to simulate the human form, but until you have a living person under your crosshairs and the authority to pull the trigger on that person, you don't know what you will actually do.

Some snipers have written in books that they always remember the eyes of the men they killed, that they have a memory of each person they shot . . . but I don't. I do remember the tactical situations, what the targets were wearing, their general appearance, but not what their faces looked like. What I can say about each one is that I positively identified them as legitimate military threats that met the rules of engagement, and I took the appropriate action on them after that.

ONE AND A HALF SHOTS, ONE KILL

Snipers train to make the first shot at a target an immediate killing shot—the saying is, "One shot, one kill." One-shot kills are possible when you're firing at targets for qualification on the range, but that ideal is not the way it actually works under combat conditions. I've made some one-shot kills, but real-world sniper teams don't deal with the exact kind of threats and the same kind of situations that are taught in school. Often the first shot misses and part of the sniper and spotter's business is to use that first miss to make a correction that results in a kill.

When we make these kinds of kills, the enemy is completely surprised. He doesn't know we've been watching him, evaluating his behavior, making a life-or-death decision about him. If we see somebody watching a patrol, for example, and he comes up with binoculars and a cell phone and seems to be reporting on the location and direction of the patrol's movements, that fits the criteria for hostile intent and we can shoot him. For example, I watched a young man in his teens casually walk to a position where he could watch one of our units; there was something about his manner that seemed odd, and, sure enough, he ducked down into a car, still watching the patrol, and came up with a pair of binos. He was safe until he produced the binos, and that was what killed him. I put three shots into him before he could get off a report, and he slumped over the wheel.

This kind of engagement was fairly common. The local insurgents seemed to think their observers could work in safety, and the hotel where we had set up our operations was right in their faces. We took a building in the middle of their hostile town and we dominated their terrain. The more we used this building to our advantage, the more the local enemy wanted to destroy the hotel and us. This resulted in several large-scale engagements.

My sniper team and Sgt. Seneca Locklear's team went out to set up a hide where we could overwatch a building where a raid would be conducted by the infantry later the same day. Alpha Company provided a machine-gun team as a security element for us. We got into our hide and began observing the building under suspicion.

Not long after we started watching, I noticed a vehicle pull up for the second time. The car looked familiar—it was a station wagon and had some distinctive features that matched a car we had seen near an IED attack a few days previously. At the time there was no way to connect the car with the blast, but here it was again and we started paying attention to it. The driver dropped off a few men outside the building and drove off—and five or six minutes later he pulled up again to drop off another few men, all of military age. There was a pattern to what we were seeing—the men always walked over to a man by the road, spoke to him for a few moments, and then moved off into an alley. Two other cars, a white Capri and a Datsun four-door taxi, were dropping men off at the same time, and between them all, they must have delivered about thirty military-age men to this particular location.

We got on the radio and reported all this. Something was obviously happening, but just what was not apparent. The man outside seemed to be pulling security, but there was nothing that would permit us to engage anybody. But when the raid was executed a short time later, the building turned out to have a large sand-table terrain model of the area around our forward operating base. These men were planning an attack on our base. We thwarted a major attack without firing a shot, just by observation.

Anybody can pull a trigger; anybody can hit a target at long range with modern weapons. I could teach a monkey how to shoot—but there is so much more to being a sniper! The art of the sniper is in being able to get into position without being noticed, to be able to observe for long periods and to know what you are seeing, to make a precision long-range shot if and when appropriate, and to make tactically useful reports by radio. A sniper's work is a lot like hunting; you have to go where the targets are likely to be, then set up your ambush and wait in an alert and prepared way. The actual shot, if there is one, is one very small part of the process.

SNIPER EMPLOYMENT

Our last six months were very successful professionally for Shadow Team. The first six months of our first deployment were not very productive; we were able to do a few engagements but were otherwise mostly misused. Our chain of command was reluctant to turn us loose and let us operate away from a larger security force. They didn't want us to be out of direct communication unless a quick reaction force (QRF) was ready to extract us in an emergency. We were on a short leash during this period and didn't do anybody much good. We were used to provide marksmanship training for the Iraqi army and sometimes as a show of force, and we helped on some clearing operations.

That changed on our first mission of the second six months. We killed three enemy insurgents putting in an IED on that mission, and the engagement validated our team with our command group, who then began to let us off the leash.

The first six months were spent in open farmland areas among a population that was somewhat friendly. Then we went to the town of Ramadi, where everybody hated us. The IED threat was high at the time and many of our missions were intended to reduce this threat. We spent a lot of time early in the deployment overwatching the population from hide sites and getting to know the patterns of the place. It didn't take too long to notice a young Iraqi man walking down the street with the clothing, posture, grooming, and swagger that fit the pattern of the guys who were placing the IEDs. You would see somebody like that and say, "Okay, something is about to go down, and that guy is involved in making it happen!" Soon another guy would join this guy, then a car would show up—the right kind of car, the kind of car we learned to expect—and all of the pieces would fall into place. Learning to understand the patterns and the subtle clues took us about a month and a half, but then we really started to score. At that time and in that place, the insurgents were very predictable.

We spent a lot of time studying the maps and overhead photographs of the town. Just by looking at these maps and evaluating the

marks that indicated insurgent activity, we were able to anticipate locations where something bad was probably about to happen. Over a
period of a few weeks, we were able to validate our team with the
chain of command, and they began to trust us to conduct our own
operations with a minimum of support. Our deal with them was essentially this: "We can sustain ourselves in our hide sites for extended periods without any help and with reasonable security—but
if we call for help, we expect somebody to come and get us out before
we can be rolled up. Let us go and we'll produce results for you!"
Once they saw what we could do, that's just what happened.

Our first real adventure began as we took over from the team that
had been in place prior to our arrival, a procedure called relieve in
place, from the 503rd. They showed us around and indicated where
incidents had happened. They had very little luck in their previous
year. During our briefing they told us the local insurgents knew
where the sniper teams were, and they were expert at avoiding detection. The team made only a few shots during their deployment, and
they told us to expect the same results.

Part of this hand-over process involved looking at a lot of photographs, and our first clue that things might not be quite as advertised was when we were handed a photo of a peaceful, quiet
neighborhood—and the photo showed an insurgent placing an IED!
We missed that the first time we looked at the photo but saw it later
when we knew better what to look for.

Not long before a large cache of weapons and munitions had been
found in an industrial area within our area of operation (AO) so we
decided to set up nearby. About 0200 one morning we took over an
abandoned building overwatching a block with many small auto-
repair shops and similar businesses, and we set up out of sight in a
building nearby.

We lay there and sweated for about eighteen hours without seeing anything clearly related to insurgents, but our suspicions were

raised by the amount of traffic going in and out of one of the car-repair garages. We called the QRF out to inspect the place, but before they could arrive a car pulled up next to one of the trash piles outside the shop.

We split the team before this so we could watch more of the area, so not all of us could see what happened next: there were four guys in the car, and one got out, walked around to the back, and popped the trunk lid. Sam and another guy were watching that direction, and when one of the guys pulled out a 155mm projectile—which was already prepared as an IED—the two of them could not believe what was happening right in front of them. They could see that a lump of plastic explosive was in the fuse well and the wires leading to the electrical blasting cap were clearly visible. All three insurgents were relaxed and cheerful, apparently joking with each other and appearing to feel entirely secure. They were only sixty meters away from us!

All of us were astounded. Somebody said, "You've got to be shitting me!" Because of the close range and the angle, we didn't have a very good firing position in our hide—we had expected targets farther out. Sam and I grabbed our weapons and went out on the roof. In the few seconds this took, the insurgents got another IED from the trunk and hid both under some trash and were on their way back to their car.

All four of us opened up with our M4s. The windshield shattered, and glass was flying everywhere. Someone methodically engaged the car, intending to disable it and anybody inside . . . and setting fire to it in the process! The driver never got out of the vehicle, the guy in the front passenger seat got halfway out before he was hit, and the third guy was in front of the car when he went down. A fourth insurgent was hit but crawled out of the kill zone when we decided to get back behind cover. We had no cover on the roof, and now we had attracted a lot of attention from the neighbors.

ROADSIDE BOMBS AND IED TEAMS

The insurgents at that time were pretty predictable, and while they're doing things differently now, here's what they were doing in 2005:

We noticed a pattern of behavior in them that indicated they were about to place an IED. It started with an old man or a young kid who inspected a hole that had been previously dug. He'd stop, look in the hole, look around, look back at the hole, and then move on. If a kid was doing the inspection, he'd usually be more secretive about it, riding up on a bike, slowing down to check out the hole, then turning around and riding off.

Ten or fifteen minutes later a car would show up and drive past three or four times, slowing down to inspect the hole again, then drive away. Pretty soon, another car would come up and stop; this was the cover vehicle. Another car pulled up by the hole itself, and a third vehicle, usually a van, stopped behind the first two. This was the rear security and casualty-evacuation vehicle.

There were typically two men in the middle vehicle—they were the IED emplacement team. As long as they were not discovered, the device would be placed and the hole covered up, then the two men would get back in their car. Two vehicles would drive off in one direction; the third would leave in the opposite direction.

There were lots of variations on this pattern, and we watched one go down one morning. It was 11:30 in the morning, and we were watching a busy boulevard in Ramadi when we saw two men appear carrying a 155mm projectile. These things weigh about hundred pounds, so one of them had the front and the other carried the back. We saw them step off the sidewalk; traffic stopped to let them walk across the roadway with their heavy burden into the median. Traffic started up again and Iraqis went about their business as if all was normal. People on foot walked by and waved at the men in a friendly way.

Sergeant H had to engage these guys, but he had to wait until traffic cleared enough to give him a clear shot. While he waited, one of the two crossed back across the roadway while the other finished covering up the round.

That first engagement in Ramadi really impressed a lot of people, including the local populace. Until then, the insurgents got to decide when American soldiers had an opportunity to see them and to shoot at them in classic gunfights. When we killed those three insurgents, they had no idea we were around. They thought they were safe, and we killed them all. The message went out to all the other insurgents that they shouldn't feel safe just because no Americans could be seen in the area—American snipers could be watching from anywhere. We changed the rules of the game in Ramadi with that first engagement.

It took a few days for the word to get out. We had two or three similar engagements right away, then nothing for three weeks. We finally found out why: our S2 intel guys were intercepting phone calls between local insurgents and their leaders, and the conversations at this time were going something like this:

INSURGENT CELL LEADER (to local cell member): "I need to have you place an IED at the intersection of A and B streets."
LOCAL INSURGENT: "No. I can't go out there."
INSURGENT CELL LEADER: "What do you mean, 'no'?"
LOCAL INSURGENT: "If I go out there, the American snipers will shoot me dead."

That is one of the ways snipers "make money" for the tactical commanders, and that is how snipers help shape the battlefield.

We shaped the battlefield in another way. In late August, a huge suicide-vehicle-borne IED (VBIED) was detonated outside a major hotel at the edge of our AO. This hotel was at a critical location and was heavily guarded. It adjoined our forward operating base (FOB), and the main supply route, MSR Michigan, passed close by the front of the building. The Marines had an AO of their own nearby. IEDs had been used frequently by the insurgents in the area, and the VBIED was an attempt to escalate the pressure on all American and Iraqi units in the neighborhood.

The explosives were carried by a dump truck that evaded detection until it turned a corner and made its run on the hotel. At that point the security forces opened up on the truck, alerting everybody in the building to take cover. The explosion knocked everybody down but, aside from some broken arms and legs, no serious injuries were sustained. Had the truck been able to get a little closer, the whole building might have come down.

While ordinarily we prefer to operate from clandestine hides that are occupied for short periods, we decided to set up a static hide at this location. On the roof of the building was a smaller utility shack that provided a commanding view of the neighborhood and was sturdy enough to provide both cover and concealment. We used a sledgehammer to punch a couple of discrete holes in the walls, then proceeded to turn the place into our little penthouse and started looking for trouble.

It didn't take long to show up. On the third day we noticed a guy acting suspiciously at the window of a building across the street; he was the trigger man for two car bombs. We saw him detonate them, and then we killed him.

That stopped the IEDs in the area immediately, including the MSR and the whole area under our observation. At the time we went into that static hide, the hotel was surrounded by enemy observers as close as two hundred meters. We began engaging these targets and taking them out. Within a few days, there were no more enemy observers across the street, but they had pulled back to about four hundred meters, where they thought they would be safer. We killed those observers, too. Then they tried it from about six hundred meters, and we methodically killed those insurgents as well whenever they appeared. After a month or so all the insurgents were pushed out to around eight hundred meters, or a half mile, from the hotel. Nobody approached the hotel unless our team decided they were safe.

The insurgents became frustrated. They couldn't engage us with direct fire because we killed them as soon as they appeared. They couldn't engage us with indirect fire because of the terrain and the friendly patrols. We shut down their VBIED missions before the vehicles could get close enough to do damage. So they tried another technique: false propaganda.

They started circulating reports through the sheiks and imams that American snipers on the top of this hotel were shooting women and children. They knew that if such claims were made loudly and forcefully enough, political pressure might shut us down.

Sure enough, we had to talk to the battalion commander, the operations staff, and others who were worried that we might be committing atrocities. We showed them all our rules-of-engagement criteria and proved our point—we only engaged positively identified military targets. Then somebody pointed out that no women or children had been shot in the area, that there had never been any bodies of women or children found during our mission. Our commander was convinced, and we went back to work killing bad guys.

THE M4 CARBINE AS A SNIPER WEAPON

The "one shot, one kill" motto of the sniper profession is a fine goal, but that is not the way it worked for us. Of course we had M24 sniper rifles, but we used our M4 carbines to make many of our kills. When you are confronted with multiple targets at the same time, you can't effectively engage them with an M24 bolt gun. The M24 lets you make very precise shots on individual targets at long range, but what we encountered were situations were we had multiple targets in front of us at various ranges, and we needed to be able to engage them all very quickly. It is essential to kill all of them, not just one or two, and a bolt gun is too slow under such circumstances. The M4s and ammunition we were issued were virtually as accurate and effective out to around eight hundred meters as the M24 and M118 ammunition.

I am a very strong advocate for the Designated Marksman program, a great idea that is paying off very well! My rack-grade M4 was modified with a suppressor, a match-grade trigger, and an ACOG sight, and it was making first-round hits at 730 meters! The Mk262 77-grain Black Hills ammunition is by far the preferred ammunition for the M4—it is deadly! It provides reliable first hit incapacitation. We've had incidents where enemy insurgents have been shot and hit in the same place at the same distance with the 77-grain Black Hills round and the standard Army 62-grain bullet; the first guy was dead when he hit the ground, the guy hit with the lighter bullet was patched up and lived.

Our battalion surgeon saw the two wounds and thought one was from an M4's 5.56mm round, the other and more deadly wound from an M24's 7.62mm round. He was as surprised as the rest of us to see how effective the heavier bullet could be in the carbine.

After that second engagement in Ramadi where we saw how well it performed, every one of the team got rid of the old "green tip" rounds and loaded up our mags with the new ammo. It was so much more effective and accurate! With our modified rack-grade M4 carbines, we were able to shoot sub-MOA (minute of angle). This combination did everything we wanted a rifle to do.

As much as we liked the M4, our primary weapon remained the M24, and we all spent a lot of our first six months war-gaming different scenarios. When we were just sitting around with nothing else to do, we discussed how we would react if certain events occurred—kind of like the immediate action drills all infantrymen conduct. These discussions helped us anticipate what we would do, for example, if something unusual happened.

Ordinarily, we wanted to have the primary shooter with the M24 and the guy next to him—normally the spotter but on our team usually a backup shooter—both on their weapons, ready to fire. The school solution has the second man on the spotting scope to help the shooter know where his rounds are hitting. That's fine if you have only one guy to shoot at and he is at long range, but within our normal engagement ranges, getting on target was not a problem. The problem was that we needed to engage three or six targets that might appear at three hundred meters for a few seconds, then disappear. We wanted to kill them all, not just one. So in these kinds of circumstances, we both fired at the same time. "On your shot," I told Sam or whoever was on the M24, "and that will be my cue to start engaging."

Our normal SOP was to go quietly into an area, be as unobtrusive as possible, and to watch what was happening without the local population knowing we were there.

We walked everywhere within our AO, a box on the map about two kilometers by two kilometers. This was somewhat unique in that area at that time. Only after we had engaged a target and needed to be extracted did we call for vehicles to come get us. Since there were only six or eight of us, the conventional guys thought we were nuts for operating this way since we had comparatively little firepower. On the other hand, we thought they were nuts because they were dependent on their vehicles and the vehicles restricted their movements and their situational awareness, and made them easier targets.

Our first mission was in support of a large battalion-sized show-of-force mission that kicked off in the middle of the night. One of the maneuver elements discovered what they thought was an IED hole—it had been prepared, but the explosive device had not been implanted. We got a call about 0400 to move from where we had been supporting the patrols to a hide site where we could watch the suspected IED hole. About two hundred meters from the site, while we were well off the road, we noticed a man walking from the direction of the hole with a shovel over his shoulder. Through our NODs, we could see him glancing around in a somewhat nervous manner, and the very early hour made us very suspicious. I called in a spot report, and they replied, "You're cleared to engage."

I had the M4 and put the laser spot on him, fired a couple of rounds, and he went down. We stayed in position, watching to see what else might come down the road, and about five minutes later we see the guy I shot is moving around. We moved up and discovered that I had hit him in the knee, not the chest where I had been aiming! Well, I tried to figure out what went wrong and realized that my primary M68 sight had been re-zeroed recently, but I had neglected to align the laser at the same time. You can imagine the kidding I got for that! I was the battalion sniper team leader, supposedly the best shot in the battalion, and I nearly miss a guy at just two hundred meters!

During our first six months in Iraq, we got only two shots, and neither were really normal sniper missions with sniper rifles. The other engagement was right after our FOB had come under mortar attack. The observer for that attack was spotted fleeing in a van and my partner and I were in position to engage the vehicle with M4 carbines. We stopped the van and a platoon moved in to grab the insurgent.

That was it for the whole six months, and then we went to Ramadi. We had heard a lot of horror stories about the place, but when we met the outgoing team, they told us that we could expect few engagements here, too.

CHAPTER SIX

VOODOO BALLISTICS: SOMETIMES ONE SHOT, SOMETIMES ONE KILL

Killing a person with a rifle looks so easy in the movies. You grab a weapon with a scope, put the crosshairs on your victim far away, and press the trigger—and down they go. "One shot, one kill" is the sniper's motto; the real world is not nearly that simple and seldom will each shot result in a killing impact.

The problem of actually placing a bullet onto a real-world human target at conventional military-sniper-engagement ranges is more complicated than voodoo medicine, and sometimes with less chance of success. At ranges up to, say, 300 meters—a long city block—a rifle engagement is pretty straightforward and iron sights without adjustment will do the job. But out beyond 400 and 500 meters, and especially past 800 meters, things really get odd and interesting.

When you send a bullet downrange at a target, say, at one thousand meters, you can't point the weapon at the target and still hit it. You will actually point it at a spot far above the target, and, even if there is not a breath of wind, off to one side. At least a dozen different factors will influence the flight of the bullet and must be considered when you design your engagement and decide just where the crosshairs should be when the weapon discharges. There is a good reason why snipers carry little data books with them, use calculators loaded with ballistic-solution software, glue data tables on the stocks of their rifles, and that is that the wide, wonderful world of ballistics is damn complicated.

One factor is, of course, the effect of gravity that will pull at the bullet the moment it leaves the muzzle. Air resistance slows the bullet as it rips downrange; the density of the air shapes its lethal trajectory, making the ballistic curve lopsided and steeper toward the end of its journey. But air density changes with variations in altitude, with humidity, and with temperature, each adding one new piece to the engagement puzzle that must be factored in by the sniper. All other things being the same, at high altitude your bullet will impact higher than it would at sea level.

The specific kind of ammunition used is another factor. There are often large performance variations between lots of the same type with the same bullet and the same propellant load from the same manufacturer. Marine and Army snipers normally fire M118LR cartridges produced by the Lake City Ammunition Plant, each built around a Sierra Match King open-tip boat-tail projectile. These cartridges are manufactured to extremely high standards, with very tight tolerances, and are carefully tested before shipping, but even so, some lots are more consistent than others. New lots are tested by units in the field. Snipers and long-range competitive shooters say that individual rifles "digest" different ammunition loads in different ways, and they are not surprised when ammunition that performs well in one rifle performs less so in another.

The temperature of the propellant in the cartridge can have a very large influence on velocity, and velocity is also connected to the shape of the ballistic curve. A cartridge that has heated in the sun and is twenty degrees warmer than a 70-degree cartridge that has been pulled from deep inside a rucksack will strike its target twenty inches higher at one thousand meters. A twenty-inch variation at a thousand meters will put you right off the target, and it is only one factor of many that will influence the fall of the shot. Snipers need to add that factor to the puzzle, especially when operating in extreme cold environments, like the wide-open spaces of Afghanistan in winter.

The one major variable, the one that will drive you nuts when trying to make a tough shot at extreme range, is wind. Even a gentle breeze will move the bullet significantly at ranges more than three hundred meters; at six hundred or eight hundred meters, the movement can be feet instead of inches. So you dig out your handy Kestrel wind-speed gauge to measure the velocity—one more factor to plug into the calculator—and it shows 10mph from left to right. Well, if you're standing on a rooftop in Ramadi or a ridge in Paktika Province, Afghanistan, that measurement is good only for the spot where it was taken—the wind one hundred meters downrange might be 22mph from right to left, dead calm at the two-hundred-meter point, 5mph at a quartering angle from the left at three hundred meters, and so on, all the way to the target. Wind is tremendously variable from one place to another, and wind has a very powerful effect on the projectile's flight downrange. Snipers learn to read the wind at intermediate distances by watching laundry on a clothesline, leaves on trees, the movement of grass at the edge of a road, the way a scrap of paper flutters across a sidewalk. From these observations they make a calibrated guess about what the wind will do while the bullet flies toward its target.

Then there is the individual rifle itself. There are about 3,500 M24s in the inventory, and each one is slightly different from the rest. No two of them are likely to have fired exactly the same number of cartridges, and each cartridge fired will leave its legacy. Every time a rifle is fired, the burning propellant, acting at high pressure and temperature, erodes the throat area of the chamber a tiny bit. The throat is a critical area of a sniper rifle's anatomy; it's the place where the bullet first engages the rifling and starts its brief journey down the bore. A 7.62mm NATO rifle, like the M24 or M40, is expected to last about ten thousand rounds before this area is so eroded that the barrel must be replaced. Heavier calibers, like the .338 Lapua and .300 Winchester Magnum (WinMag), are good only for a thousand rounds at best. As in any kind of manufacture, there are tolerances and variations in the manufacture of the barrel itself. Some barrels shoot better than others—same manufacturer, same lot, same everything—so one barrel will print a smaller group of shots than the next.

Another factor related to the rifle, and a huge one, will be if the barrel is clean and cold or warm and fouled with a thin layer of copper molecules left by a projectile. Snipers record two "zeros": one for the first shot out of the gun after cleaning (a "cold-bore shot"), another for the second and subsequent shots when there is propellant residue in the bore. A typical cold-bore shot from my M24 will hit one inch high and one inch to the right at one hundred meters, or ten inches at a thousand meters, from the point of impact made by the second shot out of the same gun, all other things being equal—something else to consider when setting up a shot.

Now, suppose you are up on a ridge in your cozy little hide and you identify a target in the valley far below. Your laser range finder measures the range at exactly one thousand meters from your position. Do you get to calculate the shot with that thousand-meter range? No, you don't, and if you did you'd miss, because the slant angle from horizontal is also a factor in your ballistic solution. If you are shooting down at a forty-five-degree angle at a target one thousand meters from your position, the effective range for your sight adjustments is just 707 meters—you'd probably hit well above your target with a one-thousand-meter sight setting. You aim low when shooting uphill or down.

All these elements make sight alignment difficult enough, but now the whole business gets really strange. When a bullet is fired, the rifling—the spiral lands and grooves inside the bore—force the projectile to rotate around its axis, and this rotation partially stabilizes it by gyroscopic effect. For example, a bullet fired in a rifle that has rifling with twelve-inch twist will spin once for each twelve inches of travel downrange, or thirty-six hundred times in one thousand yards of travel. The voodoo effect of this rotation is that it makes the bullet swim, or drift, a bit in the direction of the twist, so your projectile doesn't just curve in the vertical direction but, like a curve ball in baseball, it moves laterally as well. The phenomenon, called spindrift, can move the point of impact several inches at one thousand yards in a no-wind situation. Since there is almost always some wind, long-range sight-alignment calculation factors in spindrift as well as wind effect. In a gentle 5mph breeze the two can move the bullet two and a half feet to the right at a thousand yards, good enough for a clean miss.

If that isn't enough to make you want to find another line of military business, the whole issue of voodoo ballistics gets even worse—the rotation of the earth becomes yet another factor in long shots. At the moment the bullet leaves the bore of the rifle, its destiny is fixed. During that shot's time of flight—a second and a half or so—the earth will be rotating underneath the bullet and the place where its target was at the moment of departure will move slightly before the bullet arrives. How much that point on the ground moves in that second and a half relative to the point of aim varies with the direction of the shot and where on the earth's surface the shot is made, but it can be several inches in long-range real-world engagements. Depending on these factors, the point of impact may move up or down, left or right, from the point of aim. In close-range engagements the effect is too small to be a factor. But when you're making 2,500- or 3,000-meter shots with an M107, as some snipers have been doing, it is a factor to add in with all the others.

So how do snipers deal with such a complex set of variables when a guy with an RPG is visible on a rooftop four blocks away and he needs to be shot and killed promptly? There are actually two very practical methods.

The first is to keep the number of actual variables to a minimum. Snipers do this by carefully zeroing their weapons, that is, recording cold-bore and second-shot settings for every batch of ammunition, at both anticipated normal engagement ranges and under conditions as close to expected temperature, altitude, humidity, and other environmental factors. For police snipers, that would be at one hundred meters because a high percentage of SWAT sniper shots are at very close range. For SEAL snipers in the open desert, a six-hundred-meter zero, or longer, will insure the scope is set for something close to a routine engagement range. Zeroing the rifle automatically incorporates all the individual variables—spindrift, earth rotation, density-altitude—from one rifle to the next, one lot of ammunition to the next, and can approximate most of the environmental variables, too. This will make the weapon good to go right out of the bag for most engagements. The shooter reads the wind, estimates its effect for the shot, and either holds dead on or holds off (that is, to modify the aim to compensate for windage) if he's in a hurry. If he has a little time, he can crank some adjustments into the scope, but most snipers prefer to hold off.

If you're sitting up on a ridge and waiting for targets down below, you know well in advance that your shots will go high unless you compensate, so a practical sniper will template his battlefield in advance; that is, he'll figure out where he will probably have targets and estimate or measure the angles and ranges to those places. Then he can calculate in his head how much to hold off. If a target pops up someplace unexpected, up the hill or down, he knows that he needs to hold low either way—how much will depend on the angle and the distance, but that's why snipers spend a lot of time training at the range, to build experience and knowledge. That is also why snipers carry and maintain a detailed logbook and record of every shot fired.

Then there is the really easy way to solve the ballistics problem. The motto at sniper school may be "one shot, one kill," which is fine for shots out to four hundred or five hundred meters or so—but in the real world, especially at the longer ranges beyond seven hundred meters, you make sure your spotter is on the glass, make a shot, then make an adjustment from where the first one struck. This solution incorporates all the voodoo ballistics data in one easy solution—wind, slant, propellant temperature, barrel wear, and the rest. You just hold off to compensate for the difference between the point of aim and point of impact, then send another one downrange. At extreme ranges the bullet may be subsonic and your target may not even notice that he's under fire until the second round connects, and then it is too late for him to care.

All this relates to what happens before the trigger is pulled—the process of designing a shot that has a high probability of connecting with its target on the first try—but we still haven't pressed that trigger. The whole business of a long-range shot gets even more complicated when you look at the evolution of an actual engagement.

"Target!" calls your partner. "RPG gunner on the roof at twelve o'clock, to the left of the laundry, looking over the edge and preparing to fire."

"I see him."

"Range—one thousand meters exactly. Zero wind—no correction. Come up eight and three.* Engage!"

"Shooter up!

"Spotter up! Send it!"

It takes a few seconds to get your breathing under control, get the

---

* Eight minutes of angle plus another three clicks on the scope vertical adjustment turret.

crosshairs settled on the distant target. He's moving around, peeking over the edge down into the street where an American patrol is operating, getting ready to put his RPG into the vulnerable roof of a Humvee, a Bradley, or an Abrams tank. He moves to the edge of the roof and stands still, taking aim. Breathe. Exhale. Breathe. Crosshairs stable on center of mass. Take up trigger slack. Partial exhale. Maintain sight picture. Press, press, press . . . *blam!*

Although a shot seems to begin and end in an instant, snipers are very aware of all the things that transpire in the second and a half between the moment when the trigger breaks and the moment when the bullet comes to rest half a mile away. They know, for example, that the mechanical process of firing the cartridge takes time, and things can happen during that time. A delay of twenty-two thousandths of a second occurs between the instant when the mechanical trigger unlatches, releasing the firing pin; the pin moves forward and strikes the primer, initiating the combustion of the propellant. In that tiny fraction of a fraction of a second, a walking human target will move about an inch, and a running target about two inches—not much, but enough to begin to dodge a bullet.

The little primer at the base of the cartridge contains a tiny amount of explosive. When the firing pin finally strikes the primer and compresses this explosive against a tiny anvil, the material detonates and is consumed in about one thousandth of a second. The flash ignites some of the propellant in the cartridge, and it begins to burn rather than explode. The pressure inside the cartridge case rapidly builds, and when the pressure is great enough to break the bonds of friction that hold the bullet in the neck of the case, it begins to move forward.

Ideally the bullet will be just touching the breech end of the rifling before it is fired, and the bullet will engage the spiral lands immediately. The bullet is designed to be a perfect match with the diameter of the bore, sealing the propellant gasses as they increase in pressure and forcing the projectile down the tube.

That propellant doesn't burn up all at once. Some of it will be pushed down the bore behind the bullet, gradually being ignited and adding more pressure to accelerate the projectile off on its short, rapid journey.

All this sudden pressure and heat is a shock to the rifle and it reacts in several dynamic ways, all too quickly to notice without instrumentation, but each influencing the flight of the bullet. In one of these reactions, the barrel actually expands a bit as the bullet moves down the bore, like a snake eating an animal. The barrel whips, too, and rings like a bell. Sniper rifle barrels are free floating (nothing touches them from receiver to muzzle) so that they may vibrate freely. As the bullet is pushed down the bore and forced to rotate by the rifling, the rifle itself reacts by twisting in the opposite direction.

When the bullet is finally spit out of the muzzle, it is, even in the best rifles, somewhat unstable. It wobbles a bit, yaws a few degrees, before its rotation and gyroscopic forces make it more stable. But all the way downrange, the best bullets from the best rifles will always have a bit of yaw and will wobble slightly during flight.

As the projectile leaves the muzzle, it has been accelerated from a full stop to about 2,400 feet per second in a space of twenty-four inches. That is about 1,636 miles per hour, well over the speed of sound at sea level. Air resistance immediately slows the bullet, and as it slows its trajectory becomes steeper and its retained energy rapidly diminishes. After two or three seconds of flight the bullet is far slower and has far less energy left to smite the foe.

Until the bullet slows to about half its initial velocity, it will be moving faster than the speed of sound and creating its own little sonic boom as it zips through the air. Actually, it is more of a crack than a boom, and it is a very distinctive sound, particularly if you have ever heard it from a bullet intended for you, yourself.

But when the bullet slows enough, odd things may happen. As it goes subsonic, the bullet may become very unstable and tumble through the air end over end. This will slow it even more, and it will quickly run out of steam and fall to the ground. If you are in the vicinity of a bullet that has slowed to subsonic velocity, you won't hear that warning crack. The projectile may make a bit of noise when it impacts, but it is common for people under fire at long range to not notice near misses unless the impacts are revealed in other ways.

As it zips downrange to fulfill its destiny, the bullet slows, wobbles, drifts in the direction of its spin, is buffeted by wind currents, and may or may not begin to tumble when it goes subsonic. The amount of energy retained by the little bullet is gradually drained away until, at extreme range, you may hit a target without having enough energy left to do it much damage, and damage is what the bullet is supposed to do. This is called terminal ballistics, the dark and deadly story of what the bullet actually does when it strikes its victim.

This story of the terminal effects of rifle fire is the fundamental topic of warfare with individual weapons. If you can get past the usual squeamishness about the blood and gore, it's a fascinating topic. The behavior of a bullet on a body is a lot more complicated than you'd think. In addition, the behavior of a person who has been hit by a bullet is also extremely complicated. The study of both is part of sniper training.

When you fire at a target during training at sniper school or in most other American military programs, you are presented with a piece of paper or steel target about the size of a human head and torso. This target is about twenty inches wide and about fifty inches high. Hit that target anywhere and you normally score a kill and get credit for your shot. In the real world, when you actually fire at a human figure, the business is tremendously more complicated. You can hit a real human's torso with a bullet—sometimes several bullets— and he may not even notice. People are hard to kill.

For example, a friend of mine, a police officer, and his patrol partner were attacked by a man armed with an edged weapon and under the influence of drugs. The two officers fired on the attacker with their 9mm handguns from close range. The assailant was hit nine times, seven in the torso, before he finally fell to the ground. He remained combative until he bled out and lost consciousness en route to a hospital.

Here's another example: Many soldiers in Iraq and Afghanistan report shooting and hitting enemy combatants with 5.56mm bullets from their M16s and M4s, sometimes inflicting "through and through" wounds that go in the front of the body and out the back without immediately incapacitating their target. These targets didn't realize they had been killed and continued to fight. That's not the way targets behave during training!

Just because you put a bullet on target downrange does not mean that your victim will behave in the way intended. As with the flight of the bullet, what actually happens depends on many factors.

The ideal effect in a normal engagement is that the bullet produces a wound cavity that begins almost immediately on entry and that damages and disrupts bone, blood vessels, organs, and muscle in a fairly massive way. This massive shock to the body will begin the process of inflicting death, and will sometimes immediately incapacitate a person, but sometimes they don't seem to notice—at least, not right away.

This effect requires that the bullet have enough energy left to penetrate the layers of clothing, skin, fat, muscle, and bone that protect the organs inside the chest cavity. When maximum-effective-range figures are published for cartridges like the M118LR, part of the calculations involved concern accuracy and part concern retained energy. You may actually hit a human target at, say, three thousand meters with an M118LR bullet, but its velocity and retained energy will be so low that it will penetrate only a short distance into a body and might even be stopped by clothing.

Even when a person is shot in the torso within effective range, the immediate effect will vary tremendously from person to person. In a common reaction, the muscle groups that provide upright posture and support immediately relax and the person drops straight to the ground. Sometimes the arms will fly upward, a phenomenon one high-scoring team called the wave. Head shots will sometimes result in a violent spasm when leg muscle groups suddenly and violently contract; as a result, the person seems to jump or leap in the air.

A person shot in the torso is not normally dead and may not be unconscious. He may have minutes or hours of life remaining. Sometimes a person with such ultimately mortal wounds will recover for a bit, pick up his weapon, and get back in the fight. In the wide, wonderful world of warfare, just because someone has been shot does not mean that you can forget about him as a threat. He can still kill you if he wants, and for many of them that is exactly what they want to do as their last living act.

Even if you manage to hit a person's aorta (the large blood-carrying vessel attached to the heart), your target will have about ten seconds of potential fight remaining before his lights go out. A great deal of what a mortally wounded person can do in those seconds and minutes will depend a lot on what part of his anatomy has been damaged, the level of adrenaline in his bloodstream, and his state of mind at the moment of injury. Persons who are excited and angry can be very formidable opponents even after they've been shot one or more times.

People remain still on the ground after being shot for a variety of reasons, not necessarily because they are unconscious. Movement may be painful. The shock of the event may be immobilizing. The fear of imminent death may also be immobilizing. Blood loss may not be great, despite one or more bullet wounds, and a human target may control bleeding with direct pressure or a tourniquet. Many people can recover from such injuries to be functional for a minute or an hour or longer. Like so many things in a fight, it depends.

Only two small areas of the human body will produce immediate incapacitation when hit by a bullet, and both are challenging real-world targets at any range. The heart muscle itself is one. Hit directly, death occurs almost instantly.

The other is the brain stem. Many people have been shot in the head and survived, but the brain stem, a lemon-sized area where the nerves of the spinal column meet the brain, is the target of choice when you absolutely need to make an instantaneous kill. The preferred point of aim for such a shot, when the target is facing the shooter in a normal erect posture, is the tip of the nose. The bullet will often shatter the skull when properly placed. A brain-stem hit results in instant relaxation and immediate death.

For all other hits, death is usually minutes away. Unless the wounds are somehow controlled, a human body leaks its essential juices internally or externally, a process called bleeding out. When enough blood has been lost for the person's blood pressure to fall so far that the heart can't function and oxygenated blood is no longer delivered to the brain, consciousness is lost. The person is still not quite dead but nearly so. The heart muscle will twitch and spasm for a bit, the brain's electrical functions will fail, and then all the muscles will completely relax. Shooting a person on the battle-field is a different experience from shooting a target on the range.

CHAPTER SEVEN

STAFF SGT. HARRY MARTINEZ

Harry Martinez is a former Marine and current member of the Pennsylva-nia National Guard. He is also a police officer in civilian life. Typical of many older and more mature National Guard soldiers, Martinez brings a great deal of experience and lessons learned from his day job and his previous careers to his military assignment. He was the team leader for Shadow Four during the many months of his deployment and has many confirmed kills.

I come from a very patriotic family, it's one of the reasons I joined the National Guard at the age of seventeen, as a junior in high school, and then spent five years in telecommunications. I liked the military but this commo assignment was very boring. The older guys in the unit kept talking about men with more exciting and danger-ous jobs—Marines and Rangers and Green Berets—with a kind of rev-erence and awe. I thought to myself, *I don't want to be sitting around ten years from now talking about what other guys have done—I want to be some-body who is a real warrior!* When my National Guard enlistment was up, I changed over to the full-time Marines.

Even at the age of twenty-two, with five years of military service, the Marine recruiter had his doubts about me. I was only five feet six inches tall and weighed only 130 pounds. My parents had their doubts about me and the Marines, too, because of the rigors of Marine training. When it came time to decide what kind of training I wanted, I selected the infantry. The Marine gunny looked at me dubiously and said, "Listen, son, you need to reconsider this—I think you have what it takes to make it through boot camp, but Marine infantry is a whole other breed."

I went into the infantry and after seven months of training finally was sent to my first tactical unit. I spent my first two years in Central America training Honduran soldiers, a phenomenal experience. It was here that I first encountered Marine scout-snipers. At the time I had not even heard of them, but the first time I saw them they were wearing their ghillie suits—they looked like Sasquatches—and I was really impressed. "Who are those guys?" I asked.

"Those are STA Marines," one of the sergeants answered, "from the Surveillance and Target Acquisition teams."

I would later be invited to join the STA team, but not until we deployed and fought in the first Gulf War. I was a SAW [squad automatic weapon—light machine gun] gunner and part of the first battalion (1st Battalion, 6th Marine Regiment) through the breach. Afterward I was approached by the STA platoon and asked to become one of their snipers, an honor I quickly accepted. Although I wasn't able to get school trained at the time, it was a very rewarding assignment because rank was less important than your ability to perform, and everybody in the unit was excellent at his job. Every member of the scout-sniper team wanted to be there and do his job in a superior manner. This unit had a level of motivation that was new to me.

When the war was over, those of us on the scout-sniper team had some choices to make. Some of the guys who were in line to go to staff NCO positions left the Marines for opportunities to become Army Special Forces or Rangers, where they could continue to be snipers and remain in tactical units.

I had seen combat and thought, *I will never again see that level of intense organization and performance.* I really enjoyed my combat experience during the Gulf War, and for the first time in my life I thought, *Now I know where I belong.* Actually, I knew I needed to be two places at the same time—in the military and in law enforcement. My father had been a police officer and had told stories about catching bad guys, and that sounded attractive, too. I had the maturity, leadership skills, experience, and motivation to become a law-enforcement officer.

I went through training, became a patrol officer, and then qualified to become a police sniper. The training was done by the FBI, by the Marine Corps, and by some civilian companies staffed by former members of Delta, Special Forces, Rangers, and SEALs. Most of the cadre at these schools had previously been in the Army's Special Forces, and that encouraged me to consider reenlisting in the National Guard. I loved the Marine Corps, but it is a small service and the opportunity to go to schools is limited. That limits your opportunities for service. The Army is huge by comparison and has many more slots for the same sort of training.

While reading the reports about the battle of Fallujah, I kept thinking, *That's where I need to be!* My friends thought I was nuts, but when the call came for volunteers to be part of a Pennsylvania National Guard infantry brigade, I signed up. Not long after, I was in Mississippi training with a new brigade. This new brigade had recently been an armor unit with tanks and suddenly found themselves with a new mission.

Infantry brigades are supposed to have a sniper section, but this unit had none. Seven men had volunteered for training, and I was assigned to be the section leader. About twenty more volunteered before training began. For three weeks beginning in March 2005, Harry's Backyard School of Sniping was in session. I taught them everything I had learned in the Marine Corps and as a cop about marksmanship, field craft, tactics, and rules of engagement. We also did a lot of PT (as we call physical training). The class started with twenty-seven guys and ended with twenty-one.

I was now part of Alpha Company, 3rd Battalion, 103rd Armor Regiment, 28th Infantry Division, Pennsylvania National Guard, and in charge of a seven-man sniper section. Three of those men would quit before we got to Iraq.

While the brigade was training up for deployment, we were all told, "You can forget about throwing grenades and firing machine guns—those days of the war are over now! You won't even have .50cal machine guns because the war is not being fought that way anymore." I'd been in two combat zones by now, and I told my men that we'd learn those weapons anyway and practice with them over and over.

At last we finally deployed and ended up in Ramadi, in Anbar Province, in the middle of the night and moved into Camp Corregidor. Three of my seven guys decided that the sniper team was too dangerous and they quit. Soon after we settled in, Captain Karney came over and asked, "Have you talked with any of the snipers from 3rd Infantry Division? Why don't you go over and see what they can tell you about how they operate around here."

Our M24 sniper rifles still had not arrived at this point, but I found out where one of the Ghost team leaders could be found and looked him up. The guy was asleep when I arrived, and when he woke up, I introduced myself and said, "I'm here to get a little lessons-learned training; what do we need to know to operate in this area?"

The guy propped himself up on his elbows, and with eyes half closed said, "Don't go out in two-man teams—you'll be killed!" Then he rolled over and went back to sleep. So much for the lessons-learned!

Sniper teams at the time went out in six-man groups, moving

under cover of darkness. At the same time, the Marine and infantry units went out on patrol with no less than forty or so men, with armored vehicles for support. The Marines had already lost six snipers in the area when they were completely overrun and killed, and the same thing happened to another group of snipers during my stay in Iraq.

We settled down into a routine. My spotter was another college guy, Spc. Jarrod York, a biology major by training. Jarrod had studied life but now was an expert sniper and a lethal killer in Ramadi, one of the many ironies of Iraq. Another guy in our little group at that point was Spc. Joseph Bennett, another sharp guy and a real war machine. Joseph would take six bullets in one engagement during our deployment, but he kept fighting and lived to go back to college. Spc. Rick Taylor was the youngest guy of my team and another sharp college guy and National Guardsman. The only training any of these guys got was from me during our three-week improvised sniping school. A year later these four guys had among them two Bronze Stars, one with V-for-valor device, one Purple Heart, three Army Commendation awards for service, and another three ARCOMs with V-devices for valor.

Although we were part of the 28th Infantry Division, we were assigned to work with Shadow Team in July 2005 and did so until December. My four-man team began operating independently at the beginning of October.

I would not be alive and breathing had it not been for men like Bryan Pruett, James Gilliland, Kevin McCaffrey, Aaron Arnold, Ulysses Collett, and Sam Samuel. The fighting in Ramadi during our last six months was so intense that serious consideration had been given to assaulting the town in a massive and destructive way as had been done with Fallujah. That was not done for political reasons, but I seriously thought at this time that I would not survive the months till the end of my tour. Of the five team leaders in my 101st

Airborne sniper section, Joker Section, at that time, one was killed, one had his back broken during an attack, another was hurt while his team was being extracted under fire, and the final team leader suffered other wounds. I walked away with just a few scratches, and that was because of the lessons I learned from the Shadow Team leaders.

I was operating with Task Force Dark Eagle, a combined force of ANGLICO* Marines and Army snipers, working the south side of the Malaab neighborhood of Ramadi, near the stadium. This was a real hotbed of insurgent activity, and the threat level was so high that it had been left alone for quite a while. We set up on a rooftop while the conventional forces conducted a push through the area that would drive enemy fighters in our direction. The plan was to systematically intercept any insurgents driven out into the open.

There were eight of us on the mission that night, the six regular guys and us two new guys. Several Marine Corps helicopters inserted us into a neighborhood called Diyala. The 101st Airborne units were aggressively patrolling the neighborhood, trying to get the insurgents to come out and fight. While the dismounted infantry roamed around the neighborhood, we were in overwatch positions where we could cover them. The 101st was very good at challenging the insurgents to come out and fight, and when they did, to engage and kill them. The attitude among them was, come out and fight—we are here to clean house!

As the infantry began working their way through the area, our sniper team selected and occupied a house with good fields of observation. A family was in the home and they were collected and placed under guard. Every household is permitted to have a weapon, usually an AK-47, and this was also secured. The whole building was methodically cleared to make sure there were no hidden threats, and

---

* Air and Naval Gunfire Liaison Company.

A Marine sniper, Cpl. James "Rock" McGlynn, sights through the scope of his 7.62mm M40A1 sniping rifle from a sandbag rest in the Marine compound near the Beirut International Airport in 1983. McGlynn would fire one of the opening rounds of a war against Islamic irregular forces that continues today. *(US Department of Defense [DoD] photo)*

Spc. Theodore Amell scans the horizon for insurgent activity during a patrol near Mosul, Iraq, on March 31, 2005. Amell is assigned to Bravo Company, 1st Battalion, 5th Infantry Regiment. His M14 rifle is a relic of the Viet Nam era and not tremendously accurate, but was recalled to service because of the dire need for even moderately precise weapons effective at 500 meters and beyond. *(US DoD photo by Tech. Sgt. Mike Buytas, US Air Force)*

Maj. Charles Greene using himself as bait for enemy snipers at an intersection called "the circle of death." He's wearing an Iraqi commando uniform and a mixed bag of kit. *(Charles Greene photo)*

A US Marine fires a .50cal M107 rifle at vehicle targets during a live-fire exercise at the Godoria Range in Djibouti's northern training area August 26, 2006. *(US DoD photo by Staff Sgt. Reynaldo Ramon, US Air Force)*

Sgt. Brian Pruett watches for enemy activity. He has stripped down as much as he can to cope with the stunning heat of Ramadi, often 120 degrees. *(Harry Martinez/Shadow Team photo)*

A US Marine Corps (USMC) Marine and his spotter both assigned to Reconnaissance Detachment, Command Element, 24th Marine Expeditionary Unit (MEU), Special Operations Capable (SOC), man a 7.62mm M40 sniper rifle from a position covering a vehicle checkpoint in Iraq, during Operation Iraqi Freedom. *(US DoD photo)*

A US Army sniper team from Jalalabad Provincial Reconstruction Team (PRT) scans the horizon near Dur Baba, Afghanistan, October 19, 2006. Suspicious activity was reported along the hilltops after a medical civic action project was conducted by the Jalalabad Provincial Reconstruction Team and the Cooperative Medical Assistance team *(US Army photo by Cpl. Bertha Flores)*

Loopholes provide a bit of protection and are not as obvious in Iraq, where bullet holes are a common building decoration, as they would be here. This M24 rifle is set up to cover one field of fire during the soccer stadium fight. *(Harry Martinez/Shadow Team photo)*

Visible at the top of the windshield is the entrance hole of an enemy sniper's bullet that probably hit a bit lower than intended. This bullet passed through the cab and out the rear window before striking an Iraqi soldier manning a machine gun in the penis. Greene lined up the two holes, easily identified the site from which the enemy sniper had fired, then waited for the man to reveal himself. When he did, Greene immediately killed him.
(Charles Greene photo)

On March 27, 2003, a soldier assigned to A Company 2/505th Parachute Infantry Regiment, 82nd Airborne Division, provides security while the unit searches for a large cache of weapons in the Kohi Sofi region of Afghanistan. The soldiers are tasked to locate the weapons, which could ultimately be used against US Forces personnel deployed to Afghanistan in support of Operation Enduring Freedom. *(US Army photo by Sgt. 1st Class Milton H. Robinson)*

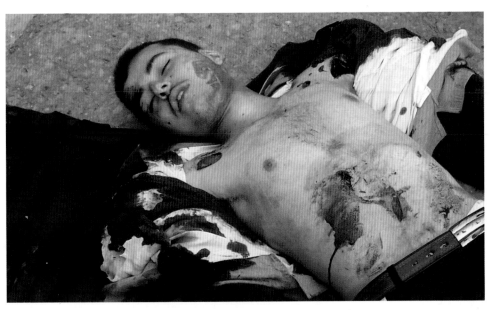

Paybacks: after Major Greene and the other two warriors were shot by an enemy sniper, the Iraqi commandos assaulted the position where the fire had originated. This young insurgent had the Tobuk sniper rifle and paid the price for shooting Greene—he has been shot at least five or six times. *(Charles Greene photo)*

Lance Cpl. Juan Vella, Sniper, 1st Battalion, 4th Marine Regiment, Regimental Combat Team 1 (RCT1), holds security with Clint Sprabary as his spotter in Al Shur, Iraq, March 24, 2003. Operation Iraqi Freedom is the multinational coalition effort to liberate the Iraqi people, eliminate Iraq's weapons of mass destruction, and end the regime of Saddam Hussein. *(US Marine Corps photo by Cpl. Mace M. Gratz)*

LEFT: Spc. Ross Henderson, of 2nd Battalion, 27th Infantry (Mortar Platoon), 25th Infantry Division, Schofield Barracks, Hawaii, watches for enemy forces while at a halt during a convoy to the Gayan District of Afghanistan on October 7, 2004. *(US Army photo by Spc. Jerry T. Combes)*

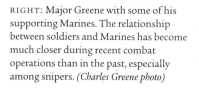

RIGHT: Major Greene with some of his supporting Marines. The relationship between soldiers and Marines has become much closer during recent combat operations than in the past, especially among snipers. *(Charles Greene photo)*

Spc. Francesco Musso, a sniper with Headquarters and Headquarters Company, 2nd Battalion, 35th Infantry Regiment, 25th Infantry Division, pulls security in Qalat, Afghanistan, October 9, 2004. The patrol was checking voting places during the Afghanistan presidential election. *(US Army photo by Staff Sgt. Joseph P. Collins, Jr.)*

A scout-sniper with Headquarters Company, 3rd Battalion, 5th Marine Regiment, 1st Marine Division, scans for insurgents in the streets and buildings along the edge of Fallujah, Iraq, during the first hours of Operation Al Fajr, November 8, 2004. *(US Marine Corps photo by Lance Cpl. James J. Vooris)*

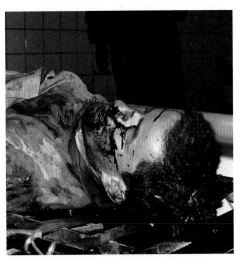

Maj. Charles Greene on the gun. Officers don't normally execute sniper engagements but Greene is not a normal officer. In this case he is an adviser to the Iraqi Army's special forces and wears the old "chocolate chip" pattern Battle Dress Uniform (BDU) of this unit. He's using an Iraqi version of the Russian Dragunov rifle, a local variant called the Tobuk. It is the same sort of rifle with which Greene himself was later shot. *(Charles Greene photo)*

Although head shots are usually immediately incapacitating, the target should normally be within 200 or 300 meters, even for the best snipers. Beyond that, the risk of a miss becomes significant and even some hits will not put a man down immediately. This man went down immediately. *(Charles Greene photo)*

US Army soldiers of 1st Battalion, 24th Infantry Regiment, scan for enemy activity from the top of a building during a combat operation in Mosul, Iraq, November 9, 2004. The regiment is on the offensive searching for and engaging insurgents. While on this offensive, the regiment received indirect fire, small arms fire, and rocket propelled grenades (RPGs). *(US Army photo by Sgt. Jeremiah Johnson)*

US Marine Corps Sgt. Michael Sistunk and Lance Cpl. Matthew Bateman both part of the Reconnaissance Marines from the 26th Marine Expeditionary Unit (MEU) Special Operations Capable (SOC), practice stalking techniques with an M40 sniper rifle during Exercise Slunj 2000. The bilateral exercise is designed to build interoperability and cooperation between US and Croatian military forces.
(USMC photo by Cpl. Rick T. O'Connor)

A US Marine Corps trooper with 1st Battalion, 8th Marines, tries to lure insurgents to show their position by firing on a target extended out over a wall and into the open during Operation Al Fajr, which is in support of Operation Iraqi Freedom. *(USMC Photo by Lance Cpl. J. A. Chaverri)*

A U.S. Marine attached to 1st Battalion, 8th Marine Regiment, 1st Marine Division, looks for insurgent activity in Fallujah, Iraq, November 10, 2004, during Operation Al Fajr. *(US Marine Corps photo by Lance Cpl. Trevor R. Gift)*

Target inspection after an engagement. The driver has been killed with a shot to the head—a neat trick when shooting through barrier material like glass. Two other insurgents were efficiently killed after Shadow Team members watched them brazenly display weapons. SOP for the team was to wait till all three were in the vehicle with the doors closed, then the driver was killed first and the passengers next. *(Harry Martinez/Shadow Team photo)*

US Army Spc. Chantha Bun, Bravo Company sniper, 1st Battalion, 24th Infantry Regiment, scans for enemy activity at 4 West, an Iraqi police station in Mosul, Iraq, November 17, 2004. Soldiers from the regiment and the Iraqi National Guard secured the police station after attacks by insurgents. *(US Army photo by Sgt. Jeremiah Johnson)*

US Marine Corps personnel with 1st Battalion, 8th Marines, look for insurgents running through the streets of Fallujah during Operation Al Fajr, which is in support of Operation Iraqi Freedom. *(USMC Photo by Lance Cpl. J. A. Chaverri)*

Spc. Kevin McCaffrey considers his options. Many of Shadow Team's kills were made with these upgraded M4 carbines rather than with conventional sniper rifles. *(Harry Martinez/Shadow Team photo)*

Sgt. Brian Pruett relaxes in the back of a Stryker armored vehicle enroute to an insertion point in Ramadi. *(Harry Martinez/Shadow Team photo)*

The pedestrian bridge over Route Michigan in Ramadi, with the infamous traffic circle in the distance beyond. Both are easily within range for snipers working out of OP Hotel and many kills have been made in the vicinity. *(Harry Martinez/Shadow Team photo)*

US Marine Corps personnel with 1st Battalion, 8th Marines, look for insurgents running through the streets of Fallujah during Operation Al Fajr, which is in support of Operation Iraqi Freedom. *(USMC Photo by Lance Cpl. J. A. Chaverri)*

Staff Sgt. James Gilliland with his tricked-out M4 carbine. It is equipped with an ACOG sight, PEQ-4 laser, sound suppressor, and bipod. The basic weapon design is now nearly fifty years old but has been modified over the years. With a good barrel and trigger and with 77-grain bullets, this light rifle will reliably kill at 400 meters and beyond. *(Harry Martinez/Shadow Team photo)*

Major Greene and his Tobuk,
scanning for targets.
(Charles Greene photo)

The 4-power scope on the Tobuk is not powerful by American
standards but incorporates a useful range-finding reticule that is
suitable for this weapon's normal maximum engagement range of
about 500 meters. *(Charles Greene photo)*

Although student snipers spend many hours learning to construct hides and use camouflage, real-world operations frequently require hasty positions. Here an M107 .50cal Barrett sniper and a rifleman with an M4 carbine engage targets from a rooftop position. *(Charles Greene photo)*

Major Greene in a typical urban sniper position. *(Charles Greene photo)*

Charming, centrally located, OP Hotel is well-ventilated and always has plenty of vacancies for visiting sniper teams. Insurgents have long known of its use by US Army soldiers and Marines but never know for sure when anybody is in residence until an IED team on Route Michigan is slain. The building has been attacked by rifle fire, RPGs, and even a massive truck bomb. *(Harry Martinez/ Shadow Team photo)*

This soldier is using a PVS-10 day/night scope mounted on an M24 rifle. The PVS-10 was state-of-the-art ten years ago but is now comparatively primitive with limited night capability. *(Charles Greene photo)*

Staff Sgt. Harry Martinez uses a Leupold spotting scope to peek over a wall during a battle at the Ramadi soccer stadium. *(Harry Martinez/Shadow Team photo)*

Two Shadow Team snipers in hasty firing positions at the edge of a field. This is the sort of terrain where the ghillie suits each sniper builds during training would have been useful, but those have been left behind. *(Harry Martinez/Shadow Team photo)*

LEFT: Staff Sgt. Harry Martinez spots for one of his Shadow Team snipers. The spotter is the key player during an engagement. He gets the shooter on the target, watches the flight of the bullet's trace through the atmosphere, observes the fall of the shot, corrects misses, and observes terminal effect more clearly than can the shooter. That is why the most experienced man is generally the spotter, not the shooter. *(Harry Martinez/Shadow Team photo)*

RIGHT: Staff Sgt. Harry Martinez on the gun. He's using an M24 sniper rifle, a simple five-round bolt-action weapon that uses a design more than a century old. These weapons are heavy, slow, rugged, and reliable. When coupled with one of the superb Leupold tactical sights, match-grade ammo, and a skillful shooter, the M24 can reliably produce first-round kills on stationary human targets half a mile away. *(Harry Martinez/Shadow Team photo)*

LEFT: There are a lot of dead bodies in this photograph made from the hide where Harry Martinez got his first real-world tactical sniper experience. Both vehicles in the center of the photo were used by insurgents before being detected and engaged by Staff Sgt. James Gilliland's Shadow Team. One man lays dead behind the van, another beside the passenger door, and several others are inside the vehicles. One has managed, despite his wounds, to get out of the kill zone, and one wounded man sits on the sidewalk awaiting his fate. A M2 Bradley armored fighting vehicle has rolled up to secure the scene and count the bodies. *(Harry Martinez/Shadow Team photo)*

then we set up to conduct operations. During the night we used the roof for observation, but as dawn approached we went back into the house to be less conspicuous. Up till this time, Sam told us, the snipers normally fired from upper stories. By shooting from ground level there was a chance that we could trick the insurgents into thinking that our fire was actually coming from other insurgents—a little confusion factor to throw them off balance.

The team leader, a staff sergeant with lots of combat experience and an excellent management style, told me, "Harry, go upstairs—we have some guys crouching down out in the field to our front. There is no reason for them to be hiding. Get up on the roof and see what is going on." I took my rifle and spotting scope and crawled into a position where I could observe the field.

Sure enough, there they were, three guys digging a hole about 250 meters from our hide. Each of them was holding a bag. One of the three was visually scanning the area, clearly a lookout watching for anything unusual. All of the three were military-aged men who met all the elements of the profile for insurgents in their dress and their grooming. But none of these factors alone or together met the criteria for us to engage them, so I continued to watch and wait. Finally, they stood up. Two of the three had a sort of package with handles, and the package was so heavy that the men had to lean against the weight. Still, I wanted to give them the benefit of the doubt—maybe the objects were some sort of farming equipment? Then the third man moved in a way that made it possible to see what was inside his bundle—it was a rocket! That was all we needed to engage.

The patrol leader, however, wanted to see for himself and we ended up bickering about whether to shoot or not. I was spotting for one of my guys, who continued to track the three guys through the scope of our M24. Finally, the patrol leader agreed that the rules of engagement had been met and that we could shoot, but by now the guys were moving away—our opportunity was evaporating. My sniper then decided that he couldn't pull the trigger; he turned and said, "I can't take the shot."

They were getting away, so I grabbed my M16A4 and hastily got into a firing position. The men were in tall grass now, with just their upper torsos exposed. I put the red dot of the Aimpoint sight on the chest of the man with the rocket and, since they were walking at right angles to us, added a little lead. There was still enough time to get into a better kneeling position, so I rested the forend (the front of the stock) on the wall and supported the butt of the rifle with my left hand. I leaned into the weapon, let out a breath, and took my shot. The man's body reacted—I hit him—so I shifted to engage one of the other two and got off a shot but couldn't tell if the second shot was a hit or not; both by now were out of sight in a palm grove.

The problem at the time was that we were all using 62-grain projectile 5.56mm ammunition for our M16s and M4s, and these bullets would go right through people who would sometimes not even notice immediately that they had been hit. I might have hit him or not—he got away in either case.

After I cooled down a bit, I went back up to the roof and took my shooter aside and told him, "Look, I really like working with you and hope to do so often in the future, but you have to respect my judgment; when I tell you to engage, you have to take the shot."

"You're right, Harry," he said. "I don't know why I did that. For some reason, I just could not bring myself to shoot that man." I really had to admire his integrity for saying that. And I also was reminded of the many stories I had heard about men being unable to kill other men.

The insurgents were smart and adapted to our patterns of engagement. They knew we avoided shooting women, so they used women when they could. They knew we would shoot somebody who kept peeking around a corner at American patrols, so they stopped doing that and just stood in the street for a while, and then walked casually off to make their report. They knew we didn't shoot children, so they used children and teenagers as lookouts.

SPOTTER UP! SEND IT!

Sniper teams spend hours and days quietly waiting for a target to present itself, very much like duck hunters patiently waiting for their prey. When operating from an established hide site, as some teams did from Combat Outpost Hotel in Ramadi, the terrain has been studied and dissected in detail. Every building, every landmark, every visible intersection in range has been named and sketched, their distances measured with the laser range finder and plotted on a terrain map.

One guy is always scanning the terrain, first with the unaided eye to get the big picture, then with the scope for objects of interest. There are normally two kinds of scopes available: the weapon sight with its variable field of view, and the spotting scope, also with a variable magnification, which will allow closer inspection of a distant object. Rifle scopes are available in many versions, but a 4.5- to 14-power is typical; the wide field provides a brighter image and wider view of the landscape, and the higher magnification provides a closer look but with a little darker image.

Snipers are very careful to avoid concentrating only on the distant buildings and people and strive to maintain what some of them call situational awareness. If you watch only the suspicious guys on the corner at 230 meters, it is easy for their friends to get in close to your hide (if they figure out where it is) and roll a grenade in the window, or get within your perimeter while you are distracted with the action on that faraway corner.

"Spotter up!" are the magic words the sniper has been waiting to hear, the signal that his partner has identified a target that meets the rules of engagement, is in range, and should be fired upon. This is the shooter's cue to get behind the gun and get ready to fire, and to listen for the rest of the spotter's report.

"Pedestrian bridge—226 meters!" says the spotter. The pedestrian bridge is a well-known landmark and terrain reference point when you're working out of OP Hotel. The shooter knows where to look and immediately swings his rifle to the bridge. With his scope dialed down into wide-field view, he can quickly take in a large portion of the structure. At the same time, the shooter glances at the elevation turret on his rifle's scope, verifies it is set on his preferred zero, and mentally calculates his hold-off for the known distance, 226 meters.

"Military-aged male, gray pants, white shirt, using binos—look behind the tree on the south side of the bridge," the spotter says.

"Military-aged male, grey pants, white shirt, with binos—I have him moving around the tree on the south side of the bridge," the shooter repeats, to verify they are both looking at the same person. "Sniper up!" he calls when ready to engage.

"Send it!" the spotter calls, confirming that he is ready to evaluate the fall of the shot. At the command "Send it!" most snipers will immediately fire.

When the weapon fires, the recoil and propellant gasses momentarily obscure the target from the shooter, but the spotter will typically have a good view of the impact. Two hundred and twenty-six meters is a very close engagement range for a sniper, close enough for a head shot and well within the effective range of a rack-grade M16 and a rack-grade infantry rifleman, but such shots are common for snipers in the urban battlefields of today. At longer ranges the spotter will be able to see the trace of the bullet as it flies through space, displacing the air and creating a momentary visible path through the atmosphere.

WIND CORRECTIONS

Although we were a part of the 28th Infantry Division of the Pennsylvania National Guard, and the 3rd Infantry Division was being replaced by the 101st, missions still had to be carried out. In December 2005, with the assistance of 1st Marine ANGLICO commanded by Marine Capt. Garrick Rard, a combined force of Marines, Air Force TACPs,* and Army scout-snipers began to operate in South East Ramadi, a section we labeled the Badlands and the insurgents called Malaab.

On our first mission, we set out on foot again under the cover of darkness, but overhead we had surveillance aircraft to support our patrol. The pilots had night-vision equipment and a map identical to ours, and they provided real-time intel on any activity during our movement and insertion into the hide site.

We were eight men strong and confident. We seized a house that allowed us to surveil Malaab from approximately five hundred-plus meters without stepping into Malaab. This area is still a hotbed of insurgent activity today; during my time there the threat level was so high that it was virtually untouched.

Exercising our SOPs, we entered the house. The family was collected and taken into another part of the house and placed under guard. The household's permitted AK-47 was secured and rendered inoperable while we remained in the house.

The house was methodically cleared to make sure there were no hidden threats, and then we set up to conduct operations. On this particular mission, we hammered through a wall and set up two loopholes using a sledgehammer. A rest plan was implemented and we basically remained at 25 percent alert. I usually stayed up during the night and would catch a nap during the daylight hours.

---

* Tactical Air Control Parties.

Although York was my spotter on paper, in the real world we shared the responsibility. That day York couldn't sleep, and he had spotted some suspicious activity inside Malaab. For the next several hours, York began to watch a group of young men hang near a corner. From their vantage point they could not be seen from the towers of Corregidor or from OP Hotel. Every once in a while, I would walk over to join York and observe.

There were four men, all dressed in athletic clothes and sneakers. One individual stood out from the rest; he was dressed in dark clothes and wore a lot of jewelry. All this information was being passed onto the higher-ups. Their response was typical: "Continue to monitor." ANGLICO gave us many advantages, including their radios, which enabled us to monitor multiple channels. York got tired and asked me to take over the weapon. Since our point of interest was well over five hundred meters, I decided to enhance my position and get as comfortable as possible.

At the same time, I enhanced my rifle position. I brought the weapon to me using these heavy pillows in order to create a real good natural point of aim. After achieving this, I started to observe Mr. Jewelry. I noticed that he would run into a courtyard and then reappear whenever a small convoy drove by on Michigan Avenue. Using his own binos, Captain Rard found another position inside the house and verbally reported his observations. Around this time, OP Hotel reported a large convoy traveling eastbound on Michigan. Mr. Jewelry quickly got up, entered the courtyard, and disappeared. As I was watching, Captain Rard was reporting out loud Mr. Jewelry's actions. I began to focus on my fundamentals. Mr. Jewelry stepped back out on the street. I checked my dope; it was set at five plus one. I started to breathe in through the nose and hold and exhale out through the lips. This would bring my heart rate down.

"He's got a black box in his hand!" I recognized Captain Rard's voice.

"I see it," I replied.

Mr. Jewelry sat down and was partially obscured by a shrub. I could see only his head and shoulders, and I could just make out his hands when he extended the antenna on the black box.

My finger completely encircled the trigger. Ted Hollenbaugh, a former Marine who was working for the FBI at the time, had shown me this technique.

I placed the crosshairs on where I thought his chest was located. As I inhaled, the crosshairs rose slightly above his shoulders. Wait.

When I exhaled the crosshairs came smoothly down and when it fell on his chest. I squeezed the trigger gently back. I watched a plume of dirt rise up into the air between Mr. Jewelry's back and the courtyard wall. Then, slowly, Mr. Jewelry fell over.

Captain Rard confirmed my observations and concluded with "Good shot."

The other men ran for cover. I did a follow-up and waited for my next target. A dump truck pulled up and positioned itself between OP Hotel and Mr. Jewelry. The driver crouched behind the wall; slowly and with great effort, he dragged Mr. Jewelry away from the corner.

To tell you the truth, I thought about killing him as well. The only reason I didn't was because it was evident they had no idea where the shot came from. If the driver had given any indication that we had been compromised I would have punched his one-way ticket to paradise.

CHAPTER EIGHT

TOOLS OF THE TRADE

This is an exciting time for the sniper community, a time of many lessons learned from real-world events and applied to tactics, techniques, equipment, and procedures. These lessons are also inducing radical changes in the weapons systems used by snipers in both the military and the law-enforcement communities.

Snipers use three kinds of weapons today—the sniper rifle, generally a bolt-action, five-shot, scoped weapon designed specifically for long-range, deliberate, very precise engagements; assault rifles for high-volume fire; and pistols.

SNIPER RIFLES

The traditional sniper weapon has long been the heavy rifle and its telescopic sight. Such weapons were in use during the American Civil War of 1861–65 and, despite being muzzle-loaders, were effective at the same ranges as modern weapons—first-round hits on a stationary man at six hundred meters and occasional hits to a thousand meters and beyond. Those early sniper rifles, like the Whitworth, were very slow to load, had delicate optics, were expensive, and were heavy . . . but, actually, the same comments can be applied to today's rifles.

Snipers call these long guns, and they are big and heavy. They are available in calibers from 7.62mm Winchester (or NATO, if you prefer) to .300 Winchester Magnum, .338 Lapua, .416 Barrett, or .50cal, among the popular options. These sniper-specific weapons generally have heavy, stiff barrels of about twenty-four inches, fiberglass stocks with adjustable butt length and cheek-comb height, adjustable triggers, and optical sights. These dedicated weapons normally have carefully selected barrels and are built by gunsmiths who specialize in their manufacture. The stocks are carefully inletted to insure that nothing touches the barrel for its entire length; the tube is supported only by the receiver to avoid any interference with the harmonic vibrations of the barrel when the weapon is fired. Many of these weapons are now designed to mount a suppressor and brackets for night-vision optics.

ACCURACY AND THE MODERN SNIPER RIFLE

The accuracy of these weapons is amazing. A true sniper rifle is normally capable of at least one minute-of-angle (MOA) precision, and many are much better. A minute of angle is the standard measurement for firearms accuracy, an angle that is one-sixtieth of one degree. One MOA is almost exactly an inch wide at a distance of one hundred yards, two inches at two hundred, and so forth, out to ten inches at a thousand yards. When a rifle shoots to one MOA, that means it will, all other things being equal, put the center of every bullet into a circle no more than one inch across at hundred yards. If you take a twenty-five-cent coin (slightly larger than one inch across) and have someone hold it up for you at a distance of one hundred paces, you're going to have a hard time seeing the coin at all, but any trained sniper should be able to hit such a target with every shot when fired from a supported prone position.

But one MOA is only the beginning of sniper rifle accuracy, and many modern weapons will shoot to one-half or one-quarter MOA under ideal conditions. A rifle that will shoot to a quarter MOA will put all its bullets in the same hole at one hundred yards, a four-inch group at a thousand. Such precision means that you can make a first-round head shot on a man standing half a mile away . . . all other things working in your favor. Quarter-MOA rifles are rare and treasured but are a luxury on the modern battlefield, where plenty of killing has been done with one-MOA weapons.

There are many factors that determine a sniper's ability to deliver a shot to a precise target—the quality of the ammunition in particular—but the fundamental factor is the simple steel tube called the barrel and the other simple components that comprise a bolt-action rifle: the receiver, trigger assembly, stock, and optics.

The standard NATO 7.62mm cartridge has been the foundation for American sniper rifles since 1966, when it began to displace the older, and in many ballistic ways superior, .30-06 round that was used by US soldiers and Marines during World War I and II. The NATO cartridge is smaller and has less propellant capacity; Marine snipers who used both weapons complained at the time that the NATO round would make reliable incapacitating hits up to eight hundred meters, but the older .30-06 was a killing machine out to thousand meters or more. The whole issue of ballistics, an important one to snipers, was explored in chapter 6.

SECONDARY LONG GUNS

Although the classic precision sniper rifle is the symbol of the sniper's trade, many teams report that they are not using them to make many of their kills. Instead, a two-man sniper team will always have an M16 or an M4 or a similar assault rifle with its high-capacity magazine and ability to deliver a high-volume of fire against multiple targets, often at close range. Some snipers carry both an M16 or an M4 carbine in addition to their massive primary weapon, the long gun. The spotter on a two-man team will typically carry this secondary weapon.

In addition, snipers and other American war fighters routinely carry pistols, and they use them. Pistols were not much more than a fashion ornament for soldiers and Marines during the World Wars, Korea, Vietnam, and the smaller scuffles of the late twentieth century. Very few war fighters had any confidence in these handguns or their ability to use them effectively. The legendary M1911 Colt .45 Automatic was considered useless by an older generation of war fighters but is beloved and used effectively today, largely because of better training in the proper use of handguns in combat. One hundred years after its initial development, the M1911 is being re-adopted by the US Marine Corps, replacing the Beretta M9 9mm. The Army still currently issues the M9, and many other pistols are in use on the battlefield. The resurgence in handgun use among sniper teams as well as all the other ground combat units is the result of urban operations that often bring warriors and enemy combatants into contact at very close range, especially in close-quarter fights where a pistol is faster on target than any long gun.

SNIPER BATTLE RATTLE

Besides the firearms, snipers carry and routinely use a lot of mission-essential equipment: binoculars, spotting scopes, night-vision optics, entry tools, radios, hydration systems, and particularly laser range finders. Even for very short-term missions, snipers will head out with their rucks loaded down with ammunition, grenades (M18 smoke and M67 fragmentation), MREs, radios, batteries for the range finders and radios, bottled water, Leatherman-type combination tools, an entry kit for breaching doors and walls, mosquito net and similar materials for building hides (customized for local conditions), chem lights, C4 explosive, blasting caps, time fuse, and fuse lighters.

THE M24 AND M40 SNIPER RIFLES

If, somehow, a US soldier or Marine from one hundred years ago could be brought back to life and shown the weapons and gear used today, he would find much of it very strange indeed—but he would recognize the M24 and M40 sniper rifles instantly, and he would know how to use both immediately and without instruction. The primary weapons of most snipers today are almost identical to the military rifles used by American war fighters in the years before World War I. They are indeed identical to the weapons used in 1966 and after because the standard-issue sniper rifles have not changed significantly in more than forty years.

There are newer weapons like the SR-25 and the SDM version of the M4 carbine, and the mammoth M107 .50cal Barrett, but the weapon of choice for both Marines and soldiers on sniper teams is a simple bolt-action rifle in 7.62mm NATO caliber.

Although they are known by different names and have some slight differences, the Army and the Marine Corps use almost identical weapons. The Army's version is the M24; the Corps' is the M40. Both are based on a Remington bolt-action, five-round receiver. Both use heavy target-type barrels of extremely high quality. The major difference is that the Marines use a short receiver that can accommodate only cartridges up to the size of the .308 NATO round, while the Army decided on a longer version that allows conversion of these weapons to different cartridges. While that may seem to be a minor point, the issue of just which cartridge offers the best performance on today's battlefields is a hot topic. American snipers are using .300 Winchester Magnum (WinMag), .338 Lapua, and many other rounds. The Army's rifles can be quickly and economically converted to these larger rounds, while the Marines are essentially stuck with the .308 NATO cartridge and its poor performance past six hundred meters.

Rifle marksmanship as a competitive activity has been a very popular military sport for well over one hundred years. Army and Marine shooters have been competing at national and international matches against civilians and teams from Canada, England, and elsewhere. Shooting is an Olympic sport, too, and both services invest a lot of effort in fielding winning teams. The idea has always been that such competition provides spin-off lessons to the common Eleven Bravo infantryman, and that's the foundation of both Army and Marine Corps sniping programs.

Prior to World War II, both services used the Winchester Model 70 rifle, a simple, sturdy design originally aimed at the hunting market. With a heavy barrel chambered in .30-06 caliber and with a match trigger and heavier stock, the Model 70 brought home many trophies and championships in the 1930s. Then, when the war began, these match rifles were shipped off to compete in combat where they performed very well, even though the men who fired them had very little training and learned what they needed to know on the job.

Those tired old Model 70s were pulled out of the Marine's rifle team's inventory in 1965 and shipped off to Vietnam along with many of the Corps' rifle team champions. Equipped with the long Unertl 8-power scope and still chambered for the .30-06 cartridge, these weapons started making kills and changing the tactical situation for Marines on the ground. At the same time, old M1D Garand rifles, the most common World War II sniper rifle, were pressed into service despite their anemic 2.2-power optical sights.

As their sniper program was getting off the ground in late 1965 and early 1966, it became obvious that there were not enough suitable weapons in the inventory to equip all the Marines who needed them. And there were problems with the existing rifles that needed to be considered when additional weapons were ordered. One of the problems was that the .30-06 cartridge, the standard rifle round until that time, was being replaced by the NATO-standard and less-powerful .308 round. Any new Marine Corps sniper rifle system would have to use the new cartridge, since the older version would gradually disappear from the available inventory. The Model 70 rifles could have been converted and rebarreled, but the cost of this conversion would have been close to the cost of a new weapon.

In December 1965, the Marine Corps Marksmanship Training Unit (MTU) was tasked with selecting a new weapon for snipers. The rifle chosen for the sniper program had to have an off-the-shelf, commercially available design because there was no time to develop something from scratch. MTU tested five commercial rifle designs—the Remington Model 600, the Model 700 in three variants, the Winchester Model 70, and the Harrington & Richardson Ultra-Rifle. At the same time, MTU evaluated seven scopes for sniper use.

After a very short period, in April 1966, MTU selected the Remington 40X, a bolt gun design then used for varmint hunting and for long-range target competition, and the Redfield Accu-Range variable power scope. Seven hundred of these were ordered in short-action receivers, barrels chambered for .308 NATO, fitted with Redfield variable power scopes. The rifle was christened M40.

The original stocks were wooden, and they warped in the high humidity of Vietnam. While not perfect, they started killing enemy soldiers at six hundred to eight hundred meters, ranges where NVA personnel had previously felt safe enough to walk around in sight of American units.

There were plenty of teething pains with the M40. The scopes fogged up, the range finder melted, and when the stock warped, the wood applied pressure on the barrel, which ruined the rifle's accuracy. The actions got loose and that degraded accuracy a bit, too.

Marine armorers and manufacturers fixed the problems one at a time, and the weapon matured; the M40A3 of today is a refined version of the rifle first issued in 1966. The stocks used today are fiberglass and are painted. They have bipods attached to the forend, and the buttplate and comb of the stock are adjustable to the shooter. Marine sniper rifles have recently been converted from Redfield scopes to a Schmidt-Bender variable power sight with a bullet-drop compensator (BDC) and close-focusing features.

SHOOTING THE M40A3

So much for the specifications and history, neither of which has ever killed an enemy except by boredom. If you want to understand a weapon, shoot it at a target that can shoot back. But we will start, as sniper students do, with steel-plate targets. Because the Marine's version of the rifle currently has a scope with advanced features, we will use the M40A3 for this demonstration, but nearly everything that follows applies to the M24 as well.

The prone position is preferred where terrain permits. Find a suitable spot, extend the bipod or use your assault pack for a support for the forward end of the stock, then slide in behind the gun. The butt of the stock is adjustable—you can make it longer or shorter to fit your own anatomy. Most snipers set it up so the distance from the crook of your arm, at the inside of the elbow, to the first joint of your trigger finger matches the distance from the buttplate to the trigger.

Millions of soldiers and Marines have been taught to line up on the gun at a forty-five-degree angle, but not anymore. The approved prone position now is directly behind the weapon, with your right leg in line with the stock and barrel. When you fire, the recoil force pushes straight back and your body resists the movement much better than before, keeping you on target and better able to observe the fall of the shot.

While you get yourself arranged, your spotter is setting up the laser range finder and spotting scope. He'll try to look right over the top of your rifle, if he can, in order to better watch the flight of the bullet's trace through the air and see its impact downrange. Get out some M118 ammunition, dig your sand sock out of the pack, and place it under the butt of the rifle.

Take five M118 cartridges and, with the bolt open, insert them one at a time into the magazine of the weapon. Push the bolt forward to feed a cartridge into the chamber, then lower the handle to lock it in position. The safety switch is at the right rear of the receiver; pull it back toward you and the weapon is on SAFE.

Look through the telescopic sight. It has five adjustments: an eyepiece control for your personal vision requirements, a zoom control from low power to high magnification, a focus control to adjust for near or far targets, a bullet-drop compensator, and one knob to adjust the crosshairs left or right and another to adjust them up or down.

Set the eyepiece by rotating the ring until both the distant objects in the scope and the crosshairs imposed over the scene are sharp. The weapon has already been sighted in for five hundred meters. Adjust the bullet-drop compensator to 400, and this will shift the crosshairs to account for the trajectory of the M118 ammunition.

The reticle shows not just a simple set of crosshairs but a series of dots spaced along both the vertical and horizontal lines of the sight. This is the Mil-Dot reticle. Each of these dots may be used to measure one miliradian* of angle, a nifty feature that permits you to estimate the range to a distant target with good precision, even without a laser range finder. At full magnification, the distance from the center of one dot to another is 3.6 inches at 100 yards or 36 inches at

---

* Miliradian is a system of angular measurement that provides an alternative to the "minute of angle" system. Both may be used to measure dimensions and ranges and are used for hold-off shots at movers, or to correct for wind or other factors using calibrated scope reticles but the actual calibration system is different. One miliradian equals a lateral distance of about 3.6-inches at 100 yards; one minute of angle equals about one inch at 100 yards.

1,000 yards. This is handy to know because a standing soldier will be about 72 inches high. If you use the reticle to measure the apparent height of a man you'd like to shoot at, and you put the bottoms of his feet on the crosshairs and the top of his head lines up with the center of the fourth dot, you know he's 500 yards away and you can adjust your scope's BDC accordingly.

Your initial target is a steel plate representing the head and torso of a man; it is suspended from a frame out on the known-distance range. "Come up fourteen minutes plus three clicks," the spotter calls, and you dial in the change. This is done by rotating the turret on top of the scope to the amount specified. Make sure that you and he are talking about corrections from the weapon's zero, not your last engagement. SOP for most snipers is to dial the scope back to its normal zero, typically at six hundred meters, and then make the corrections from there. "No wind correction," he calls again, so that stays on its six-hundred-meter setting.

The foundation for precision shooting is the ability to control variables, to tuck yourself into the rifle exactly the same way every time, to have your cheek kiss the comb of the stock in exactly the same place with exactly the same pressure, to have exactly the same distance from your eye to the scope, to embrace the grip with your shooting hand precisely the same way, one shot to the next. Your trigger finger enters the trigger guard only when you are ready to make the shot—a small safety ritual taught to all modern war fighters. The position of your index fingertip on the curved steel of the trigger is part of your personal ritual, always the same from one shot to the next if you expect to control the placement of your bullets on their targets from one shot to the next.

When you make precision rifle shots at long range, you become aware of forces and factors that nobody else on the whole wide battlefield will notice. Your heartbeat and the pulsing of the blood through your body, even at rest, will make the rifle twist a microscopic amount, but enough to move the crosshairs a few inches, back and forth, on your target half a mile away.

Every breath will move the weapon even more, so breath control is part of this deadly art. Snipers have different techniques for dealing with the movement induced by breathing, but the standard method is to take several moderately deep breaths, then momentarily stop breathing during the middle of the inhale/exhale cycle—a respiratory pause—and then make the shot.

Making a precision shot, then, takes time and methodical concentration. When the sights are set and aligned, the crosshairs steady on the target, and breathing is under control, you press the trigger directly, smoothly, and deliberately to the rear. If you've done everything correctly, and the gods are with you, the 175-grain projectile will launch from the weapon at a speed of about 1,800 miles per hour, fly through the air for about a second, and strike the target within a couple of inches of your point of aim.

Consistently putting a bullet within a few inches of point of aim, shot after shot, is an art and a craft, and sometimes a bit of magic. Precision long-range marksmanship is only one part of the sniper's deadly art, but without it the other skills are useless.

EVOLUTION OF THE M24 AND M40 BREED

After forty years of experience with the basic Remington 700 receiver, American snipers seem determined to keep using this simple and sturdy foundation for their weapons for another few decades. There has been some loose talk about using Knight's Armament's SR-25 as a replacement for the bolt gun, but the sniper community has so far shouted the proposal down. There is very little to jam, break, or get out of alignment with a bolt gun, and the Remington design has proven itself faithful and dependable.

While the idea of switching to a self-loading weapon has produced objections, there are few complaints about the possibility of using ammunition with better reach and terminal ballistics. The 7.62mm NATO round has been developed to its maximum potential, and its rated eight-hundred-meter maximum effective range is just not good enough for a lot of snipers today when targets are presenting themselves at ranges of one to two thousand meters. The result has been that Navy SEALs, Army Rangers, Green Berets, and many other members of the community are buying bolt guns that fire hotter cartridges and sometimes larger bullets.

An example of this evolution is the trend toward two very powerful cartridges: the .300 Winchester Magnum (commonly called WinMag) and the .338 Lapua. Both combine larger case capacity with heavier bullets that zip downrange much faster than the NATO round and retain much more energy when they smite their victims over half a mile from the muzzle. Army Rangers are currently using the WinMag very successfully in combat and took first and third places with it at the Sixth Annual US Army International Sniper Competition.

These hotter cartridges and heavier projectiles have the virtue of improved ballistics, but at several costs. One is that the barrels burn out much more quickly than with the M118 NATO cartridge. Weapons firing the M118 need new barrels after ten thousand rounds; the WinMag and Lapua are good for no more than one thousand rounds and sometime less.

Ranger snipers don't care. They have unit armorers who can quickly replace the worn tubes with fresh ones every year or so, and the improved reach and punch are worth the trade-off.

Both cartridges deliver noticeably more recoil, but snipers aren't sissies and this is not a significant battlefield issue, either.

The Army has long considered converting all its sniper rifles to the .300 WinMag cartridge—the reason the M24 has used the long version of the Remington receiver since it was introduced so long ago. It hasn't happened yet, but there are certainly a lot of sniper rifles now used, mostly by the special-operations community, with this powerful round.

Remington produces all the Army's M24s as complete weapons systems in both 7.62mm NATO and .300 WinMag. In either version, the rifle with its scope weighs about fourteen pounds. The barrel is hammer-forged stainless steel with a black powder–coat finish. The standard trigger is adjustable from approximately one- to eight-pounds pull, and the butt of the stock is also adjustable to suit the user with two inches of travel.

While the receiver group and barrel have not changed much in design over the decades, the stocks and sights are undergoing radical changes. Instead of the simple traditional design, a fiberglass copy of the wood version used in the 1960s, Marines are mating their M40 short-action barreled receivers with highly adjustable McMillan stocks. Other users, like the Army's Ranger Regiment, have selected a design from the British company Accuracy International. These composite-material stocks have the virtues of being extremely strong and dimensionally stable while also having ergonomic designs that shooters generally prefer.

MONSTER RIFLES AND ONE-MILE KILLS

The advent of a whole family of large weapons designed for the heavy sniping mission transformed the sniper mission beginning in the 1980s and 1990s. Heavy sniper rifles are normally based on cartridges intended for heavy machine guns, the standard of which is the .50cal design of the brilliant John Browning. These are special weapons with special roles, but they have been spectacularly effective in reshaping the battlefield.

As an example, early in the invasion of Iraq, Sgt. James Hernandez made a shot that changed the reputation for snipers among both friendly and enemy combatants. His spotter noticed a Fedeyeen fighter standing in the open about two thousand meters from their position. From the man's behavior, he seemed to be taunting the Americans while encouraging other enemy fighters nearby by acting as if he were untouchable, at least by small-arms fire. Hernandez's platoon sergeant was standing next to him and said, "Shoot that guy!"

"I can't see him," Hernandez replied, but his spotter walked him onto the target. It took five or six rounds, but he finally connected with the man, blowing his arm off.

The shot surprised everybody—the enemy soldier, the sniper platoon itself, and even Sgt. Hernandez. Snipers suddenly acquired more respect from both sides of the battle. Their own commanders started to take them off the leash and let them make their own decisions about what and whom they could engage, and radio intercepts revealed that the enemy chatter was saying, essentially, "Don't go out on the street—the American snipers will get you!" Three sniper teams with their heavy rifles shut down enemy activity in one whole sector of the city.

The .50cal projectile is big enough and fast enough to use against all sorts of targets at ranges far beyond 7.62mm range. As an example, during the battle of Falluja, the loudspeakers normally used to call Muslims to prayer were being used for a more sinister purpose, to tell the local insurgents where American patrols were operating. These announcements helped enemy soldiers attack or escape, so a decision was made to turn them off. Navy SEAL sniper teams used their Barretts to fire at the speakers at a range of three thousand meters, over a mile and three quarters, destroying them and removing one resource for the enemy forces.

THE LEARNING CURVE

Jon Wiler and Ed Harper were snipers within the a recon platoon of the 101st Airborne. Just before the initial invasion of Iraq in 2003, both were told that they would trade their M24s for the M107 Barretts. Although they had received some training on the .50cal rifle during sniper school, that was years in the past for both. They got a brief refresher class on cleaning and disassembly and told to get ready for war.

Wiler and Harper headed off to the range with their new toy. Neither were especially impressed with the weapon at the time, but that would change. For one thing, the M107 was almost as big as Harper and weighed nearly as much. Wiler, a taller soldier, ended up carrying it much of the time.

Their unit was trucked up from Kuwait and into position for the attack on Samara. The first few days were a learning experience for all concerned, on both sides of the battle. Sgt. Hernandez's one-mile hit was a confidence builder for the Barrett teams. Wiler and Harper, along with all the other M107 teams, started thinking that despite the Barrett's intended role as a weapon for engaging hard targets like vehicles and structures, perhaps it could kill enemy personnel at extreme range as well.

Five days into the fight, Wiler and Harper were sent forward. They hooked up with the rest of the recon platoon and were assigned a sector that included a hospital. They selected a firing position that looked like a large pile of dirt, which on closer examination turned out to be donkey manure. There was no other suitable cover in the area so they held their noses and set up the gun.

"We hadn't operated as a .50cal team before," Wiler says, "so we were figuring it all out as we went along. Ed got on the gun and I set up the spotting scope directly behind him. We knew there would be a lot of blowback to each side when the weapon fired and, considering what was going to be blown back, I wanted to avoid as much of it as possible. We learned everything the hard way!"

Jon quickly noticed several men hanging out of an open window of the hospital at about the seventh-floor level. One, wearing what

appeared to be a military uniform, was using a handheld radio to report activity on the street below. Beside him was another man
dressed in typical Fedeyeen attire; the two of them seemed to be enemy forward observers.

"See that?" Wiler asked Harper. "Hospital building, seventh floor?"

"Got 'em," Harper responded.

They began to plan to engage. Without a laser range finder, the
team had to use their training and judgment. The only tool available
was the Mil-Dot reticle in the spotting scope and in the sight. This
reticle works well when an object of known size is visible and closer
than about a thousand meters. Beyond that the system begins to be
guesswork.

"Okay, Jon," Harper asked, "how far do you think that is?"

"Ah . . . how about eleven hundred meters?"

"Sounds good to me. Now, what about the adjustment?" Neither
knew much about the scope or the ballistics of the weapon-cartridge
combination, so Wiler suggested using the first dot on the vertical
part of the crosshairs for his hold-off.

While they were considering all this, an enemy mortar air-burst
round detonated very near their manure pile, raining bits of steel all
around. Then they started taking ineffective small-arms fire, apparently directed by the men in the window. Wiler called in a report and
got an authorization from the battalion commander to engage the
spotters the next time they appeared.

It would be the first lethal engagement for either sniper, and both
were tense with the responsibility of putting the crosshairs on a living human being. Wiler began to coach Harper: "Okay, Ed, just relax and take the shot when you're ready. Watch your breathing.
Relax . . ."

When the pair appeared again, Harper made the shot, the muzzle
blast producing a cloud of manure that momentarily obscured the
target. Wiler recovered in time to see the bullet impact far below the

window—they had miscalculated the distance to the target. Both targets disappeared.

Wiler and Harper stayed in position throughout the morning. Around noon they traded places, and Wiler almost immediately saw the two men again. This time they were both in uniform. He hesitated and then fired, using the third dot from the center. The two men's bodies overlapped from Wiler's position, and the bullet struck one and then the other. They both collapsed into the room.

BIGGER IS SOMETIMES BETTER

Thirty-caliber projectiles have been the standard for snipers for many decades, but part of the development of the current art and technology of the mission is based on the idea that larger projectiles can be fired from shoulder-held weapons, and these larger projectiles can accomplish a lot more damage on the target than the traditional 175-grain full-metal-jacketed bullet. The smaller round, for example, is pretty well spent by the time it reaches a thousand meters downrange and may even be tumbling through the air. Such a bullet doesn't have enough volume for any effective amount of explosive, either, and an explosive charge can be useful for some sniper engagements.

The M2 .50cal Browning Heavy Machine Gun (HMG) has been part of the American arsenal since just after the end of World War I, and it has been so successful that it has been changed very little over the years. Part of that success is its cartridge, the .50cal BMG, a combination of a practical projectile for long-range engagements and a case with enough propellant capacity to push it out the bore with enough energy to smack military targets effectively up to a mile and more downrange. It has, in a practical way, not been surpassed in all that time and its popularity is higher than ever. Here's why:

All modern military rifle projectiles leave the muzzle at about three thousand feet per second, plus or minus a couple of hundred fps. The little 5.56mm bullet fired by the M16 is only 150 fps faster than the 12.7mm projectile of the .50cal, and the 7.62mm projectile of the M118 sniper ammo is even slower, but not by much. There, however, the close comparison stops.

The BMG cartridge case has the capacity for ten times as much propellant as the 5.56mm and five times more than the 7.62mm. The .50cal bullet is about ten times heavier than the 5.56mm and five times heavier than the 7.62mm. The .50cal starts with ten times as much energy as the 5.56mm and about five times more than the 7.62mm—and on the battlefield, retained energy counts.

The virtues of all these details become plain when you shoot an M24 beside a TAC-50 or other .50cal heavy sniper rifle. At ranges out to six hundred meters or so, both will typically shoot with about the same degree of accuracy, around one MOA. But the .50cal will demolish the engine block of a vehicle at that range, bringing it to a halt, while the 7.62mm will hardly have enough retained energy to punch through the sheet metal of the hood, and it will certainly not destroy the engine block's cast-iron core.

By six hundred meters the 5.56mm bullet is beginning to run out of steam as air resistance slows it down; the 7.62mm is still very lethal and has not dropped much but is slowing down, its trajectory arcing substantially. The mass of the heavier bullet helps the BMG projectile retain its energy and resist wind deflection at such ranges. Beyond one thousand meters both smaller bullets are nearly spent while the BMG, when fired by skilled snipers in suitable weapons, can make good on the "one shot, one kill" tradition to 1,500 meters and can put down enemy targets reliably even beyond that.

SOTIC AND THE BEGINNING OF US ARMY
HEAVY SNIPING

I had my first encounter with the .50cal sniper rifle in the late 1980s on a visit to SOTIC, or the Special Operations Target Interdiction Course, which is part of the John Fitzgerald Kennedy Special Warfare Center and School at Fort Bragg, North Carolina. SOTIC is the place where members of the whole special-warfare community go to acquire and refine sniper skills. It was and still is a place where Rangers, Green Berets, SEALs, and members of the many other communities attend a series of programs that are even more demanding than the standard USMC and Army sniper schools. The place was named at a time when the term "sniper" was something of a dirty word, so "target interdiction" was used instead and remains a vestige of the old kinder, gentler, politically correct US Army.

We were introduced to a sniper team in full ghillies, one with an M14, the other with a monster rifle that was entirely new to me. As it turned out, it was new to the team and everybody else, too—the Haskins .50cal sniper rifle had just been born a few years earlier. Although heavy-caliber, man-portable rifles like the .55cal British Boys Anti-Tank rifle saw extensive issue during World War II, such weapons were not considered very useful because of their tremendous recoil, poor armor penetration, and limited accuracy. Americans who wanted to engage targets at distances beyond the eight-hundred-meter effective range of the M40 or M24 used the M2 HMG with a telescopic sight and set for single-shot fire.

The Haskins I saw at Bragg very closely resembled the Boys rifle—long barrel, sturdy bipod, hefty muzzle brake, bolt action—and was obviously a heavy weapon. Unlike the Boys rifle, I learned, the Haskins had a very good recoil-absorbing mechanism within the stock assembly, and you could fire the weapon without detaching your retinas or breaking any of your larger bones.

The M500 Haskins was the Army's sighting shot for a heavy sniping rifle. It had some virtues and some vices that were worth trying
out, but the design was not suitable for the missions the Army had in
mind. One hundred and twenty five were purchased during the
1980s, and some saw combat service in Grenada and Panama. Among
the weapon's virtues was excellent accuracy out to two thousand
meters—a mile and a quarter—plus moderate recoil, sturdy design,
and acceptable weight. What was not acceptable was the very slow
loading process that required removal of the bolt, fitting a cartridge
to the bolt, and then replacing the whole assembly back in the receiver before firing. If the recoil was acceptable, the firing signature
from the muzzle blast was not; the Haskins produced a cloud of dust
with every shot that advertised to the world, "Here I am, shoot me!"

But it was a start. It got a lot of people in the special-ops community thinking about the possibility of two-man teams being inserted
deep into enemy territory and then engaging so-called hard targets
like radar vans, anti-aircraft systems like the nightmarish ZSU-23-4
fielded by the Soviets and their allies, or parked helicopters or fighters, light armored vehicles, or any high-value target that needed to be
serviced without the help of combat aircraft. At the time, the whole
role of covert operations was in turmoil and exciting disarray because it was apparent to all the special operations forces (SOF) players that the battlefield of the future would emphasize small groups
or individuals conducting covert operations that did not resemble
the kind of warfare for which America and the other NATO nations
had been preparing.

Rather suddenly, a lot of people who operated crystal balls and
tried to anticipate the missions of the future began to see teams of
two men, perhaps with long hair and beards, sneaking into a foreign
nation and working a little black magic before sneaking back out,
looking very innocent the whole time. Such missions were imagined
to include disabling aircraft with precision long-range fire, and the

Haskins proved that the .50cal cartridge, with its high-explosive and armor-piercing projectiles, could do such missions and hit such targets reliably at ranges of a mile and beyond. Even better, the Haskins could be easily disassembled and stuffed into a golf bag or other inconspicuous container, carried in a rucksack without attracting much attention, then put back together once the sniper team reached its final firing position. Once assembled, the Haskins would hold its zero, the team could launch its projectiles from a discreet distance, then take the weapon apart and make a stealthy retreat while the opposing team was wondering what happened to their radar van or aircraft.

Using the Haskins, American sniper doctrine began to develop and the people who write doctrine began to imagine the opportunities available beyond the old 800-to-1,000-meter limits. The weapon demonstrated just what the .50cal cartridge and its big projectile could do against point targets rather than area targets, and the search for a practical heavy sniping weapon got into high gear.

About the same time a competitive target shooter and machinist named Ronnie Barrett designed a new weapon around the .50cal cartridge, a rifle he christened the M82 based on its year of development. The M82 is a recoil-operated semiautomatic with a ten-round magazine. A combination of a good muzzle brake and the spring-loaded mechanism provides very good recoil damping. It is a weapon you can shoot comfortably all day . . . or at least until noon because the back blast from the muzzle is still substantial.

The M82 was not intended to be a one-MOA weapon that could make head shots at a mile, at least with the standard ammunition available for the M2 HMG. With such ammo, it is a two- or three-MOA rifle that is primarily intended to punch holes in enemy vehicles, crew-served weapons systems, bunkers, plus the usual parked aircraft and any ZSU-23-4s that are within a mile or two of the sniper team. The Swedish army bought the first ones and the US Army bought some in time for the first Gulf War, where they got a good workout and proved the concept to everybody's satisfaction. The current version, the M107, is very similar to the original—almost five feet long, weighing thirty pounds. This is not a weapon for sissies.

As with any sniper weapon, half the issue of accuracy depends on the ammunition, and most military Barrett rifle shooters today are using thirty-year-old, Vietnam-War-surplus, machine-gun ammunition. These rounds were never manufactured to sniper rifle tolerances—they were intended to be sprayed at the enemy rather than fired carefully at individual targets. Variations in this ammunition add another MOA or so to the Barrett's angle of diffusion, and that adds up to about a thirty-to-forty-inch group at a thousand meters. This is perfectly acceptable if you want to disable a vehicle with a high-explosive incendiary (HEI) round to the engine block, but your chances of a first-round hit on a man at that distance are maybe one in four.

Although never promoted as a sub-MOA weapon by Barrett or anybody else, when fed high-quality, match-grade .50cal ammunition, even the M82 or M107 will shoot close to the one-MOA sniper standard, and one report claims a 7.5-inch group at a thousand meters.

With a ten-round magazine, an M82 or M107 sniper can keep sending rounds downrange until one scores or the target ambles off. Since the .50cal projectile is subsonic at long engagement ranges, the target will not be alerted by the hypersonic crack of the bullet breaking the sound barrier; he will hear the crunch of the bullet only as it impacts the ground and may not even realize he's under fire.

So what's this huge rifle like to shoot? Once you get over your apprehension about the recoil and the muzzle blast, it is very interesting. For one, you can accurately and routinely smack vehicle-sized targets a mile away, and with HEI ammunition each hit is marked by a bright flash as the projectile impacts.

Most US Army snipers become acquainted with the Barrett at Fort Benning's Burroughs-Left range, one of many in the Harmony Church area of the installation, a great place to learn how to operate a TOW missile, an M2 Heavy Machine Gun, or other long-range infantry weapon. Burroughs is a vast space with derelict tanks, trucks, and artillery pieces rusting at ranges out to almost two thousand meters from the firing line. The easy targets are old eight-inch cannon only a few hundred meters downrange, well marked by thousands of impacts from .50cal and larger weapons. Farther out are more demolished trucks and artillery, and at the extreme edge of the range, almost at the tree line, is an elderly and much-abused M48 tank carcass that was a technological marvel half a century ago but now serves only as a target.

As with other sniper rifles, the weapon is best fired from the prone position. It is possible to fire from a supported-sitting position using a wall or Humvee hood, but prone is highly preferred. You get behind the gun, body on line with the barrel, right hand on the grip and left hand supporting the butt of the weapon. The magazine for the M107 has a ten-round capacity, but experienced shooters normally load only eight to prevent overloading the magazine spring and to avoid the resulting stoppage. Insert the magazine in the well just forward of the trigger guard and rotate it up and into place; the latch will click, securing the mag. When the rangemaster calls "The range is hot!" you are allowed to send rounds downrange. Pull the operating handle on the right side of the receiver back against the heavy spring tension, then let it go. A big, bright HEI round will feed into the chamber with an authoritative *klunk*. The safety switch is on the left side, under your thumb, just above the grip; move the indicator from SAFE to FIRE, and you're ready to shoot.

The distant tank at 1,800 meters—a full mile—is a good test of the weapon. With your come-ups dialed into the scope, place the crosshairs of the sight on the target's center of mass, the tank's turret ring right in the middle of the vehicle. From the prone position and with your left hand supporting the butt of the stock, it is easy to lock the sight onto the spot where you want to place your bullet, even at that great distance. Report, "Shooter ready!"

"Send it!" your spotter responds.

Trigger control is one of the fundamental component arts of sniping. You must press the trigger while keeping the sight picture perfectly aligned. When the M107 fires, your shoulder gets a gentle push no worse than from a 12-gauge magnum duck gun. The muzzle blast is anything but gentle, your body is thumped by the momentary wave of pressure directed backward by the brake on the end of the barrel, but it is very tolerable.

That muzzle blast kicks up some dust and gravel, which quickly clears. If you put your body in line with the gun, directly behind the barrel and scope, the recoil will not displace your view much. You can watch through the scope as your bullet smacks the iron hulk at about two thousand feet per second, about a second after it left the weapon. A momentary flash of white light marks the impact a few feet forward on the hull, about five feet from your point of aim. That works out to three minutes of angle from your point of aim, just about what is expected from the weapon and the thirty-year-old ammunition you just fed it. Fire again with the same point of aim and you may hit the turret, the rear of the hull, or even the turret ring under the crosshairs.

THE LONGEST LONG SHOT: CANADIAN SNIPER TEAM'S RECORD KILL

One measure of the sniper's art and craft is the distance at which he is able to deliver effective fire. Carlos Hathcock made a confirmed kill at 2,286 meters (2,500 yards) in 1967 using a standard M2 .50cal Heavy Machine Gun on which had been mounted a telescopic sight.

Then, in March 2002 during Operation Anaconda, Cpl. Rob Furlong and Master Cpl. Tim McMeekin, a sniper team from the Princess Patricia's Canadian Light Infantry (PPCLI), made a confirmed kill on a Taliban machine gunner at 2,430 meters, the longest documented sniper kill on record. The team was part of a larger nine hundred-man Canadian contribution to Anaconda, an epic campaign to destroy the Taliban and al-Qaeda forces in Afghanistan's Shahikot Valley, and with them were three other PPCLI snipers: Master Cpl. Graham "Rags" Ragsdale, Dennis Eason, and Cpl. Aaron Perry. On 3 March, the snipers, with their huge rucks and huge rifles, boarded CH-47 Chinook helicopters for the ride into battle. With them was American army Sgt. Zevon Durham.

Anaconda was a huge operation that was designed around US Army Special Forces and indigenous Afghan fighters as the primary force. Their objective was to destroy the Taliban in what had been until then a sanctuary. US Marines and other combat units were included to provide support for the main effort. On the ride in nobody was entirely certain what they would encounter.

The helicopters took heavy fire approaching the landing zone at dawn. They skimmed in through the mountainous terrain, then put them down and out on the ground. Enemy gunners and mortar crews were waiting, and they greeted the teams with direct and indirect fire while the Canadian snipers quickly set up their weapons and prepared to return fire. Perry, Eason, and Ragsdale formed one three-man team built around a single McMillan TAC-50 rifle. McMeekin, Furlong, and Durham formed a second team around another TAC-50.

Perry and his team moved under fire to a better position higher up the slope, then set up their weapons and optics and went to work. The Taliban were brave and experienced, but their weapons and skills were badly outclassed by the Canadians. One by one the teams identified targets, lased the range with their Vectors, made their come-ups, and fired. They killed the enemy soldiers methodically, one at a time, at ranges up to nearly a mile, and routinely with a single shot from the big .50cal rifles.

When competent and well-equipped sniper teams are used properly, they can make a huge contribution to the fight. The Canadians quickly established their credentials as competent and well equipped, and they soon found themselves being hauled from one problem spot on the battlefield to another, putting out fires that suppressed individual enemy fighters and their crew-served mortars and machine guns, at engagement ranges that were far beyond their training or doctrine. Perry made a kill on an enemy artillery observer at a lased 2,310 meters, just a few meters short of Hathcock's legendary record.

Corporal Furlong was shooting a McMillan TAC-50 rifle, a bolt gun chambered in the same .50cal cartridge used by Hathcock's weapon and so many others before and since. The McMillan is one of a new breed of heavy sniping and target rifles that are designed for extreme precision at extreme range; it will shoot half-inch groups at one hundred meters and five-inch groups at a thousand if fed suitable ammunition. Canadian forces selected it as their standard long range sniper weapon in 2000. Corporal Furlong's successful shot would not have been worth attempting with a conventional weapon firing conventional ammunition, but he and the Canadian forces anticipated such engagements when the weapon was adopted. But the Taliban in eastern Afghanistan probably didn't know anything about the TAC-50 in March 2002.

Perhaps that was why the enemy fighters were so casual when they were observed in the mountains of eastern Afghanistan. The terrain was barren and exposed and, with no American or Canadian units visible, it must have appeared to them that no rifleman could possibly harm them from the closest available cover and concealment over a mile from their position. That turned out to be a fatal error.

There were three enemy soldiers out in the open, each loaded with weapons and ammunition, working their way to an al-Qaeda mortar position another few hundred meters away. Furlong and McMeekin were prone on the frigid ground, the spotter using his Vector laser range finder and the shooter watching through his weapon sight. McMeekin called the range: "Twenty-four-thirty meters!" Even at full magnification, a human target is very tiny at such a range, and the team had three of them from which to choose.

All seemed to be reinforcing a mortar position further up the mountain. Two of them carried what seemed to be ammunition; the third had a rucksack and an RPK machine gun. Under such circumstances, the man with the RPK is automatically designated the priority target because he is the greatest immediate threat to friendly forces—the machine gun can be brought into action where it is and its projectiles have the range to deliver area fire (although weak and not very effective) against the Canadians even at this tremendous distance. Furlong chambered a round, put the crosshairs over the man with the machine gun, verified the switch was set on the FIRE position, and began the sequence to make the shot.

"Stand by," Furlong called to his spotter, to make sure he was ready to call the shot.

"Send it!" McMeekin answered.

The TAC-50 made a tremendous boom when fired, but the enemy fighters didn't seem to notice and they may not have even heard the report, which was more than a mile and a half from their position. They did not seem to notice the impact of the first round when it struck the ground nearby. McMeekin and Furlong made their corrections, adjusted the scope, and repeated the cycle.

"Stand by!"

"Send it!"

Boom! The second round impacted the gunner's rucksack, and this time the enemy noticed but did not react. "Where did that come from?" one of them probably wondered.

"Stand by!" Furlong called again.

"Send it!" McMeekin answered again. *Boom!*

Four seconds after leaving the weapon, the huge projectile came arcing down and this time hit the Taliban gunner in the abdomen. No consolation to the enemy soldier, he had just completed his part of establishing a new world record for the longest sniper kill, surpassing Carlos Hathcock's record kill by about ninety meters.

During the nine-day operation nobody gave a lot of thought to the matter of record books, but many Americans present were deeply impressed with the huge contributions of these very few Canadians to the overall effort. In the process, the PPCLI snipers earned the admiration of the Americans whose operation they were supporting.

In an unusual gesture of honor to soldiers of a foreign nation, American Army commanders recommended that each of the five Canadian snipers be awarded the Bronze Star for their performance on the battlefield.*

EVEN BIGGER THAN FIFTY

The .50cal BMG round is big, but it's not the biggest or most potent caliber on the sniper's battlefield. Russia has its own version, the 12.7×108 round, and builds some exotic weapons around this cartridge. South Africa's very creative arms industry has developed weapons around two monster cartridges, the 20mm×83.5mm and

---

* This story should have a happy ending, but it doesn't. All five Canadians were soon back in action against the Taliban, supporting Operation Harpoon. On their return after five more days in combat they were advised that one of them had been charged with mutilating an enemy corpse. Instead of being honored for their valor and professional conduct during Anaconda, all five were isolated, interrogated, required to give DNA samples, and had their gear searched and some of it confiscated. Presentation of the Bronze Stars was delayed by the Canadian government while the long investigation continued. In the end, and too late, the charges were dropped for lack of evidence. The witch hunt, however, embittered all five and has left a vivid scar on the Canadian armed forces generally and the Canadian sniper community in particular. A counterinvestigation by the Canadian armed forces ombudsman is studying the charges and the way they were investigated. All five ultimately received their American decorations, too little and too late to compensate for their ordeal. The whole story was covered in the 15 May 2006 issue of *McLean's* magazine in a story available online, "We Were Abandoned," by Michael Friscolanti.

14.5 × 114mm Russian heavy machine-gun rounds, although the rifles to fire them are so heavy that they become essentially crew-served weapons.

Several European manufacturers have designed weapons around the Russian heavy machine-gun rounds. Technica, a Hungarian arms company, has produced a line of such heavy sniping rifles, and Steyr-Mannlicher has developed what seems to be the ultimate magnum rifle cartridge, the 15.2 × 170mm, and a rifle to shoot it. The Steyr weapon is called the Infantry Weapon System (IWS), and it fires a sabot projectile at extremely high velocity, about 1,500 meters per second. It can punch a hole through conventional rolled-steel armor plate an inch and a half thick from 1,000 meters. This performance would defeat many common armored vehicles in use today and is what the old Boys Anti-Tank rifle was intended to do during World War II.

At the request of an American government client, Barrett has adapted the M107 design to fire a 25mm cartridge, a heavy weapon designated the XM109. The 25mm round is under development but is planned to offer a warhead with a fuse that can be programmed to detonate at a specified distance downrange, a portable version of an artillery proximity round. Such projectiles would be ideal for antipersonnel use against groups of enemy or targets behind walls or similar cover where an airburst would be highly effective. The large projectile has enough volume for such a fuse and for shaped-charge warheads that could defeat vehicle armor much better than the traditional kinetic-energy armor piercing (AP) projectiles normally available for the .50cal HMG.

THE SURPRISING DMR

What is the least likely sniper rifle on the battlefield? It is the little M4 carbine or its nearly identical twin, the M16 rifle carried by hordes of American soldiers and Marines. The tiny 5.56mm bullet in its green-tip version has been notorious for poor external and terminal ballistics, and many war fighters have stories of making hits on enemy personnel during combat and having them keep fighting. Now when you shoot somebody in combat, you want them to stay shot, to go down and stay down. That does not always happen with the 62-grain bullet when fired in the M4 or M16.

But as Marines and soldiers began to operate in urban areas and sometimes got into very close-range fights, the M24s and M40s were useless—sometimes fatally so. The M4 was the weapon of choice because it was compact, had high-capacity magazines, and was just the ticket for close-quarter battle (CQB). When a heavier bullet, the 77-grain projectile, was used, insurgents began to take notice and went down for keeps instead of ignoring hits as they had previously done.

As part of the Designated Marksman program, some rack-grade weapons were modified by the Army Marksmanship Unit's shop at Fort Benning, Georgia, with heavier barrels and match-grade triggers to produce what has been called the Designated Marksman Rifle (DMR).

These weapons have become extremely well respected, especially when used with the heavier bullet. Many teams are reporting a majority of kills with these secondary weapons, and the old complaints about stopping power have been changing to rave reviews. Although the 77-grain bullet is not very good at barrier penetration, when used against an exposed human target the projectile often begins to tumble on impact and creates a very substantial wound channel that normally puts the target down on the ground permanently.

CHAPTER NINE

CPL. JAMES "ROCK" MCGLYNN: PSYCHO WARD'S FIRST BLOOD

The modern era of combat sniper operations might be said to have begun in 1983, when Marines were finally authorized to return fire against Hezbollah and other militia fighters operating in Beirut, Lebanon. One photograph of a left-handed sniper on a rooftop during that conflict has been frequently published in books and articles about the era, but normally without identifying the Marine behind the gun. That young rifleman was Cpl. James "Rock" McGlynn. When the rules of engagement were finally relaxed and force was met with force, he and other members of his STA platoon's sniper section were the first to take a measure of retribution for the bombing of the Marine Corps barracks and the deaths of over two hundred Marines.

I did three floats in the Mediterranean as a rifleman for Bravo Company, 1st Battalion, 8th Marines, and was called "gungy," or "gung-ho." I always was highly motivated. I wanted to fight and was always the first one into the mud when we were doing drills or exercises. This was noticed by my NCOs and I was promoted to lance corporal quickly. Then, when we got back from our first float, quite a lot of the guys in the STA platoon were at the end of their enlistments and they were getting out of the Corps. This produced eight open slots in the platoon and I wanted to fill one of them.

When I checked up on what was required, everything was against me: you couldn't be left-handed—and I am left-handed. You had to have fired Expert on your last qualification, and because of some medical issues during boot camp I had not scored well enough for Expert. But I put in for sniper training anyway, and perhaps because of my motivation, my platoon and company chain of command approved and sent my application up to Battalion. Ultimately I went to the school at Camp Lejeune and did well—third-highest score overall out of twenty-four in the class—despite not matching the written qualifications.

Being a left-hander, I discovered during the course, turned out to be an advantage instead of a handicap. Since the forend of the weapon was normally supported by a sandbag or something similar, a lefty can maintain his firing hand on the grip, his cheek welded, and his firing position while operating the bolt with his right hand, something that a right-handed shooter cannot do.

The school taught some things that I still use. One was the KIMS game that developed the memory skills so important for the observer's mission. Even today, while driving around, I will note and memorize license plates, then recognize them weeks later, a habit taught at sniper school.

After some additional training we ended up in Lebanon in July 1983. An escalation of tension between the factions competing for control of the city began about that time. As the Israelis prepared to pull out of the country, our mission as Marines was to train the Lebanese army to take over manning the checkpoints that maintained some order and control in the city. This army was composed of men from Muslim and Christian factions, and trying to train them was a bit like trying to train a bunch of kindergarteners—each faction was loyal only to its own community instead of to the overall mission. Fighters from Syria and elsewhere were infiltrating the city and becoming active. It was a kind of Wild West environment and getting wilder day by day.

Sniper fire from the various militias gradually increased during the first couple of weeks of October, making life dangerous for everybody around the airport. Our rules of engagement permitted engaging hostile targets only if we were being actively engaged ourselves, and only with specific authorization from higher up.

The faction facing us were Shiites and their organization was the Amal, or Hope, militia. Their local commander was a young man who went by the name of Abu Rabia. We called him Castro because of his appearance and the way he dressed. We had orders to kill him on sight.

The Amal snipers were pretty sophisticated and well trained. For example, we noticed one old lady hanging laundry on a line on the roof of one building a few hundred yards away. At first this seemed a normal and innocent activity, then we noticed that as soon as it went up, she took it down again, walked back off the roof, then came out again and hung the clothes up all over again. During this same time we could hear somebody firing individual rounds at Marines nearby, but could not identify the source. Then we started looking more carefully at the woman and realized that she was walking by a loophole in one wall, and after watching the loophole, we finally saw a muzzle flash; she was working with a militia sniper and helping him conceal his shots.

October 14, 1983, was a key day for the Marine Corps mission in Lebanon. We had been stationed at the airport, keeping it open. I was on guard duty at the Battalion Landing Team compound gate when one of our NCOs, Sgt. Allen Soifert, was driving a jeep along the airport's perimeter road and the vehicle was fired upon. The sergeant was killed, the jeep flipped over, and several Marines were injured.

The battalion commander was in the area at the time and saw what was happening. An ambulance with a red cross attempted to get to the vehicle but was fired upon. Our commander, Colonel Geraghty, then had to send in an AMTRAC, an armored vehicle, to get the dead and wounded, but at the risk of coming under fire by RPGs.

Colonel Geraghty was enraged by this event. It was his last straw. He called for all available snipers to report to Charlie Company's area. There were four of us—Rutter, Bush, Moore, and myself. Another team of two Marine snipers were already in position.

When we got there, he took the leash off and gave us the authority to kill any civilian with a weapon, any Lebanese army uniformed personnel wearing a red armband or red headband (both recognition symbols for one of the militia factions), and Castro if we saw him.

The six of us killed three militiamen that afternoon, and that seemed to quiet the locals who had been firing on us recently.

At the time, the Marine infantry platoons still had to operate under the old rules of engagement. That meant that they had to radio up the chain of command for permission to fire, and by the time they got it, their targets would be gone.

Rutter and I had an assigned firing position. We called it the Psycho Ward. We moved in and stayed through the night. Frank Roberts, one of the snipers who was already in position, identified an area of militia activity that he had spotted. It was centered around the shell of an abandoned little restaurant called Café Danielle in an alley facing us. Frank told us that people often fired on Marines from this place so we started observing it.

We could see a few people with AKs and RPGs in the area of the café while Rutter and I set up our rifles. We figured the range at four hundred yards. There was no wind. We both made sighting shots to confirm the range. Mine was right on; Rutter's rifle had been set for five hundred yards and needed a little correction.

The Amal militia knew exactly where we were, of course. At 0915 one of the militia fired at us, still thinking that we couldn't fire back— wrong assumption! The alley was full of them. I selected one wearing a blue tracksuit and shot him. He dropped to the ground, limp.

At 0945 I killed an RPG gunner. He came out of Café Danielle in an area we called Hooterville with an RPG on his shoulder and an

AK-47 in his hand. He was wearing a helmet liner on his head and when I hit him, his head snapped back and his helmet liner went flying. I hit him right in the heart.

"You got him, Rock!" Rutter yelled. "You got him, man! He just fucking dropped!"

Right after he went down, a red Mercedes came flying up to where he fell. The doors popped open and two guys, both wearing red armbands, got out and started lifting the RPG gunner and dragging him to the car. My partner killed one of the pair, and another Marine sniper team about hundred meters away noticed what was happening and fired at the other. This shot missed but shattered the windshield. The driver panicked, put the car in reverse, and stomped on the gas in a desperate effort to escape. In the process, he ran right over his buddy, the guy Rutter shot. We laughed at him.

Prior to 14 October, the militias fired on Marines pretty much whenever they felt like it, without fear of effective retribution, Then the gloves came off and the whole area was quiet and peaceful for a week. On 23 October, our barracks was attacked by the suicide bombers and 220 Marines plus 21 other servicemen were killed.

My sniper partner and I were in our firing position at the time of the explosion. I felt the ground shake, but there was nothing special about that; it happened all the time as a result of bombing or artillery. I sat up and looked in the direction of the Beckka Valley to see if there was any cloud of dust or smoke. Rutter also looked around but in the opposite direction. "Holy shit, what's that?" he said. I turned around and saw a huge cloud of smoke and dust, just like an atomic bomb, where the barracks had been.

CHAPTER TEN

SNIPER'S REVENGE: THE MAGNIFICENT BASTARDS AND THE SNIPERS OF HEADHUNTER TWO*

For anybody who thinks that snipers are safe and secure from enemy counter-sniper missions, there is the sad lesson of Headhunter Two, a four-man team from Echo Company, 2nd Battalion, 4th Marine Regiment (a regiment known within the Corps as the Magnificent Bastards), killed on 21 June 2004 in Ramadi, in a way that caused a lot of reevaluation of sniper tactics and techniques. It also created a desire for vengeance. It took two years, but those tactics were changed and the vengeance achieved.

Headhunter Two was one of three four-man sniper teams in the platoon, led by Cpl. Tommy Lynn Parker and including three other young Marines, Lance Cpl. Juan Lopez, Lance Cpl. Pedro Contreras, and Lance Cpl. Deshon Otay, working out of Combat Outpost on the east side of Ramadi. They headed out the gate about 0100 and moved to one of the three OPs (observation posts) routinely used by Marines in the city, a home that was under construction, only about eight hundred meters from Combat Outpost, and inserted themselves into the structure, setting up on the roof as was their routine.

---

* This information is based on a Naval Criminal Investigation Report obtained by *Marine Corps Times* and *Marine Corps News*, from interviews with Marine snipers from Echo Company's scout-sniper platoon involved in the incident, and other documentation.

What actually happened on that rooftop and when is uncertain, but it has been the subject of a lot of speculation and a Naval Criminal Investigation Service (NCIS) inquiry. The evidence suggests that Headhunter Two selected their overwatch positions and set up their radio and gear according to unit SOP. They started making routine radio checks every thirty minutes, calling back to Echo Company—call sign Porky—to check in with a normal situation report (sitrep). Sometime during the morning the team apparently went to 50 percent security with two men on watch and the other two relaxing; such a routine is normal on sniper teams because it is impossible to stay fully alert and observant for more than two or three hours at a time.

The sitreps from Headhunter Two back to Porky were called in every half hour, just as they were supposed to be, until sometime in midmorning when one was missed. The last entry in the radio log, when it was discovered in Lance Corporal Lopez's dead hand, was 0730. Missing a scheduled radio contact was nothing unusual then or now; radios fail, batteries quit, and Radio-Telephone Operators are sometimes busy with other things, so the Marine on radio watch back at the Echo Company TOC was not immediately worried at the missed call.

By now two other sniper teams from Echo Company were on the job, both at the ever-popular OP Hotel right down Route Michigan from Combat Outpost. Porky got on the horn and called Headhunter Three: "Have you had comms with Headhunter Two?"

"Negative," replied Sgt. Jason Finch.

Local SOP at the time was that you could miss three radio checks, but if two hours elapsed since your last sitrep, the quick reaction force was going to come out to your position for a welfare check. Porky didn't wait two hours to investigate the problem; fifty-one minutes after the last contact, he diverted a patrol from Echo's 2nd Platoon, already on the street, to the sniper team's position, just as a precaution.

They arrived about 1130, set up security around the building, and then two Marines headed upstairs to check on the team.

All of them were shocked by a scene of carnage. The four Marines had been killed, three execution-style, and were sprawled on the roof. There was blood everywhere. All had been shot and one had his throat cut. The team had clearly been caught by surprise. Parker and Contreras had apparently been asleep, Parker with his boots and body armor off, Contreras wrapped in mosquito netting. There was not much sign of a struggle except for one curious discovery—one of the men seemed to have thrown his knife at the attackers.

All of Headhunter Two's weapons and sensitive gear was gone— two M40A1 rifles, four M16A4 rifles, about twenty-four 30-round magazines for the M16s, eight M67 fragmentation hand grenades, one PAS-13 thermal weapon sight, and a PRC-119F secure radio. The loss of the Marines along with the loss of these weapons made this a double catastrophe, one which the Marine Corps scout-sniper community would lament for many months.

The patrol leader got on the radio and made his report to Porky. The radio operator back at Echo had the sad duty to report what happened to Headhunter One and Three. Sergeant Finch was still on radio watch when the call came in: "Headhunter Two are all KIA," Porky said. Finch couldn't believe he heard the transmission correctly. "Say again your last transmission," he called back.

"Headhunter Two are all KIA," he heard on the H250 handset.

It took Sergeant Finch a few moments to collect his feelings, and then he passed the word to the other Marines at OP Hotel. They took it hard, retreated into themselves for a few minutes, and then, like good Marines, got back to their mission. Later that night a couple of insurgents made the mistake of being within range when they used AKs to spray a passing convoy. Headhunter One and Three killed both, the beginnings of a long series of paybacks.

The killers brought along a video camera and recorded the carnage.

Adding insult to injury, images of the dead snipers were gleefully broadcast almost immediately across Arab-language television. The broadcast made Marines sick and furious.

That would normally be the end of the story, but not this time, not for Marines. Immediately there was a lot of introspection and after-action-review kinds of discussion, and that produced some useful lessons-learned. Parker, it turned out, had been the only school-trained 8541 on the mission, the other three were regular Marine grunts. That kind of ratio wasn't unusual then or now in the Army or the Marines. Lots of guys on sniper teams are learning the business, waiting for a school slot to open up, and they are often excellent war fighters. But all were young and of lower rank and less experience than is common for a sniper team. Parker was an E-4 and the others were E-3s; an E-5 sergeant will lead most sniper teams, so there was speculation that inexperience might have been a factor.

There were all sorts of possible factors and all sorts of questions, guesses and speculations. How could Marines be killed this way, without getting off a shot? Headhunter Two's story could only be told by the blood and the bodies on the roof—three Marines with bullet holes in the head, another with multiple wounds to the torso, some scattered gear . . . all just clues, with no real answers to all the questions. There was speculation that insurgents dressed as construction workers were able to approach the team without being challenged, then managed to shoot them at close range—but that was initially just speculation. According to the NCIS report, as quoted in *Marine Corps Times*, a senior NCO put responsibility for the massacre on Corporal Parker for "letting his guard down." Parker's wife, on the other hand, reported that he had complained to his chain of command about improper employment, untrained personnel assigned to sniper missions, and—a cardinal sin in the sniper business—being sent to the same place, by the same route, at the same time . . . helping the enemy predict when and where the sniper team could be attacked.

Then, after the attack, it was discovered that a cell phone conversation specifically authorizing the attack on Headhunter Two had been intercepted. The details of this intercept—who intercepted it, how it was processed—remain classified. Scraps of information included in the NCIS report and obtained by *Marine Corps Times* indicate that the actual identities of some of the hit team were discovered, and that American investigators have had contact with one of the key players, who was then somehow able to disappear. The whole thing was an intensely bitter experience for Marines generally and Marine scout-snipers in particular.

Chalk up one victory for the insurgents? Not if you are a Marine. The incident was never forgotten, its lessons never ignored. There were immediate changes in sniper-mission tactics, techniques, and procedures, including some for which Corporal Parker had asked. One of these was to make sure more school-trained, 8541-qualified scout-snipers went out on each mission. Both Marine Corps and Army sniper schools used the deaths as a teaching point. Sniper employment officers, platoon leaders, platoon sergeants, team leaders, and team members themselves all took a long look at how they conducted business and made some changes. One of the changes was that commanders sometimes became even more cautious, even more risk averse, even more likely to keep a tight leash on their sniper teams. SOP in many units, as a result, is to never send out a sniper team without a security element of four to twelve infantry, a tactic with its own tactical problems since it is hard to be covert with sixteen guys in a hide instead of four.

Then, at last, payback time: Almost two years to the day Parker and Headhunter Two were killed, Sniper Section Four from 3rd Battalion, 5th Marines—known as the Darkhorse regiment—set up in a hide alongside a highway west of Habbaniyah. The view from one window of the hide showed the divided highway, a small store, and a dirt frontage road. This position offered good observation for activity around the store as well as on the highway. Sgt. Kevin Homestead, an infantry Marine from Kilo Company, was on the scope.

Inside the hide the Darkhorse snipers monitored radio traffic on their battalion net. Nearby were some Amphibious Assault Vehicles (AAVs) on a routine patrol of the area. At 1145 hours the team noticed movement inside a black Opel sedan parked in front of the store. The vehicle had tinted windows, but the sniper and spotter were able to see somebody inside the vehicle operating a handheld video camera and using it to record images of the Marine AAVs as they lumbered down the road. Homestead and the snipers could see that this recording was done covertly, with the camera partially hidden, but not well enough. Using a video camera to record military subjects is a capital offense in Iraq right now, and the snipers prepared to enforce the law. They didn't know it at the time, but the man with the camera was Ihab Mohamed Abbas, an insurgent from Ramadi whose life was about to be violently terminated at the age of thirty-one years.

The engagement range from the hide to the vehicle was short, only about 220 meters. Although neither the sniper nor the spotter could see who was using the camera, it was easy enough to calculate where he had to be, over on the left side of the vehicle behind the driver's seat. While they continued to observe, the team's RTO called up the AAVs with a quick sitrep about the covert surveillance.

Then the team noticed something unusual—the stock of a weapon leaning against the right side rear window. While the AAVs were still nearby, the team watched Abbas reach for the rifle—a scoped bolt action—and chamber a round, sealing his own doom.

Engaging a target through auto window glass is notoriously difficult because the barrier tends to deflect and shatter a projectile, but the Darkhorse sniper had a plan to deal with that issue. He calculated his point of aim as the center of a small fixed triangular piece of glass next to the rear passenger door window. His gun-target line was directly through this small aperture, but he could not be certain that the barrier would not deflect the projectile on impact. Instead of relying on the first bullet to do the job, he decided to fire three rounds, the first to defeat the barrier, the other two to defeat the man with the camera and the rifle.

Perhaps Abbas was intending to step out of the car and pop a round or two at a crewman's head exposed in one of the AAV hatches, perhaps using the roof of the car as a support. Whatever his plan, he didn't even get the door open. Three quick rounds through the tiny window struck him in the chest. He rolled over on his side and bled out. Abbas probably had ten seconds or so to ponder his own death as his blood gushed onto the upholstery and his blood pressure dropped. Then his lights dimmed and he lost consciousness and died, not knowing that he had achieved fame as a sniper killed by another sniper.

About this time, Abbas's partner—forty-one year old Faris Mohamed Abid, another Ramadi product—strolled up to the car. From inside the Marine's hide, he seemed pleased and cheerful about the three shots he and the rest of the neighborhood had just heard, probably assuming that his associate had made the shots at the Marine patrol and had ducked back in the car.

Abid opened the door and got behind the wheel, closed the door, and probably asked his now-nearly-deceased buddy about the shooting, but Abbas undoubtedly wasn't talking. Abid was turned around, his feet across the front seat, perhaps trying to look at his partner in back when Sergeant Homestead put three bullets from his M16 through the right-side window and into him, too. Faris Mohamed Abid leaned back against his door and died.

One of the Marines on the team had called up their boss back at Kilo Company, call sign Samurai Six, with a spot report after the first engagement. Soon a squad of Marines arrived at the store to check out the car and to add a little muscle in case there were any more insurgents nearby looking for trouble. What they found was amazing.

Inside the car, along with the bodies of Abid and Abbas, the Marines made a wonderful and bittersweet discovery—Corporal Parker's M40A1 rifle, the one captured by whomever killed Headhunter Two. The original Unertl scope was gone, replaced by a Tasco hunting model, but it was the long-missing sniper rifle from the Ramadi rooftop two years previously. In the chamber was the round Abbas was about to fire at the Marines in the AAVs. For all that time a Marine weapon had been used against Marines, and now it was home.

There was more. Inside the car was a hidden compartment that held all sorts of insurgent treasures: a hand grenade, a Browning 9mm Hi-Power pistol with a magazine and ammunition, a Bushnell laser range finder, a second video camera complete with charger and blank tapes, a full magazine for an M16, two sets of fraudulent license plates for the car, several audio cassettes, and about seventy-five 7.62mm NATO rounds for the sniper rifle. Later on, when the haul was analyzed by the S2 shop, the videotape revealed five minutes of coverage of the AAVs with lots of close-ups of the commander's hatch.

Several little coincidences helped provide a bit of closure for the whole Headhunter episode. A check of serial numbers confirmed the identity of the M40A1 rifle. It had been in the Marine Corps inventory for many years and had been used in combat, coincidentally, by Darkhorse Marines in the first Gulf War before being turned over to the Magnificent Bastards. It was a Darkhorse Marine who killed the insurgent who was about to fire it, and the driver, Abid, was killed by a former member of that same battalion.

The last round chambered in the M40 has been recovered and preserved. Its bullet was pulled, the propellant and primer removed, and the bullet replaced, to be kept as a little bit of history.

That cartridge will probably be the last one chambered in M40A1 Serial Number E6546973. The Magnificent Bastards are glad it has been recovered but have avoided taking it back because of its tainted history. This rifle has a sad history and has probably killed Marines, and no Marine wants to use it again. At this writing, there is talk of putting it in a museum. Sgt. Maj. James Booker, Two-Four's battalion sergeant major when Headhunter Two was killed and himself a career 8541, was quoted as saying, "There are evil spirits on it . . . but I would like to see it preserved and sit in a place of honor."

CHAPTER ELEVEN

SERGEANT ROB: SPIDER-MAN IN SAMARRA

Sergeant Rob (we give his first name only, at his request) was deployed to Iraq for a year and served on a sniper team in the northern city of Tikrit and also in Samarra. He currently maintains a blog, Sniper's Eye (sniperseye. blogspot.com).

One of the things that made our team a bit different from others was our technique for stealthy insertions and extractions. Other teams cut locks and broke open doors and so did we, but we also infiltrated the hard way—we climbed up the outside walls and gained entry like cat burglars or Spider-Man, often without the people inside the buildings knowing we were there. On our team, climbing ability was essential, and if you couldn't do it you were dead. We did some crazy things during operations—jumping from one rooftop to another, scaling the side of an apartment building using the drainpipe, walking along outside ledges just a few inches wide. Climbing was important for us because it is so important for snipers to infiltrate and extract without being detected by the enemy.

Our daytime missions were conducted a bit differently than the nighttime insertions, but they, too, involved a lot of climbing. We wanted the insurgents and their supporters to know we were out in the city with our rifles, prowling around and looking for targets, but we didn't want them to ever know exactly where we were. We seldom bothered with walking down a street, instead, we hopped over walls, climbed under and over fences, moved through yards, across the tops of buildings, and always moving in unpredictable directions and unexpected places. The insurgents have a big network of people who do nothing but watch for American and Iraqi army patrols and who call in reports on these patrols to insurgent headquarters, but we moved in ways that made it almost impossible for anybody to track our movements and intercept us.

Unlike Special Forces and similar SOF snipers, we were not allowed a lot of latitude about how we set up our gear or our missions. I was attached to a conventional infantry battalion where the command group didn't cut snipers any slack—we were just like everybody else as far as they were concerned, infantrymen with a long gun.

Although this forced us to carry gear that we would otherwise have left at the FOB, we were at least permitted to set up our vests in a way suitable for somebody using a bolt gun and firing from the prone position. Our SOP was that the shooting side of your vest was kept entirely clean of pouches and gear. And, the other side of the vest would only have two or three M16 magazine pouches and another little pouch for a Motorola radio. Setting up the vests this way was necessary because we did so much climbing and we needed to move quietly.

Moving quietly was an art form for my section. I've scaled the outside of a building like a cat burglar, entered the house from the second floor, and moved through the house while a family is watching television in an adjacent room. I could walk right past them and they would not notice! We could, and did, move through an occupied residence, get up on the roof, spend a day or more in position, and only when we left did the occupants know we were there, and only then because we said "Good-bye!" on the way out. Being a sneaky bastard is on the top of the sniper-skill set list!

Climbing was part of this, and it ought to be part of the training at sniper school. For example, during one nighttime insertion in Samarra, we selected the roof of a two-story house for our hide site. A truck was parked beside the place and we used that to get up to a ledge on the side of the residence, then climbed from there up to a balcony. From there it appeared to be a dead end, with no obvious route to the roof. But after a while, I noticed that the side of the wall had decorative projections that could get us to the next balcony. It was far enough up that I had to jump to reach it, and then I had to pull myself up enough to reach the framework of the balcony. I climbed up and over, and from there got to the roof.

Now this is tricky in more than one way. When you're climbing, you don't have a weapon—somebody has to hold it for you, except for your pistol. While I was climbing, the other guys had to pull security and hold my rifle. Once I got to the roof, they handed up my M16 and I took over the security role at the same time I was helping the next guy get up. Of course, all this is extremely dangerous, but it is also a great deal of fun; the adrenaline rush is fantastic! But if you need your weapon while climbing, you are screwed! And the thirty-five pounds of gear on your vest—the ammo, the Individual Body Armor (IBA) plates—make climbing so much harder. That weight makes it easier to fall, and if you fall you are totally screwed that way, too!

FAILING THE TUG TEST

You could get hurt so many ways, some of them very unexpected. As an example, late one night around 0200 hours two other guys and I were about to insert into a hide site we had selected on the roof of a home. It was summertime, and nobody in Iraq sleeps inside because it is so hot; they set up beds on their roofs or patios where it is a little cooler.

Our route to this building required that we move through the yard of the house next door, and as we got to the gate, we could see the people asleep in the front yard. We slipped into the yard and up to a brick wall that had to be scaled before we could get to the hide. This wall was about five feet tall, and I was going to be the first one up and over.

Now you have to understand that in Iraq the quality of construction is just awful, and that you can't trust the strength of a building unless you test it yourself. We did that by tugging on anything that we intended to use as a climbing aid or handhold—we called it the tug test. So I gave this wall a tug before trying to climb it, but I guess I didn't try quite hard enough.

I jumped up, got one leg over the wall, and then the whole thing just collapsed underneath me! I hit the ground and watched as all these bricks started falling toward me like a bad dream. The crashing finally stopped about a half second after it started, but it felt like an eternity. The wall was now a vast pile of rubble that stopped inches from my feet. If I had fallen closer, it would have crushed me. But there I lay, looking at the hole in the wall. Beyond the hole were my two teammates, both looking at me and saying, "Dude, are you all right?" Of course, all the noise woke the Iraqi family up and perhaps the rest of the neighborhood, too. So much for our stealthy insertion!

SPIDER-MAN'S BIG ADVENTURE

When replacements for the sniper section arrived, each had to be trained and prepared before they could go out on missions by themselves, and we had our own local standards for this training that was unlike anything in sniper school. This started by taking each of them on a tour of the city that went through backyards, up the sides of buildings, across roofs—the most difficult route imaginable, with an emphasis on climbing.

Late one night another guy on the team and I took three new replacements out to see the town, and it was a memorable experience for all concerned. We decided to make it full of monster climbs and impossibly dangerous maneuvers. These replacements found themselves two stories up in the air, standing on a ledge about five inches wide, and then they had to move about ten feet along this ledge with their backs against the wall. At the end of the ledge was a gap of three or four feet between the ledge and the roof of a house, and our new guys had to make a leap of faith as well as an actual leap to get a leg over the parapet, then scramble across the gap to the other house. It was dangerous, but we got all the guys over and nobody fell and nobody got hurt. Now it was time to go home.

Of course we never returned by the same route we came in on because that would have made it easy for the enemy to track us and set up an ambush. So I took the new guys home by a different set of rooftops, yards, walls, and alleys. The hard part of the evening was over, I thought, but not quite. We got to a place where you had to jump over a wall, hang from the top as you maneuver your feet onto a ledge that was on your right side, then use the ledge for footing to turn around, and move across a roof and away, all about two stories in the air. I went first, got over to the next building, and then started pulling security for the other guys.

Well, one of the new guys was ready to go. He handed me his rifle and jumped over the wall. I heard a funny *swoosh*ing sound and looked over the wall to see what the new guy was doing. He was hanging by his fingertips, twenty feet in the air, from the ledge where his feet were supposed to be! "Holy shit!" I said. "You've got to be kidding me—this is the easiest part!" He obviously wasn't going to last long, so I reached over and grabbed the vest handle on his back and hauled him over to the ledge where he was supposed to have landed. Once he was safe, I asked him. "Dude, are you okay?"

His eyes were wide and he looked like he'd seen a ghost. All he could say was "Yeah!"

BIG SURPRISE FOR THE POSTER BOYS

Most of our missions involved total boredom. Our whole team could go months without anybody firing a shot, months of watching roads and streets without anybody placing an IED or displaying a weapon. The boredom of it all was exhausting. Then, at last, a company commander came up with an idea for a mission that was so sure to produce action and excitement that all five team leaders were ready to fight each other over who would go.

Here was the mission: Wanted posters for many high-value targets were routinely pasted to walls around Tikrit, and just as routinely somebody came along and ripped them down. Our commander's idea was that we would go out and overwatch some of these posters right after they went up, and, instead of shooting the people who tore them down, we'd just put a bullet into the wall as a way of saying, "Don't touch that!" Nobody would be killed, but anybody who did this—and we anticipated a lot of people would try—would get the surprise of their life.

Two sniper teams of three men each were selected from the five in our platoon. Sergeant Rick was the team leader of one team and I was the leader of the other. We headed over to the Charlie Company tactical operations center and were greeted by the company commander.

"Matrix One! Matrix Eight!" the commander said, greeting us by our call signs. "Are you guys ready for some fun?"

"Hell, yes, sir!" I said. There are not a lot of ways to have fun in

Tikrit when you're a sniper. We took off our helmets and IBA, dug out our notebooks, and got ready to receive our op order.

We stood around a large table in the TOC. An overhead photograph of the city* was fastened to the table and covered with an acetate overlay that allowed it to be marked up during mission planning and then erased.

"All right," he said, "we want to place posters of high-value targets we're looking for around the city, but we want them to stay up longer than twenty minutes. So, where do you guys think we should put them?"

Since we had spent so much time watching the city, Rick and I had strong ideas about suitable locations for the posters. "How about here," I told him, pointing to one intersection, "and over here," indicating another, which we knew from past experience had a lot of foot traffic. An apartment building across the street that we had used weeks before offered excellent fields of observation and would provide reasonable safety.

"Sounds good," the captain said. "Now, can you guys stay out there for a day or two, or does the S3 have something else planned for you?"

We expected this, and had no intention of staying out there once we had made our little statement. As experienced enlisted Army soldiers, we knew exactly how to manipulate officers, especially company commanders, and were ready for him. "Well, sir, I think we have to do a mission with one of the other companies as soon as we're done with your poster mission." I said this with a deadpan expression that I had been practicing my whole Army career.

"Hmm . . . well, all right," he said. He knew how the game was played. Even though he wanted to keep us for a while and was

---

* These overhead views are accessible to anyone at no cost on the Internet through Google Earth (earth.google.com).

suspicious about what I told him, he took the hint. "Red Six is downstairs waiting for you."

Red Six was the platoon leader who'd be working with us on the poster op. We went off to meet him feeling smug and successful, like two bad boys who had been caught but talked their way out of detention. If there had been a chance of anything productive resulting from a longer stay in the hide site, we'd have happily agreed to it and never mentioned anything about other plans for us.

Downstairs we huddled with Red Six, made all the coordination decisions and discussed how we would infil and extract, when we'd leave and when we'd get back. When we were finished with this part of the planning, Rick and I walked back to our quarters and spent some time prepping our gear, loading assault packs, checking weapons, and bringing the other guys up to speed. There was just enough time left for a few hours' sleep, so we racked out for a while. Very early the next morning, right at the appointed time, we assembled back at the TOC with all our guys and all our gear.

Tikrit was peaceful and quiet at that hour, and still cool. It was too dark to see the shabby buildings, the graffiti, the derelict cars. The residents were still in bed someplace instead of driving like maniacs on every street and road. If you could get past the stench of garbage and sewage, it was kind of nice as the eastern horizon grew lighter. I dumped my gear on the first Humvee and climbed aboard. The other guys finished preparations for the mission and listened to the sounds coming from M16 magazines being inserted in their well, the electronic squawk of radios being tested, and the gentle rumble of the diesel engines of the two vehicles in which we would ride.

My unit used a special kind of Humvee completely unlike those armored versions you see on the news. Instead of all the reinforced doors and add-on kits, our Humvees were completely stripped of all body work—no doors, no windows, no armor. Instead of being more vulnerable, we were actually more secure against most threats this way because we all had clear fields of fire in a 360-degree radius. Anybody who wanted to try taking a shot at us was likely to be engaged effectively well before he could get off his first shot.

With everybody in place and weapons oriented outboard, our convoy moved out. In a few minutes we got to our objective. Rick and his two guys bailed out of their Humvee, and I yelled to the platoon leader up front, "This will do, sir! Let me off here!"

The Humvee only slowed a bit. We slid off the back, hit the ground running, and sprinted to the entrance to the apartment building. My two guys, Walter and Brian, beat me to the building and slid into the stack at their assigned positions. I took the point, as planned, and we moved inside.

We all had our PVS-14 night-vision goggles (NVGs) attached to our helmets, turned on and adjusted, and we flipped them down into position. Without the NVG, you were virtually blind inside the building; with them, you were inside a surreal green world where everything looked weird but bright enough to navigate and, if necessary, to fight in.

I led the stack up the stairs, clearing the building methodically as we had been trained to do, setting up intrusion alarms and booby traps behind us. At the top floor we found our destination, an apartment on the fourth floor we'd used weeks before. I tried the door handle—locked! If we had had more time I would have picked the lock, but the QRF was due on the street soon and would begin putting up those posters. Instead, I just put a boot forcefully into the door just above the lock and was rewarded by a satisfying crash as the door burst open. We stormed in and cleared the place, making sure no threats were within, then quickly began to set up our gear.

Walter, Brian, and I took one of the bedrooms. After you've set up an urban hide a few dozen times, it becomes almost automatic: you make it easy to see out and impossible to see back inside, you set up the room so you can observe for long periods without undue fatigue, and when you fire, you shoot from a very stable platform. We did this by partially opening the windows, partially closing the drapes, and using the furniture of the abandoned apartment to make ourselves comfortable. The windows were already filthy, and that helped a lot. Within a few minutes we had our gear out of the rucks, and radios and weapons set up in position. Right on cue, the QRF guys arrived in the street below.

The guys in the street were supposed to know where we were, but you know how it is in any big organization—somebody doesn't get the word, and in military operations, he's the guy that can get you killed. While I was watching the posters go up, one of the soldiers on the street below spotted me through his night vision system and stopped, not recognizing me as friendly. I quickly used my NVG infrared illuminator to put out a few flashes to give him a clue, stepped back from the window and keyed my radio handset. "Red Six, Red Six, this is Matrix One—we are in position and signaling you with IR flashes, over!"

The soldier below raised his M16 and put his PEQ-2 laser sight on my center of mass! I was furious and closed the window, then yelled into the radio, "Red Six, tell your fucking men we're up here and to quit lasing us like we're fucking goddamn Hajji!"*

Friendly fire is a recurring issue for sniper teams, and the guys we replaced had a technique for situations like this. They always hollered something like "Fucking retard!" or an equivalent phrase that the local insurgents wouldn't know, and that worked for them. It would have worked for us, but it would have also compromised our position and aborted the whole mission.

The QRF circus took their bows and exited stage left. Act One was complete. We waited for the sun to come up and the locals to begin their day.

---

* "Hajji": One of many slang expressions for enemy insurgents.

Act Two began right after sunrise. A man walking down the street noticed the wanted posters, approached the nearest one, and began yelling something about it and generally ranting and raving. Brian was on the gun at the time. He said, "I got one!" and flipped the safety switch from SAFE to FIRE.

"Wait till he grabs it," I told him. He could talk all he wanted as long as he didn't try to take it down, but we knew, of course, that he wouldn't be able to resist. It was amusing to see him rant and rave for a few moments. Then he reached up to grab the edge of the poster, and that's when Brian fired.

He put the bullet into a glass sign for a kebob shop that was just above the wall on which the poster was pasted. The glass shattered and began to rain down on the man's head. The pieces were too small to hurt him but the experience was obviously a huge surprise. He recoiled in shock and panic, quickly spun around, searching for the source of the shot that had been placed about a foot above his head. He shook off the fragments, left the poster where it was, and hurried down the street. Mission accomplished, on this guy at least.

"Target," Brian quietly reported.

"Roger," I quietly answered.

There was a long intermission until late in the morning when four young men walked down the street in our direction. They had the swagger and sass of boys in their late teens or early twenties out on the town without adult supervision. One of the guys was more animated and full of himself than the others—the leader of the pack. I knew we would have trouble with these guys, and I was right.

Now I was on the gun and got set to make a shot. The leader of the "poster boys" saw the posters on the wall and went into a variation of the same infuriated act presented by our first guy. I put the guy in the sight, crosshairs well over his head, and watched. This was an extreme angle shot, and I wanted to avoid actually hitting the young man with my shot, so I decided to put the first round well over his head, if he actually tore down one of the posters. Sure enough, he ripped one of them down violently.

I put a bullet into the roof of the building well above him, a friendly little word to the wise. He didn't get the message and actually didn't seem to notice anything unusual. Now he trooped down the sidewalk to the next poster.

The noise of my first shot was trapped in our room and damn near deafened me. Some teams have sound suppressors for just this sort of thing, but not us. My ears were ringing and hurt from the noise, a distraction that almost broke my concentration. We train to push through distractions and focus on the target. I focused on the target. "Don't do it, buddy!" my spotter said under his breath.

The guy was kind of tall. As he moved to the next poster, I selected a spot just over his head, another glass sign, for my intended point of impact. He grabbed the top of the poster. "Fine, then!" I said and pressed the trigger.

The bullet hit exactly where intended. The sign exploded in a cloud of tiny fragments of broken glass, which suddenly began to rain down on the surprised young man. Instantly he forgot about the poster and whipped off his jacket, pulling it up over his head to ward off the broken glass. His buddies were back down the sidewalk. Until now, they thought his act was hilarious. Suddenly they were all terrified. Their leader threw his hands in the air, shedding some of the glass on his clothing, and ran back to the group.

The little group quickly conferred and bravely decided on a course of action: they sent the littlest, youngest member of the group down the sidewalk to search for us. The poor little guy was frightened but he crept up toward the posters, looking around at windows and rooftops, hoping to spot us. Of course he didn't.

"Some friends that kid has," I observed.

"What a bunch of idiots!" Brian laughed.

With the neighborhood stirred up, and with our point forcefully made, it was time to give the QRF a call to see if they would kindly come and pick us up before somebody actually got hurt. Maybe the commander actually had something else for us to do!

CHAPTER TWELVE

BRYAN PRUETT: SLOW IS SMOOTH AND SMOOTH IS FAST: OPERATION QWAHETAS

Bryan Pruett was a sergeant and one of four sniper element leaders on Shadow Team during the unit's first deployment.

"Qwahetas" is a word we invented, a made-up term with an Arabic sound that we used to signify our own particular kind of mayhem or havoc when we inflicted it on the local enemy. While planning an operation, we decided to name the mission Operation Qwahetas because the building we intended to use was located near a plain white wall where Sam Samuel had spray-painted "Qwahetas" while on a mission in downtown Ramadi one night not long before.

It was a three-story building on Route Michigan that had a front side that was pretty much in view of the Ramadi Inn (a.k.a. OP Hotel), the static hide site where we almost always had a Shadow element as well as a platoon from Alpha Company, 2nd Battalion, 69th Infantry Regiment, 3rd Infantry Division. Behind the building was an alleyway that was out of view from the hotel. The great thing about the alleyway was that it enabled us to see far enough down the road to where we could have eyes on a vital intersection that was constantly being planted with IEDs.

The plan was that I and my two team members would be at the hotel for twenty-four hours, and on the morning of day three, around 0200, Sam "Samuel" and his guys would walk out to OP Hotel and we would link up and head to Qwahetas for another twenty-four to forty-eight hours. This also happened to be Sam's first mission since returning from block leave the day before.

So 0200 rolled around and Sam and his guys showed up. We began to run through everything, do our radio checks and check our gear, making sure we had a chain and lock ready to lock the door behind us, bolt cutters for the lock and chain that was most likely on the door already, food, water, and snivel gear (comfort items like gloves, gaiters, and warm clothes).

Once we got down on the street, I decided to halt things for a second and called back upstairs to the third Shadow element that was going to stay at the OP Hotel. It was headed by Harry Martinez, a National Guardsman from Pennsylvania who was working with us. I had Harry shoot out a streetlight that was really doing us no good other than exposing our movement through the area.

After that was over we radio-checked with battalion back at Camp Corregidor and with the CP* in the OP Hotel, and Operation Qwahetas was officially underway. It was a pretty short trek to the building, and we had good overwatch security being provided from the hotel almost the entire way.

I want to relay what it felt like walking down these streets on these missions. First, we all look like robots, and our movements at this point had gotten downright precise in every aspect; every head turn was sharp and with a point and every gaze was intensely focused. Our senses were at extreme levels, which I suppose is what happens when you're in survival mode.

Every step we took seemed so loud, especially when we kicked

---

* Command post.

debris or sloshed through a sewage puddle in the road. Night vision gave us an unbelievable advantage, but we were exposed to anyone who knew their way around the city and was able to find a small area to pop off some shots at us. So, fluid movement was of the utmost importance, along with not stepping on any bombs.

On top of all this there was the fratricide issue. Ramadi was not a nice city, to say the least, and the majority of the US soldiers and Marines in the area would do just about anything to avoid walking around the city streets with nothing but a radio and seven friends to cover your ass. So as we walked or ran through these streets three or four nights a week, I always wondered how many half-asleep American soldiers were in some nearby building with itchy trigger fingers and no knowledge that we were in their area of operation.

We reached the door of the building, set up a hasty security perimeter, cut the chain, filed everyone in, rechained the door from the inside, and began to clear the building, all within a couple of minutes.

I recall being very pleased with our swiftness in doing this and I remember thinking briefly about how good we were getting at these operations at this point as we flowed right through every stage with ease and no worries. Everyone knew their job and nothing stopped. "Slow is smooth and smooth is fast" was a motto that my very first company commander instilled in us, and I could see exactly what he meant as we rolled from stage to stage in this mission.

Me and the other guy secured a lock on the front door. The entire building was cleared by the time the two of us made it upstairs. We quickly began searching for the best observation area overlooking the intersection we were tasked with this night. As fate would have it, the only place where we were going to be able to overwatch that area was blocked by a cinderblock wall. Luckily we had two rock hammers and a sledgehammer between the eight of us.

We beat and banged and chiseled on this wall for more than two hours in the early morning between roughly 0300 and 0500 hours. This was definitely way too loud and strenuous, but we had no choice at this point. Our only other option was to call the higher-ups and ask permission to find another hide site, which would have posed more danger and probably not given us the view we needed. So we decided to stick it out and take our chances. The good thing here was no matter how much noise we made, the insurgents couldn't move in on us because of the overwatch being provided by the OP Hotel boys. Eventually around 0530 we had our loophole. We then set up a rest plan for the guys, and two people got on the gun and spotting scopes. We rotated out a couple of times, I had gotten a little catnap in along the way, and around 0830 I was back on. Sam was up with me, and I told him to go ahead and take the gun, since he had been gone, and I would get on the spotting scope for him.

At around 0900 traffic was picking up a little bit, but we had no real action in the area we were watching. The eyes started getting a little tired, and the body was definitely feeling the effects of sleep deprivation, but once again survival mode was in high gear.

As a sniper you want to set your gun up about three to four feet behind your loophole or possibly even farther, providing you are still able to view the area you need to view. We were set up about five feet away from the wall with our loophole, and we had a piece of mosquito net hanging up on the inside of the wall to make the hole and ourselves less visible.

Due to the lack of activity, Sam had taken his eyes off the gun for a bit to look just with his eyes at the areas closer to us. The intersection we were watching was about seven hundred meters away, so we had a lot of area in between us and the target zone to scan. I always had the worst time taking my eyes off the scope, because I just knew as soon as I did some guy would walk out with an AK-47 and I would miss him altogether. Luckily that was the case on this particular day—at about the time Sam was looking at a building across the

alleyway from us, I saw two guys come strolling out into our intersection carrying a 155mm artillery shell with lots of wires sticking
out—an IED.

"Smoke that motherfucker, smoke their fucking asses." That was
all I could mutter at the time. Sam paused for about two or three seconds before he realized what I was talking about. He quickly reposi-
tioned the M24 and began taking aim on these two assholes, who
were strolling through traffic with this bomb heading for a hole in
the road. They had no idea that they were getting ready to have a very
bad experience.

The scope was already dialed in—a seven minute plus two clicks
correction—which put us right on target. Now Sam waited. He already had the scope where he needed it; now he only waited on them
to stop walking and bend over to put this bomb in the road. "Wait,
wait, wait one . . . smoke his fucking ass!"

Bang. That was what it sounded like in our little home away from
home that morning right after those two guys paused long enough
to cover up their bomb with a piece of cardboard.

"Gut shot to the guy on the right and his buddy ran behind the
market," I reported to Sam and whoever was on the radio relaying
the information back to battalion at Corregidor. The guy's buddy
never showed his face again, and the guy somehow managed to
crawl and hid himself behind a building, where he later bled out
and died. Due to the traffic in the area we were unable to get another clear shot on this day, but luckily Sam made the first one
count. That single shot and that rock hammer to the wall and that
walk to the building and the chain on the door and "Slow is smooth
and smooth is fast" all led up to this. What we did was secure this
intersection for American soldiers to travel on for at least a month
before anyone would have the balls to come back to that area with
another bomb.

This was the first time we had ever run Qwahetas and we weren't sure if it would work out. There were a few variables that we weren't sure about but we drove on with the mission and we tried it anyway. Even when the cinderblock wall showed its face we drove on right through the son of a bitch, and it paid off. After this mission I knew something that I hadn't really thought about before: we were actually good at what we were doing. We had become professionals at something that is so unimaginable to your everyday person. I have to say, it was a feeling like no other.

CHAPTER THIRTEEN

SPC. AARON ARNOLD

I got the majority of my kills with the M16, not the M24. In fact, the weapon I ended up using was half mine, half the Army's. The barrel of my issued M16A5 SDM rifle was bent when I slipped on rubble during a clearing operation. I fell down a flight of steps to the concrete floor and landed on the rifle. I had purchased an upper receiver-and-barrel assembly with my own money to replaced the damaged assembly, and I used that for the majority of the time afterward. This barrel came from DPMS, a civilian weapons manufacturer, and was shorter than the regular M16 barrel, so I had a weapon that was as compact and convenient as an M4 but with the accuracy of the M16 with a heavy barrel.

The number-one tool we had in Iraq was the M16 with the ballistic capabilities of the 77-grain ammunition. We took ours to the range and discovered that these weapons were making consistent first-round hits on man-sized targets at eight hundred meters using ACOG sights. That is better than the normal M16 and 62-grain bullet, but the real difference came when you shot somebody with one. When you shoot somebody with the standard green tip rounds, the bullet just goes through them without much immediate incapacitation. But when you shoot somebody with the 77-grain bullet, the effect is entirely different. They react in a characteristic movement we called the wave—the arms fly up, the knees buckle, and the whole body flinches as the person is knocked down violently.

The 77-grain bullet has great penetration, too. I shot one guy through the windshield of a car and hit him in the head, right where I was aiming, killing him instantly. If I had been using the lighter bullet, I think it would have been deflected.

INTERSECTION TWO NINER SIX

The insurgents were very active around a water tower and street intersection we called Two Niner Six. Big IEDs were going off near this intersection daily, and we knew that the emplacement teams were really busy there. We had a chance to get some action at this location.

We infiltrated at night: Sam Samuel, Ulysses "Cooter" Collett, and I as one team, plus a squad of infantry guys for security. We selected an abandoned house that seemed to have good fields of view. Sam and Cooter set up an outpost (OP) on the lower floor; I went upstairs and set up another with a different sector.

After twenty-four hours in this place we had seen nothing. The operation had been planned to last only one full day, but the three of us felt that the location was too good and something would go down if we only waited a bit longer. Our platoon leader asked if we wanted to stay put another day, and so we did.

Later in the day, a sedan pulled up in my sector. Three guys got out, and they were wearing black masks! I had heard of insurgents doing this but never thought I would actually see somebody be so stupid! The men popped the trunk and pulled out an IED, an artillery shell. They carried the shell to a hole by the side of the road.

While they were doing this, I positioned myself and the two security guys with me at a window. Our firing positions were a few feet back from the wall. One of the guys had an M240 medium machine gun and I put him on one side of me. The other was a squad-designated marksman from Able* Company.

"I will initiate the ambush," I told them. "I will engage the guy in the car; you engage the guys at the hole with the machine gun. That way we won't all engage the same targets."

I killed the guy in the passenger seat with the first shot. The M240 gunner opened up on the men at the hole, but his weapon jammed after firing only about five rounds. The other rifleman and I started engaging the rest—the driver and the men with the IED. We put three down; one ran away toward a mosque.

Five minutes later, the guy came back and began peering over a wall at the IED site where his three buddies lay dead on the ground and in the car. I got one shot at him and probably got a hit on him, but he disappeared again.

A crowd showed up and began milling around the car and the bodies. Our rules of engagement authorized us to shoot anybody removing anything from the scene, but not if they were just looking. We put a few rounds over their heads to scare them off, and most of them left—all except for one guy who began taking things from the trunk, where the IED had been. When he tried to run off with something from the car, we shot him, too.

Now that the whole neighborhood was aware of where we were and milling around down on the street, it was time to collect our gear and go home. But with all those people from the mosque nearby, and an unknown number of insurgents probably preparing to attack us, it was time to call for some support. We got on the

---

* Ordinarily, A Company would be called Alpha, but within 3rd Infantry Division this was often modified. Arnold's battalion used the old World War II terminology for its A Company, partly in homage to the valor of the unit of the same name as depicted in the much-loved film *Band of Brothers*.

radio back to our CP and asked for the tank company to roll over to our location and provide some protection. The commander of the tank company turned us down flat—he was afraid that his tanks would be attacked. Considering how much armor his guys had and how little we were wearing, this seemed odd; we always thought the tanks were our reliable quick reaction force, but apparently not.

But Alpha Company's commander heard our call for help and sent his guys and their Bradleys out to get us. We had worked with them before, and they were a superb infantry unit. A short time later, Alpha Company showed up, cleared the area, and carried us home in their vehicles. They brought along explosive ordnance disposal guys, too, and they took care of the IED. At the same time, while the infantry was clearing the site, they recovered weapons and cell phones from the vehicle. After that mission, we knew that Alpha was the one company we could trust to help us out of a jam.

FIRST BLOOD

When we got to Iraq and began operations in the Baquaba region, I was one of the four guys in the section who had never been in combat. The sergeants had either been in OIF 1* or Afghanistan or they'd had some experience with shooting at people and being shot at themselves. The four of us were pumped up and wanted to shoot somebody—that was, after all, our job. We were bored out of our minds and sitting around one day and the conversation went something like, "Man, I can't wait to kill somebody!"

One of the sergeants in our section overheard the discussion. He said, "You guys don't know what you are talking about, and you

---

* OIF-Operation Iraqi Freedom

don't know what you are going to feel like after you kill a person. This is not something you should want to do!"

These comments were not reassuring and made us all feel a bit guilty about what we had been saying. Of course we had some mixed emotions over the issue, but what we had been saying was actually consistent with Army doctrine for sniper employment. Our mission was to kill people, and we were taught to do so without remorse. Suddenly, one of our own leaders was discouraging us from wanting to do our mission. "Maybe he's right," somebody said after the sergeant left. "Maybe we will feel awful when we actually do kill a person."

This encounter was troubling for me and lowered my confidence. Later in the evening I went over to the room where two other NCOs were talking. I told them about the discussion and how it made us apprehensive about what we'd feel when we finally made a shot. "I'm kind of nervous now," I told them, "after thinking about how we're going to operate. You guys have done this before—I am going to be the weak link on our team; I have never been in combat. I don't know how I will react."

"Don't worry about it," Sam Samuel said. "Your training will take over and you are going to do what you were trained to do." Then he paused for a moment and added, "And, honestly, as long as you are following the rules, it is kind of fun!"

After that I thought, *Well, I guess I don't need to be scared—I will just do my job the way I am supposed to.* My first engagement came not too long after that, when Staff Sgt. Harry Martinez and I killed several insurgents who had multiple IEDs. Both of us were excited and pumped up immediately afterwards, doing high fives and congratulating each other on successfully taking those guys out.

After that it became more businesslike—not fun, exactly, but professional. And when one of our guys was killed by an IED, we got more serious about it—payback time. My attitude was, when I saw a guy planting an IED or doing other clearly insurgent behavior, I needed to kill that person or he was going to kill a bunch of us. I was not going to let that happen.

There is a rush when you have a successful engagement. It is an adrenal rush, exciting. You wait so long in your hide, and when you get a chance to make a shot on somebody who is your enemy, there's something awesome about it. There are times when taking a life saves the lives of others.

I have never had bad dreams or bad feelings about any of the people I killed. That is because I positively identified each and every target before I pulled the trigger. You sometimes hear that a sniper can recall the faces of every person he has shot, but that has never happened to me. The stories you hear about that sort of thing has always seemed to be Hollywood, or overly dramatic, to me. Of course different people are affected by such things in different ways.

Trust is very important within military units, and once trust is established those units can conduct very successful missions. But trust has to be earned, and we earned ours the first time Shadow Team went out with Able Company's Blue Platoon. Their platoon leader, a lieutenant whose call sign was Blue One, loved the way our section worked on that first successful engagement. From then on, all the platoons in Able always asked for us to go out on operations with them. Their attitude was, "We want to go out with you guys because you always find some action, and we want to be part of it!"

One of the reasons for our success was my team leader's insistence on doing things properly and not cutting corners. When we constructed a hide, we did it just the way we were taught in sniper school. We used mosquito netting to make the hide hard to see into, used tables to get good lines of sight, searched for good window locations, and avoided using the roof. Other teams were much more casual about these things: they just stayed back from the window and didn't use the nets. I think that was part of the reason these teams didn't make many kills.

OP HOTEL

Most of my kills came from OP Hotel, a static hide. The insurgents knew exactly where we were, but they couldn't get at us very easily, even though they tried. The building was attacked by a vehicle-borne IED on one occasion and that made a mess, but we still used the location.

In a static hide, the enemy knows where you fire from, what you can see and not see. We used OP Hotel so much that it was always equipped with a lot of things that we needed to bring in to a different place—sandbags, for example, were already available at OP Hotel, along with shooting platforms designed for the location. Despite the enemy's knowledge of the site, we felt comfortable there. Insurgents would occasionally spray the building with AK fire, but it was ineffective and not much of a threat.

The vehicle-borne IED attack on OP Hotel did change our operations a bit. It shook us up. After that, we concentrated on taking out the enemy scouts and spotters; if you saw a guy using binoculars, you killed him. A guy using a cell phone or a video recorder from a roof overwatching the main supply route or our location would also be killed—those were the guys doing reconnaissance for vehicle-borne IED attacks on us.

The attack was very sophisticated, and we all assumed al-Qaeda was involved in the planning and execution. Prior to the attack, nearby insurgents provided what we call support by fire, that is, machine-gun fire directed at our building to get our heads down. Then came the suicide bomber in a truck loaded with explosives. The driver tried to ram into the building but got caught on a concrete barrier at the curb. The truck rolled over before detonating, and although OP Hotel was damaged, the blast was dissipated and the bomber killed only himself.

REACH OUT AND TOUCH SOMEONE

The insurgents had a good idea of what we could hit from OP Hotel with our M24s and M16s, and they learned to stay outside that kill zone when doing anything obviously out of line with our rules of engagement. But outside those limits they seemed to feel safe enough to conduct their ops under our observation. The M24s were normally dangerous to them up to thousand meters or so—all the way down Route Michigan, past the water tower, to the vicinity of the big mosque. That changed when we started using the M107 Barrett .50cal rifles.

Staff Sgt. James Gilliland was observing the area to the north of OP Hotel. This part of the city was light industrial, with many small workshops and garages. We had good observation of this area from the upper floors of the building and he spotted one of the big blue vehicles we called bongo trucks. The truck parked at a spot beyond our normal engagement range. Several men got out, and he saw them start to unload several IEDs.

From the crow's nest on top of OP Hotel we had a great view of this activity, and Sergeant G (as we all called him) grabbed the Barrett and began to engage. His first shot went downrange properly, but the second round failed to feed—the rifle had jammed! Someone else had been using it, sand had gotten into the receiver, and the weapon wasn't cycling. He went through the normal immediate action drills, tried another magazine, and got another shot off. Then it jammed again.

I got down next to him on the right side of the gun, stripped the cartridges out of one of the magazines, and fed one into the chamber by hand. He pulled the operating handle back, let it go, and the bolt locked up as it was supposed to. He fired and was getting good hits on the IED team and their vehicle. We had never trained to do this maneuver, never thought of it before, but we invented the drill on the spot, and it worked! The M107 is not supposed to be a crew-served weapon, but we made it one on this engagement.

The Barrett was never intended to be as accurate as the M24, and it isn't. It isn't as reliable, either, but it has its uses. We found that for us the best ammunition was tracer rounds. We'd been told to avoid this ammo because it burns out the barrel faster than other types, but we thought it was a bit more accurate. It had the other advantage of being easier to see where it hit, and that was a big help.

Those tracer rounds were helpful in one big engagement we had not long after the bongo-truck incident. The Marines had set up an OP like ours at the edge of their sector, and both overlooked a structure we christened the Gay Palace. This palace was a seven-story building and much taller than the Marine OP, and the insurgents used this advantage to frequently fire on the Marines.

We could hear the gunfire even though the range to the building was about 2,500 meters, around a mile and a half. Sam, Cooter, and I were up in the crow's nest, watching through our spotting scopes as the insurgents ran around on the roof of the Gay Palace firing RPGs down on the OP. As soon as it became apparent what was happening, Sam jumped behind the Barrett and began firing at the insurgents. The range was extreme and because of the atmospheric conditions it was very difficult to see the bullet's trace.*

Sam switched to tracer ammunition. The projectile has a small cup at the base of the bullet filled with phosphorus, and this compound burns for about a second as the bullet flies downrange, making it easy

---

* "Trace" is the sniper's term for the momentary disturbance of the air caused by the passage of the bullet. The phenomenon lasts only a fraction of a second but can sometimes reveal the point of impact on a distant target. It is most apparent early and late in the day, or during periods of high humidity.

to follow. Cooter and I spotted for him and helped him adjust for the range and wind. Sam started pumping bullets into the windows facing the Marines. Even at this tremendous distance, he was putting round after round right into the windows of the place—awesome shooting!

SNIPER PERSONALITIES

A sniper needs to be bold without being reckless. You need to be able to tell others what you intend to do, including officers, instead of asking permission. This requires boldness, especially with some officers, if you want to run missions that are successful. You have to be willing to take calculated risks to achieve these missions—a two- or three-man sniper team going off by itself in a dangerous place like Ramadi needs to be bold and self-confident. Our section wanted to be a lot bolder in our operations than our officers wanted, but Staff Sergeant Gilliland was able to show that we could execute our mission successfully and stay alive at the same time.

Even then, some of the staff officers were uncomfortable about the way we operated. But when somebody commented to our battalion commander, Lieutenant Colonel Rogoman, that Sergeant G was "dishing out business," the colonel answered that he was a "free-roaming radical," and it was meant as a compliment to him and the whole section's aggressive style of operation. Given the opportunity, we were bold, but it took the commander to help us be successful because the staff officers seemed to think of us as a bunch of cowboys.

CHAPTER FOURTEEN

JOSEPH BENNETT: TRAFFIC CONTROL FROM A DISTANCE

Spc. Joseph Bennett, affectionately known as Joey B to the team, was one of the 24th Infantry Division Guardsmen chopped to Shadow, and later to the 101st Airborne when they took over control of Ramadi. Bennett, unlike some other snipers, grew to admire the M107 Barrett .50cal and became Shadow's expert on the gun, especially on its use against vehicles. During a six-month period, he destroyed between sixteen and twenty cars and trucks with the rifle, mostly with the exotic Norwegian Raufoss Mk211 HEIAP (high-explosive/incendiary/armor-piercing projectile). Although the M107 was not intended to be an antipersonnel weapon, Bennett demonstrated that it could stop people as well as vehicles with similar devastating effect.

There was a traffic circle about eight hundred meters to the west of our position, and when we first started working in the area, cars would pull to the side of the road, and guys would get out and fire their AKs at us. The AK is really only effective to about two hundred or three hundred meters, so we were pretty safe from them. They, on the other hand, were not very safe from us.

At first we tried returning fire with the M240 machine gun, but that was not the ideal weapon—it could hit them and their vehicle well enough, but it could hit a lot of other people and vehicles in the area as well. We tried our M24s, of course, but these targets were at the edge of its effective range against personnel targets, and the M24 was not effective at all when used to stop cars or trucks. The Barrett M107 was perfect for these targets.

We were able to use the Raufoss Mk211 rounds for the Barrett. The bullet has a small amount of Composition B explosive in the tip, a tungsten penetrator, and an incendiary filling. When the projectile hits a hard surface, the result is an explosive blast combined with a kinetic energy penetrator—lots of fragments, lots of fire and flash. One hit on a vehicle will normally set a car on fire. I knocked out a lot of vehicles with this round.

Some of the vehicles were empty and abandoned alongside the main supply routes (MSR). People would drive up to the side of the road, park their cars, and walk away. They had been warned about leaving vehicles in such locations, and when we noticed one that had not moved in a couple of days, it was considered suspicious and a possible vehicle-borne IED. Insurgents often used parked vehicles for their attacks. My job on the team was to take them out with the Barrett.

It didn't take much, just one or two shots, and the vehicle usually caught fire. Then we waited to see what would happen next. Sometimes they just burned out, but several times they were loaded with explosives and I got massive secondary explosions.

I also engaged a lot of moving targets with the Barrett. Our OP was hit by a truck full of explosives driven by a suicide bomber. After that, we were told to immediately engage any trucks that turned onto Route Michigan. It wasn't necessary to destroy them—a shot into the bed would wake up the driver and remind him of his mistake. Most of them stopped, turned around, and took another route.

But it took more than warning shots for some people. On one

occasion, two of our Bradleys were patrolling in the area. I saw a car behaving oddly—it would come around a corner, apparently for the driver to look at the Bradleys, and then pull back out of sight. This happened several times. Then it pulled out again, and one of the passengers got out with an RPG and started to fire at the Bradleys. It happened so quickly that I didn't have time to tell my spotter, Rick Taylor, what was happening; I just started to engage. The car was at nine hundred meters, about half a mile. The gunner with the RPG was my priority target; I fired at him first and missed—the round went a little high. He was on the far side of the vehicle from me so I had to put the round through the door in order to hit him. I shifted my point of aim a bit and fired again, hitting him with the second shot. The bullet went through the door, exploded, and shredded the guy.

Then I began to put rounds into the car itself. The driver must have been nervous about the whole engagement, because when the first round smacked the wall across the street he panicked and stalled the engine. I aimed at the driver through the passenger-side window, fired, and hit him behind the wheel, turning him into a mess.

We always thought that the Raufoss round would not explode if it hit the soft tissue of a human body, but I made a snap shot at a guy once at a range of only three hundred meters; the bullet apparently hit his hip because it exploded and blew him apart.

I engaged so many vehicles that we started a list of all the makes and models of cars and trucks that we shot with the Barrett. It seemed an awful lot of them were Caprice Classic sedans, but I always wanted to destroy a GMC Suburban and never did. Waiting for one to show up and do something that met the rules of engagement became a running joke on our team.

On my last mission before we went home, I was set up near one of the entry control points (ECP), or roadblocks, at the outskirts of the city. I wasn't overwatching the ECP but had a primary sector in another direction. Rick Taylor noticed something suspicious among the cars waiting to go through the checkpoint and reported to Sergeant Martinez, "Hey, I just saw a guy walk up to a car waiting to go through the ECP, throw a suitcase in the back, then walk away."

Harry took a look at the situation and called to me, "Joey, bring your Barrett over here."

The other shooters and I shifted our positions and moved our rifles to the side of the hide facing the ECP. The range to the checkpoint was only about two hundred meters, so we were very close. Harry called our lieutenant with a spot report on the incident. "We'll send the Iraqi Army guys over to check it out," he said.

There was some miscommunication about the situation and the Iraqi soldiers failed to check out the car. But while we were waiting, the Iraqis waiting in line suddenly started to abandon their cars and run away from the ECP. We couldn't figure out exactly what was happening, but it seemed to be dangerous. Then the driver of the car with the suitcase came back, got into his car again, and started driving closer to the soldiers manning the checkpoint. When the Iraqi soldiers started running away we were all sure that he was a suicide bomber. Somebody ordered, "Engage!" and we began to fire up the car.

I put one round through the windshield, hitting the driver, and then shifted to the car to try to immobilize it. Even though the driver was hit, the car kept rolling forward. I put a couple of rounds into the fuel tank, setting it afire, and another into the engine. This stopped the car, and the door fell open and the driver crawled out. My shot had taken his arm off but he managed to crawl away from the vehicle and away from the ECP. The Iraqi soldiers still at the checkpoint saw him at closer range and said that he had been hit multiple times and was bleeding heavily but was still able to get away. About that time the explosives in the suitcase detonated, but far enough away that none of the soldiers was injured.

Moving targets are really hard to hit. When you try to hit a vehicle moving at forty or fifty miles an hour, you have to hold off eight or ten mils—off to the edge of the reticle.

Running people are just as hard to hit, or more so. The first guy I missed was at five hundred meters, and I shot at him with a M24. I was very upset about the miss, but my sergeant reminded me that running targets are very hard to hit. We train to hit moving targets at sniper school but not at ranges beyond five hundred meters.

I was a huge fan of the Barrett and always wanted to take it out. Not everybody on my team felt the same way. Of course it is not as accurate as the M24, and it is a lot heavier. In urban warfare, the weight is an issue because I had to carry my M16 and M203,* all the ammunition for weapons, water, and food, in addition to the Barrett and its ammunition—about fifty more pounds. After I did this a few times I decided to break the Barrett down and split the load between my partner and me, and that helped. Carrying this load under normal circumstances is not a big deal, but if you ever needed to run with it, all that extra weight would certainly slow you down. Jumping over a wall with a Barrett in your ruck is not easy, no matter how big you are!

Our section had two M107 Barretts available, and one of them was used as a backup. This weapon was nearly new and exceptionally accurate; Barretts are supposed to be two- or three-MOA rifles, but this one would shoot one-inch groups at hundred meters, or one-MOA. Some of the rifles seemed to shoot better than others, and this one was excellent.

The M24 is really an easy rifle to shoot compared to the Barrett. You could take a kid and put him behind that rifle, and he could shoot amazing groups with just a little training. The Barrett takes more work to use effectively. Shooting a guy at three hundred meters

---

* The M203 is a 40mm grenade launcher attached below the barrel of the rifle.

with a Barrett is awesome, but most of my targets were beyond eight hundred or thousand meters. Hitting a human being at that range with that rifle takes experience and training—and a good weapon.

The Barrett was such a good psychological weapon: when fliers were printed warning people to avoid digging in the road, the piece had a photo of a person with a shovel on one side, with crosshairs superimposed on his chest. The clear message was that if you were digging a hole in the road, you would be shot. The flier was very effective.

JOKER TAKES OVER FROM SHADOW

When the 101st Airborne took over from 3rd Infantry Division, we then went to work for them, and they were very strong advocates for the M107. When we went out on missions, they always told us to bring our M24s and a Barrett, too. The .50cal rifle is a very intimidating weapon. The Barrett is also a very effective weapon, too—one of the most effective small-arms weapons used by American infantry.

From the top of our barracks building on an old agricultural university we could watch a street we all called North Stadium Way. Shortly after the 101st showed up, the guys in the tower spotted some suspicious activity on a road nearby. They could see a car stopped in the road and several men doing something on the far side of the car, apparently using it to screen their activity. The TOC called down to our unit on the radio: "Get a Joker team up on the roof and see what's going on."

While Sergeant Hughes went to the roof with his Barrett, I went down to my weapon locker and got my Barrett, too, they called Harry and told him what I was doing so he could alert the tactical operations center that we'd have two guns available. Hughes was in full uniform but I was just wearing a light fleece jacket, civilian running shorts, and a pair of shower shoes. I climbed up to the top of the building and went into action dressed like that, with the Barrett in one hand and a can of ammunition in the other.

We had a better angle on the car from our location, and we called up the tower to report, "Those guys are still digging in the middle of the road." We put the laser range finder on them and measured the range at a bit more than nine hundred meters.

"Continue to observe," the tower radioed back.

Sergeant Hughes's spotter was watching through his 40-power spotting scope while we studied the situation through our rifle scopes. It wasn't clear what the men were doing until two of them got up from their digging, went to the trunk of the car, and got out two mortar rounds; now we knew for sure they were planting IEDs. Under the old Third ID rules of engagement, we were authorized to open fire immediately—but to be safe, Sergeant Hughes called the TOC for clearance. "Engage!" was their response, too.

The insurgents were partly hidden again on the far side of the car, but we lined up on them anyway and put our bullets right through the car, hitting the men. Hughes and I fired a total of twelve Raufoss rounds, setting the vehicle on fire immediately. From our position we could see at least two of the men go down and stay down, dead. Other rifles and cartridges will kill a person at nine hundred meters, but the Barrett M107 is the only weapon that will shoot that far, punch through both sides of a car, and still have enough energy to make a solid kill.

CHAPTER FIFTEEN

STAFF SGT. TIMOTHY LA SAGE, US MARINE CORPS

*T*im La Sage is a career Marine who was recovering from his wounds when these stories were recorded.

My unit was 2nd Battalion, 5th Marines, 1st Marine Division, and our sniper platoon was part of Weapons Company. I had sixteen Marines who lived with me at the combat outpost, and another four in the platoon who operated out of a place we called the Snake Pit, another outpost on the other side of Ramadi, closer to headquarters. Although the guys in the platoon were mostly young, new Marines, we had done three intense training events that got everybody up to speed.

Our platoon ran multiple missions every night, with great success. We had the confidence of our command and that had a lot to do with our success.

At first, the command required us to go out with at least a squad of infantry Marines as a security element. But these guys couldn't sit still and couldn't be quiet while we were in our hide, so that didn't make us secure at all. We said to the command, "Look, we want to do things differently. Instead of twelve noisy infantry Marines, we will go out as a group of eight or twelve snipers and provide our own security!" This suggestion was approved and it worked out very well. All of us knew how to be still and quiet, we could communicate with each other, and we had enough firepower to deal with most insurgent threats. It also meant that we had enough snipers to watch a wider area and to engage multiple targets at the same time through what we call sim fire, or simultaneous fire, when multiple snipers shoot at the same time.

This policy of sending several sniper teams out as one unit really paid off because we could cover a much wider area, we could provide our own security, and because we could coordinate our engagements in a way that would be impossible with a single team and a squad of infantry. Communications between the teams had a lot to do with it.

Once in our hides, perhaps in the same room—sometimes on different floors of the same structure—or at other times in different buildings in the same neighborhood, we established our sectors, told the others what we could and could not see, and began methodically studying everything and everybody in view.

Each of us has an assigned sector, and these sectors overlap substantially. We spend hours watching these sectors and talk among ourselves quite a bit, reporting any suspicious activity to the other teams immediately. Having several people observing an individual or an event from different angles and comparing notes among themselves really helps understand what is going on.

There are often a lot of people on the street in Iraq and we watch them all, looking for suspicious behavior. "See that guy at the intersection: clean shaven, running shoes, white shirt and grey pants? He's just standing there, not crossing the street; keep an eye on him," somebody will report. To keep track of him we give him a name—John Wayne, perhaps—and we give a name to the intersection and to many of the terrain reference points so we can keep track of it all. John Wayne might amble off for a while, then come back later, and when he does, the name we gave him makes it easy to identify him again.

Our sniper rifles all have variable-power scopes, so I dial mine back to the widest field of view. This gives me some magnification and also lets me see what the other guys are seeing in their sectors. If one of the other guys calls, "Hey, check out the guy standing on the traffic island—he's been there too long," I can easily swing my weapon over and zoom in to take a closer look at the person.

There were many times when our teams were completely out of sight of each other and yet were watching the same target, and another team can see something from their position that is masked from mine. They will call on the radio to give me a heads-up about what is going on in their alleyway, suspicious men walking in my direction, for example. We keep these reports brief for the routine things so that when something really important happens, like a truck that suddenly stops in the path of an oncoming convoy, we get the word out without delay.

For example, we had Lance Cpl. Jared Hubbard and Cpl. Jeremiah Baro as one shooter-spotter team, Grimaldi and Blair as another, plus myself, all in a position overwatching one of our Marine outposts. A taxi pulled up to our front but out of sight of the outpost. In the back were two guys, and the driver up front. Both guys got out, opened the trunk, and pulled out the components of an RPG— the launcher and the rocket itself—and they started assembling them so they could fire at the outpost.

"Hey, do you guys see the taxi at my one o'clock, four hundred meters?" the first one to see it called to the others.

"Got it!" the others said when they've got eyes on the vehicle.

Here is how we make a sim shot: If we have three shooters, for example, the team on the left will automatically engage the left-hand target, the team on the right will engage the right-hand target, and the team in the center will take the middle target. This is just common sense, but we establish and practice this tactic during training so that we don't have to discuss who shoots whom in the few seconds available to make our shots.

"Do you see the two guys at the back with the RPG?"

"Roger, got them" was the answer. We all knew now that we were going to engage, and that we would have to do it quickly, before they took their shot and got away. The big problem with the way a larger unit would handle such an encounter would involve a lot of chatter back and forth. Talk takes time, and the longer you wait the more the situation changes. So when we engage, only one guy does the talking. Depending on how close the teams are to each other, one guy begins the engagement by calling,

"I have control, I have control, I have control!"

We each know which man is our target, so that is not even discussed. The sniper making the call begins a countdown: "Five, four, three, . . . ," and everybody squeezes off their shot on "two." When done this way, there is just one *BOOM,* and nobody can tell how many shots were actually fired or where they came from. We fire on "two" because if we were working with an entry team, they would fire their diversionary devices on "one" and make their entry after that. Even when we don't have an entry team involved, we fire on "two" so we are always consistent.

Thinking these things through and deciding how we do things in advance makes us much more efficient and effective. Before we decided on this commonsense approach to assigning targets, we had incidents where one guy in a group would be shot multiple times while another guy was not engaged and escaped.

During my first deployment to Ramadi, there wasn't a single Marine in front of me and my team. My platoon and I were on the leading edge, a hell of a place to be. (I was also the lead element during the invasion in 2003. We led the way with 2nd Tanks and hit Baghdad. One-Five was getting mass casualties, and we went in as the regimental combat reaction force [a sort of fire brigade] to stop the enemy reinforcements team).

In Ramadi we had a chance to really execute our mission, and we learned a lot about building hides and staying invisible from an enemy who knows approximately where you are. For example, I might make a shot from the kitchen of a house, but through the living room window; the insurgents might look into the living room but not be able to see two rooms deep into the house where I was. There is an art to it all, and a process that you learn as you do it—how to use mosquito netting, how make loopholes, and all the rest.

"GUNFIGHTER'S PARADISE"

Working in Ramadi involved urban sniping techniques. There were some rural areas in our area of operation, but the action was in town, and we did a lot of urban patrolling and sneaking around town late at night. During the past several years urban sniping has really blossomed as a part of the sniper's business, and a lot of talent and skill has been pumped into figuring out how best to work out of buildings. We've had to learn how to enter buildings not by kicking doors down and making a lot of noise, but by stealth and setting up a hide without being noticed by the neighbors. In a rural hide you have lots of options for things like rear security, but when you're in a house the options are different. We've all learned a lot of lessons from our first tours and applied them to the ones that follow.

Ramadi had a lot of foreign fighters from Syria and elsewhere, along with the locals, who were looking for a fight, so there were plenty of opportunities for sniper teams.

COMBAT OUTPOST

We were working out of a combat outpost on the east side of town, isolated from the larger force on the west side. Besides our sniper team, two companies of Marines were assigned to the outpost. It was a dangerous place—we were attacked by mortars and RPGs every day, and the six little buildings in the complex were pretty well targeted by the enemy weapons.

These attacks targeted the little structure by the main gate used by the guard who controlled the entry point. One of the rounds managed to knock down a high-voltage power line right across the gate, trapping all the Marines inside. This created a dilemma—how to shut off the electricity without waiting hours for somebody to come out and figure out what to do, so I got the call to come and shoot the line down. I set up about a hundred yards from the pole and made the shot, dropping the wire just about the time our battalion commander arrived on the scene to see what was happening. It was an unusual application of sniper skills.

AR RASHEED HOTEL, RAMADI

A standard technique for sniper teams is to tag along with a foot patrol that is going near a place we wanted to set up a hide, then drop off and find our own place to operate for a day or so. One of these locations was the tallest building in town, an empty and abandoned eight-story hotel. Once inside we chained the doors and locked them to prevent visitors, set up M18 Claymore command-detonated mines to cover the lobby, and made sure the lower two stories were off-limits to everybody while we were using the building. In the event that any of the insurgents breached the doors and got inside, we could take care of them with the Claymores covering the stairways.

We put one team on the third floor. They could engage any targets exposed in the neighboring buildings, none of which were over three stories high, and they also served as our security element, ready to pop the Claymores in the event of an attack on us and to shoot anybody who might try to climb in through the windows. My team went up to the rooftop, an excellent position because of its visibility and fields of fire.

This was a very productive location and we had targets all day— guys setting up IEDs in the vicinity, entirely unaware that we could watch what they were doing and kill them before they could do any damage.

The rooftop was high enough that we could see the major high- way, known to Americans as Main Supply Route (MSR) Michigan, very clearly and for a good distance in both directions. During the afternoon we noticed a convoy approaching down the MSR and, at the same time, a man jump into a pickup truck and drive quickly off toward the highway. About eight hundred meters from our lo- cation, he stopped at the side of the road, got out, and began fran- tically digging a hole that we knew had to be for an IED. He was too late, however; the convoy was moving at great speed and came up on him long before he was ready to emplace his explosives effec- tively.

He managed to detonate some sort of explosive just as the convoy passed, but it just created a large cloud of dust and smoke without doing any damage. We watched as he jumped back in his truck and quickly drove between two of the Humvees, one of the methods of attack used by insurgents intending to commit suicide with a vehicle-borne IED.

The Humvees couldn't fire on the guy without hitting each other, so I lined up and took a shot at him at 675 meters. Shooting through glass is always a chancy option because once the bullet hits the sur- face it can deflect in any direction. The broken glass can be more ef- fective on the target than the projectile itself, but I was lucky. The bullet went through the windshield, killing him. His truck rolled to a stop. The convoy drove around the pickup and got to a safe distance. We got word later that when the vehicle was checked, the guy indeed had one IED he was trying to bury and another he was going to use in a suicide attack. There was nothing in this to make us pull out of our position. We stayed on mission and didn't hear much more about it over the radio. We didn't even know at the time whose convoy was involved.

A few days later, however, I heard that an Army brigade commander was looking for me, specifically and by name, at our battalion headquarters on the other side of town. Normally, this is not good news, but we were running missions every night and I had other things to think about.

When that brigade commander finally found me, he came up and said, "I just wanted to say thanks!" and he gave me one of his brigade's coins.* He'd been near the pickup when I killed the driver, and he thought I had probably saved his life.

There was a lot going on within range, and we had targets the whole time we were in the hotel, which was a couple of days. The local insurgents liked to make quick little harassing attacks on Marine positions all along Route Michigan. We had guys in sandbagged bunkers and buildings, and the insurgents knew where all these positions were. They liked to sneak up to within a block or two of these places by way of the back streets, then pop around a corner, let loose with a few rounds from an AK or an RPG round, and disappear.

Knowing how they operated, we set up five or six blocks back from Route Michigan and waited. Sure enough, the insurgents would show up, moving into position for one of these little attacks. We could see them pulling up in their vehicles only a block or so away, pulling their RPGs and AKs out of the trunk, loading their weapons, thinking they were safe and secure while getting ready to take their shot. Well, they were safe and secure from the guys out on the high-

---

*Over the past twenty years or so the Army has developed a new tradition, the unit coin, presented as a token of appreciation or acceptance into the family of a brigade or similar organization.

way, but not from us on the rooftop. It was almost like cheating—they were easy shots, only a couple of hundred meters.

People ask me, "What's your most difficult shot?" They assume the longest ones are the most challenging, and they can be difficult, but the ones at fifty meters and less can be worse. When you shoot at somebody that close, his buddies are going to come looking for you, and they have a much better idea of where you are hiding. When you take a shot at somebody five or six hundred meters away, nobody can tell where it came from. When you're shooting from some family's house, using their porch or roof to kill somebody in the neighborhood, your location will be pretty obvious, and you can expect people to come looking for you.

That is what happened while we were in the hotel. We killed a lot of guys trying to emplace IEDs, and the local insurgents figured out where we were. About 1700 hours we got a call from our unit saying that they'd intercepted insurgent cell-phone traffic talking about a plan to level the hotel while we were in it.

Not long afterward, we noticed insurgents attacking the hotel from the streets below. They tried to get inside, and that would have been okay with us because the door was booby-trapped and would blow up in their faces if it were opened. Then the Claymore would have taken care of a lot of them on the stairway if any were left for a second wave. But the insurgents couldn't breach the door, so they did the next best thing—they got a chain and locked us inside!

We got a call on the radio about this time from our unit on the other side of town, telling us to pull out of the building and extract. We called back to report the obvious ambush set up around the hotel. Things were getting interesting.

One of the bad guys got a shot off at one of my snipers who was in his hide on the roof and put a bullet about two inches from his head. The enemy shooter must have been a trained sniper, because we couldn't see him and the range was a good six hundred meters to the closest possible hide—he was a lot better than the typical AK shooter. So now we had a sniper engaging us from someplace nearby, and the enemy scurrying around on the street below.

We popped smoke on the roof to mark our position, called for support, and then started tossing blocks of C4 explosive with fuses cut to eight seconds from the roof into the alley where we knew the enemy was waiting. Our Humvees rolled up right afterward and poured machine-gun fire down the street as we rolled up the Claymores and unlocked the chain on the door. Only then did we discover that we were locked inside and we had to do something that was probably unique—we had to use C4 to breach our way *out* of a building instead of *in!*

THE SR-25 SNIPER RIFLE

Some die-hard snipers have the attitude that it's "a bolt-action rifle or nothing." But in a target-rich environment, a weapon with just five rounds in it is not suitable for the job. I was very pleased to have a weapon with a twenty-round quick-change magazine that could be used in a close-in fight with a crowd and that also had the precision to make long-range sniper shots.

It was handy one time when we got into a running battle with some insurgents and had to use a technique called an Australian peel* to pull back while returning fire. A bolt-action gun is nearly useless during such maneuvers because of its five-round capacity and very slow rate of fire.

The SR-25 has a sound suppressor that comes off easily, and the suppressor was very useful. The weapon closely resembles an M16, too, and that helps make you look just like another infantryman instead of a sniper, another useful quality.

---

* A heavily choreographed disengagement maneuver.

Despite being blasted by an IED, the SR-25 held its zero and continued to function for me. I did have one problem with the firing pin during a fight—I pulled the trigger and the hammer fell, but the pin didn't hit the primer hard enough to fire the round. The immediate-action drill didn't fix it so I had to disassemble the weapon while under fire, pull the bolt and reassemble it, and then it fired.

I used an SR-25 most of the time, but I was the only one in our platoon who did. The issue of firepower was often discussed in the platoon, and its importance had been proven earlier when Baro and Hubbard got into a fight with a large number of insurgents. They were carrying their M40s slung on their backs but also had M16s. The M16s let them fight off the attack and gain ground on the enemy. They were both written up for awards for the action.

So we all realized we needed more firepower than the M40s could provide. The SR-25 is a 7.62mm sniper rifle that looks like an M16 and offers better volume of fire than the M40 but with approximately the same accuracy. The other guys in the platoon carried both an M40A3 sniper rifle, normally in a bag slung on the back, and M16s while inserting and extracting. These guys carried up to twelve magazines for the M16, and that gave us plenty of firepower to fend off an attack.

PLANNING AND EXECUTING MISSIONS

Here is how my Marine Corps sniper platoon conducted business: we were part of a weapons company, and these companies always get chopped up and parceled out during actual combat operations to support the whole battalion. Every time we deploy, it takes a week or so for the command to get over being timid about how they use us. Snipers are often viewed as cowboys who are not under the same kind of control as everybody else. We like to take the initiative and to design our own missions, and that does not give some commanders a warm and fuzzy feeling. But after the battalion has a week or two of being attacked by IEDs whenever they go out on patrol, and when you tell them that you can help fix that problem for them, commanders will generally give the snipers a chance to show what they can do. After another week or two of IED-emplacement teams being successfully engaged and fewer successful attacks on the patrols, you're much more likely to be allowed to go out at night and conduct sniper operations the way you want.

Since we were working out of a combat outpost on the other side of the city from the rest of the battalion, I got to brief the infantry companies that rotated in and out of the outpost about local conditions. These briefings occurred before each night's patrols, and they included information about which Army units were also operating in the area and what convoys were scheduled to move in or out. This permitted us all to avoid conflicts with these other units or, sometimes, to use these other units for drop-off insertions. Alternatively, we sometimes just crept out of our outpost in the middle of the night and inserted on foot.

So our battalion gave the sniper platoon the green light to do anything reasonable, and I could not have asked for a better relationship. The company and battalion commanders told us, "If you can take out just one IED team, you're doing us a favor, and if you get more, even better! What do you need from us?"

"More ammo, more demo, and help us with the insertions," I answered, and they tried to give us anything we needed.

Snipers tend naturally to be meticulous, so our mission planning used any information available. That included intel materials like videos from the unmanned aerial vehicle (UAV) Predator, reports on where people congregate at night, information on the specific house we intended to use, and when the last time one of our patrols was in the immediate area of our intended hide. All of this was just commonsense mission planning.

Mission planning for snipers is really simple. You make some decisions about where you want to make your shot, then work backward from there. If you want to shoot at, say, four hundred meters and you have a good idea where a target is likely to present itself to you, that tells you where to look for a hide site. The final element is how to extract yourself from the position. This is all pretty simple stuff. But it was important to insure that the line platoons and companies had not previously been stomping around in the same area because that normally disrupts the neighborhood. For that reason we never wanted to follow behind another unit's patrol operations.

DEUCE GEAR—TIM LA SAGE

During peacetime, the Marine Corps has traditionally been strict about making each Marine carry and wear the same equipment—the stuff we call deuce gear. On real-world deployments, however, that policy is modified and guys get to carry what they actually need for their particular mission. In my platoon, I was very careful during the issuing of my patrol order to make every guy list each item in his pockets, except lint. That includes a basic load of things like first-aid kits, canteens, and as many M16 magazines as he can carry—ten to twelve being typical. Each guy had his M16 with an ACOG or similar sight. The M16s and the ammo were enough to keep us in the fight if attacked until a reaction team could get to our position and reinforce our little group.

One of the great things for us was the introduction of 77-grain Black Hills ammunition for the M16s. This heavier bullet was much more accurate and lethal than the standard round. To give an example of the defects of the standard round: I was in a fight with four insurgents at close range and put the first guy on the ground with a hit from an M16 loaded with the standard 62-grain ammo. While I was engaging the other three, the first guy got up and shot me, hitting my vest. The vest saved me but I was amazed that you could shoot somebody and have them go down, get back up, and shoot *you*!

USMC SNIPER TRAINING AT UNIT LEVEL

The success of our sniper platoon had a lot to do with the way we prepared guys to go to the Sniper Basic Course, and here's how we did it. First came the indoc days, when Marines who had an interest in becoming snipers had a chance to try out with us. If they seemed to be smart enough and able to handle the physical training, their names went on a list of prospects. When we had enough names on the list, we set up our own month-long scout-sniper school right in our local area, a program we called a scouting package, that was run by those of us in the sniper platoon. This was not intended to be a substitute for the basic sniper course but preparation for it and for combat operation SOPs.

The difficulty of our course was intended to create success during the stressful times of the actual Scout-Sniper Basic School. Week One was PT, learning to stalk, building ghillie suits, and more PT. Week Two was PT, stalking, and observation. Week Three included mission planning, more stalking, more PT, and lots of fieldwork. Week Four was mission week, where we secluded ourselves in the depths of De Luz Canyon, Camp Pendleton. Some of the Marines would drop themselves from the program, and then we would take the remaining to the range. That way we would not waste ammo on Marines not likely to make the platoon.

(Our graduation rate for Scout-Sniper Basic School was exceedingly high compared to other units.)

MY FINAL SNIPER MISSION

The day I was wounded, 4 November 2004, Baro and Hubbard were killed.* They had been best friends in high school, had joined the Marines together, and came into the sniper platoon together. They were from Clovis, California, and the other wounded guys and I were able to attend their funeral. It was a moving experience. The funeral was held in Fresno, and as the hearses drove to the cemetery in Clovis all the intersections along the way were shut down, the local fire and police departments turned out, and the roads were lined by people paying their respects. I have never seen anything like it.

It happened right after the big push on the town of Fallujah. My team was assigned to do preraid surveillance on a building that was supposed to have some top-level insurgents who had, we were told, escaped from that battle and come to Ramadi to hide out at a relative's house for a while.

Eight of us headed out late on the night of the third and moved very slowly and deliberately toward our intended location. When we are moving covertly it can take us much of the evening to travel five hundred meters or so as we sneak around in the shadows. Early in the morning of the fourth, about two blocks from our planned hide site, we needed to cross a secondary road. This street wasn't one of the big highways through the city, but it was well traveled and we approached it carefully.

Our route had taken us up a dark alley to this street. We halted in the shadows to watch the danger area before crossing. I sent the first two men across to set up security on the far side of the road. Then Baro, Hubbard, and I moved across. The other three provided rear

---

* Cpl. Jeremiah H. Baro, 21, 2nd Battalion, 5th Marine Regiment, 1st Marine Division, I Marine Expeditionary Force. Killed in action 4 November 2004 in Al Anbar Province, Iraq. Buried alongside his childhood friend and fellow sniper, Lance Cpl. Jared Hubbard, 22, of the same unit, killed by the same IED.

security for us from the alley and would come across once we were on the far side of the danger area.

We got about halfway when an IED detonated. It apparently was a chain of artillery projectiles connected together and sufficiently large enough to destroy an armored vehicle. We had been standing pretty much on top of where the explosives were buried, and the three of us were thrown some distance by the blast. All five of us were wounded. The two point men had been facing away when the IED went off and took shrapnel in their backs and legs.

When I landed, it took me a few moments to recover, and then I moved over to check up on my guys. I checked the first one and got no signs of life. Then I crawled over to the second and got the same indications.

There was a lot of confusion and yelling until we sorted out the details. It took a few minutes for all the dust and smoke to clear and for the two point men to recover enough to get functional again and to start communicating with me. Both of them had been wounded pretty badly, with around ten wounds in each of them. Each wound was about the size and shape of an eye. I had to do a lot of yelling just to get a response from them, but by the time the dust began to clear both were able to move back to the rest of us in the middle of the street. This simple process probably took five minutes. I began CPR immediately and was trying to gather everyone at the same time.

The eight of us couldn't stay out in the middle of the road; we had to find cover right away in case there was a follow-up attack. While two of my Marines started breaching a courtyard gate, I started CPR on one of the guys. When the Marines finally breached the gate, we all started pulling bodies and gear inside, where we consolidated our position and set up a defense.

One of the point men was our radio operator, and he had taken some shrapnel in one arm. The bones of the arm were broken in three places and he had about ten other wounds in his back. We got the radio off him and things got busy.

Somebody took my tourniquet from the pouch on my left shoulder strap and put it on the wound on my leg. At the same time I was doing CPR on one of the most badly injured men. I also had my pistol in one hand and was trying to keep an eye on the gate in case we had unwelcome visitors. One of my Marines (the one with the shattered arm) was trying to establish communication over the radio, and after a few tries he was able to talk to somebody at our battalion TOC.

Our original mission had been to do surveillance for a raid, and the rest of the raid force had been ready to launch about the time we got hit. Once we were compromised, the force commander kicked off the raid. There are a lot of moving parts in a mission like this and, not surprisingly, there was a certain amount of confusion. We spent about ten minutes on the radio trying to get somebody to come to our location and extract us, but nobody showed up right away. We kept trying to patch guys up, continued the CPR, and kept waiting for somebody to come and collect us from this little courtyard.

About forty minutes after we were hit, I finally got word that the reaction force was trying to find us and they were lost. We popped our flares and smoke grenades to mark our position. About forty-five minutes into the event, two Humvees finally arrived in the area, but they still had trouble figuring out where we were. I had to use my flashlight to show them where we were, and then they told us on the radio to come out and get aboard. I had to explain that we were in no condition to move out to where they were waiting, and they needed to come to us in the compound.

Only one of the two Humvees was set up to carry passengers and it had four aboard; the other was already full up. Both of the critically wounded were placed aboard alongside the two deceased. Both vehicles departed, leaving four of us at the compound; one had shrapnel to the chin. My legs were badly damaged.

The house we had chosen was occupied by a husband and wife. They came down and tried their best to be helpful, bringing water and apologizing for the attack. We learned that they had previously lost their daughter to another IED; she was killed when a blast aimed at an American convoy also injured Iraqi bystanders.

A couple of other Marines showed up, along with our platoon leader. (Our platoon commander was one of the original eight on patrol with us.) There didn't seem to be any other way out, so we had to borrow the family's car to try to get us out of there. I radioed battalion and told them what we were doing, then placed an IR strobe beacon on the roof and put IR chem lights around the vehicle, and hoped nobody would shoot us.

The reasonable thing to do seemed to be to move to where the raid force would be and let them manage the rest of the extraction from there. We drove about halfway to where we knew the force should have been. Since we didn't have positive communications with them, we decided that the smart thing to do would be to get out of the car and move the rest of the way on foot.

A couple of Marines from the raid finally drove by and we waved them down. I must have been quite a sight—pants ripped up to the crotch and covered with blood, no shirt but body armor, and with three sniper rifles in my hand. Fifty minutes or so after the blast, the adrenaline was wearing off and I could feel my wounds. When these guys got a look at our injuries, they locked up their brakes and loaded us all aboard for a ride back to our battalion.

Once back at the unit, I had to turn in the weapons and radios and deal with the gear accountability issues before the medics checked me out. When they finally pulled back my pant leg and saw the hole in my thigh, they quickly launched me over to the Army field clinic, where I was put on a Blackhawk back to Baghdad.

An awful lot of recent sniper missions are defensive in nature, and that can be a problem. It is sometimes the result of risk-averse commanders who are afraid that small sniper teams will get rolled up and then embarrass everybody by having their heads cut off on al-Jazeera television.

One of the things we did to take the offensive was to use fixed known sites like OP Hotel as bait. Marine patrols would often use this place—they would move in, set up shop, and spend a night or so in the building. Every insurgent in town probably knew the Marines were at this location. We knew that insurgents would sneak up to within three or four blocks of the place and then pop around corners to take shots at our guys. Our trick was to find a house five or six blocks away, on the back side of where the insurgents were probably going to show up, and wait for them. They might have good cover from the Marines in OP Hotel, but we had great shots at them.

We tried to take the offensive every chance we got. We even put on our ghillie suits and worked out of a city park. Rather than tag along with a raid force, as was the practice in some battalions, we would go out ahead of a raid and set up in a hide a day or so before the mission was launched, and that let us feed back intel on the location that helped with the plan. Once the rest of the force kicked off, we were in position to take out a key target, for example, and could engage any leakers trying to escape.

My snipers and I did our best to educate incoming sniper teams from the Army and Marine Corps to actual conditions in the area. One of the lessons we all learned from the deaths of the sniper team from 2nd Battalion, 4th Marines, was the necessity for good rear security and maintaining our diligence.

Successful sniper operations in Iraq require adaptation; you are not going to be putting on your ghillie suit very often. You need to learn to use things like laundry for screens, learn to shoot from two rooms deep in a building. You need to have an immaculate security system that includes M18 Claymore mines and guys doing nothing but watching for attempts to attack you.

CHAPTER SIXTEEN

SGT. JON

Jon served in the 82nd Airborne Division. He is out of the Army but still an important member of the sniper community. He is Barrett Firearms' training manager and is closely involved in the development of the company's new weapons and in the training of tactical personnel to properly employ them.

Before he deployed, he was part of the 82nd Airborne Division's Long Range Surveillance Detachment, whose intended mission had been to go far behind the enemy lines and be a recon element for the division commander.

SNIPER'S EVE: BARRETT .50CAL

My platoon's missions often involved providing security for foot patrols operating in the city. One of these missions in particular was dramatic. It occurred on Christmas Eve, 2004, so somebody decided to call the operation Sniper's Eve.

The plan was for the infantry to secure one of Saddam's palaces in Baghdad, a place we called the Pleasure Palace. It was in one of the worst neighborhoods in the city. The 1st Cavalry Division had been trying to clean the insurgents out of the complex for months without success—but we did it in one day. The rules of engagement for this particular mission were pretty liberal—anyone with his face covered or walking around with a weapon could be engaged.

Another time, I was set up in a ten-story building and observing one of the major streets when we noticed that something was happening below. Cars were stopping and traffic was backing up. We started hearing gunfire and explosions. The insurgents had discovered that a force of Kurd security personnel was in the area, and they had mounted an attack against them with their AKs and with rifle grenades. We could see both from our position. The Kurds wore distinctive green uniforms and black body armor while the insurgents wore civilian clothes. I could see three insurgents trying to use a wall for cover while firing their AKs down the street at the Kurds.

We had permission to engage. Although I could see all three men, parked cars blocked my view of their whole bodies, and only their heads and upper torsos were visible. My weapon at the time was the M107 Barrett .50cal rifle. I shot the first in the head, the second in the chest, and the third escaped.

The insurgents routinely come back after such engagements to try to collect the bodies, alive or dead, so I waited and kept up a good scan. Sure enough, pretty soon some of them tried to sneak up and pull the bodies away. When they did I saturated the area with the rest of the rounds in the magazine. The spotter for our M24 team watched this go down from about half a mile away. He initially thought the impacts were from RPG rounds detonating on the street, but then he figured out it was just me and my big gun.

I don't normally tell war stories about the things my unit and I did in Iraq; they sound too incredible, they sound like bragging. But we were over there early when snipers had more freedom to operate than was the case later, and we had a good, proactive platoon leader, too. All that allowed us to do amazing things.

THE INITIAL INVASION OF IRAQ

While waiting in Kuwait for combat operations to begin, we reorganized our platoons. Originally the platoon had been composed of three recon teams with a sniper team of two men attached to each, but that was changed when we got the Barretts. Just before deployment we were issued the M107, shown how to zero the weapon, disassemble and clean it, and not much more, but we would learn the rest soon enough. The platoon was reconfigured into three M24 teams and three M107 teams, and I got picked for one of the .50cal teams. Under the new organization, each team was now attached to one of the companies—Alpha, Bravo, or Charlie companies, each of which now had a 7.62mm team (M24s) and a .50cal team (M107s). I was assigned to 2nd Platoon of Charlie Company.

I had quite a bit of experience at that time, both in reconnaissance and as a sniper, and I thought at the time that the Barrett was a piece of crap. I had fired it years before, in 1999, while at the Army Sniper School at Fort Benning, Georgia.

Ed Harper and I teamed up as shooter and spotter, respectively, and we took our rifle out to zero it and see what it could do. Ed was only about five feet five inches, and the M107 when disassembled and stored in its bag is not much shorter, so I ended up carrying that with my load of ammo and gear—110 pounds, more or less.

When the assault began, our unit was part of the attack on Samarra, and even though we were an airborne parachute organization, we made our attack while riding in trucks. The ride lasted all night, and we entered the city from the west. Combat operations began later the next day.

I had a radio and 120 rounds of M8 armor-piercing incendiary (API) ammunition, most of it in the original cardboard boxes and the rest in four loaded ten-round magazines. This ammunition was ancient—the head stamps were from just after World War II, during the 1940s.

Ed and I quickly settled into a routine. Our initial job was to provide security for the unit, so we spent our days up on a rooftop watching for enemy activity, ready to shoot anybody attacking us. During the first couple of days we stayed in the trenches outside the city. Ed and I could see Iraqi soldiers moving around through our weapon sights and spotting scope, but they were far off in the distance, out of effective small-arms range.

As the companies began to conduct combat patrols, looking for enemy units, Alpha Company reported contact from the north of their position. We could hear them firing off to our left—they were in a firefight with two men in an ambulance! The Iraqis were using ambulances to transport weapons and ammunition, knowing that we would not normally fire on one, but the men in this one pulled to a stop and began firing machine guns at one of Alpha's squads— a fatal error. Two Kiowa helicopters showed up and we watched as they fired two rockets each into the ambulance's machine gunners and the Iraqi position in a building nearby, an awesome sight.

COMBAT COOK

There were not nearly enough trained snipers available to fill out the 7.62mm teams, so two of our cooks were used as snipers! One of them was a former Marine who had been trained as a sniper in the Corps—but now he was a cook in the Army, and we really had our doubts about him. He was a tall, lanky guy, a heavy smoker, and had been working as a cook for some time. But he and his partner got into heavy contact very soon after we started operating in the area, and this team made more kills than anybody else in the company. The cook-turned-sniper killed three enemy soldiers at point-blank range with his M16. He was injured in a vehicle accident not long after that, went back to the States to recuperate, then rejoined us—and he went right back to his old job as a cook. He got no decorations and little recognition for his accomplishments, and that was too bad. It takes a special man to go directly from being a cook to an effective sniper, then back to being a cook again.

CHAPTER SEVENTEEN

KEVIN McCAFFREY

Being a sniper involves making decisions about people's lives. In sniper school you are taught many things about target detection and engagement criteria and all sorts of other things related to the mission, but when you are out in the real world and behind the gun, things look different and those decisions are not so clear. Making a decision to shoot someone is not simple and is not taken lightly by any of us. Within our team, though, some people were more willing than others to shoot, and this was a source of some friction among us.

I really wanted to make a kill and came close one time when I saw a man doing something at the side of the road. He had a shovel and looked like he was digging a hole for an IED. Using a shovel on the side of the road was something that met our rules of engagement; the locals had been warned against this and the man should have known better. But he didn't seem to be in a hurry, and I decided to wait a bit before killing him. After a few more minutes of observation, it was clear that he was not digging a hole—he was just burning trash and using the shovel to build a pile of garbage. This taught me to very carefully analyze my targets, to be patient, and to be 100 percent certain when I did decide to pull the trigger.

The importance of patience and certainty was demonstrated to us when I very nearly killed an innocent man. We were on a mission in the center of the city, in what I call a fresh hide, a place that had never been previously used by snipers. Using such a place meant that the locals had no idea that Americans were in the area and any insurgents were likely to be off their guard and easy to identify. We and other urban sniper teams use other hides that are very well known to the locals, and such hides tend to be less productive as well as more dangerous.

Our Intel section had reported that this area was extremely dangerous and that about forty IEDs had been emplaced on the road we were watching, with more being added all the time. There were plans for a patrol in the area and we were sent to check it out, to see what was actually going on.

Since this hide site was new and we had infiltrated it undetected, we were able to watch activity that was entirely open and natural on the street. Our engagement criteria at the time were based on the use of many objects and behaviors. Of course we would shoot somebody on the street with an IED, an RPG, and many other kinds of weapons. But the local population had been warned to avoid using binoculars, for example, to observe convoys or patrols, or to use video recorders to tape military units and their activities. Terrorists have been using cameras for years to do their reconnaissance and to document their attacks, and camcorders are normally recovered when insurgent vehicles and safe houses are searched. Cameras, cell phones, binoculars, shovels, and many other ordinary devices could, under the right conditions, meet the criteria for engagement and death.

We were in this hide site and I had been on the gun for a couple of hours. I was tired and just about ready to switch off with my spotter when a black Mercedes pulled around the corner on the street below. Any time you see a car like that—new, clean, expensive—it is out of place and suspicious all by itself. People in Iraq can't afford cars like that, and where there is evidence of wealth there is also likely to be something illegal going on.

The first Mercedes was followed by a second and this really got my attention. The sunroof of the second vehicle was open, and standing up through the sunroof was a man with a video camera—and the camera was pointed directly at our hide site! This was really amazing because normally the insurgents do their videotaping much more covertly, and this guy was recording us right out in the open. My spotter and I quickly discussed what was happening—the man clearly had a video camera, he was pointing it right at us, and it looked just like he was taping us.

"Spotter up!" my spotter called, letting me know he was on the scope and ready to watch me kill the man in the car.

"Shooter up!" I answered, confirming that I was preparing to fire.

"Send it!"

Although the situation met all our criteria for firing, I waited a couple of seconds, continuing to monitor the activity, and I am glad I did. Something about the situation made me hold off on taking the shot, and I wanted to make extra certain that killing the man was really justified.

Just as I was taking up the slack on the trigger, with the crosshairs centered on the chest of the man with the video camera, a third Mercedes drove around the corner. Standing through the sunroof of this vehicle were a happy bride and groom, just married, smiling and waving into the camera.

I took my finger off the trigger and turned to my spotter. "Can you believe we almost killed the videographer for this couple's wedding?"

I kept thinking about the situation for the next few days, reviewing what we did and didn't do, because I had come so close to killing the man. If I had fired before the third car turned the corner, it would have been perfectly justified and met our rules of engagement;

two seconds later, it would have been entirely unjustified and in complete violation of our ROE. One lesson my team and I got from the incident was that you have to be *sure* when you pull the trigger, and that is not something that you can easily learn at sniper school. Making such judgment calls is one of the things that separate a responsible sniper from just any guy behind a gun.

As a sniper you want to make a contribution, and we do that by killing people that deserve to be killed. For a while I was not able to make such a contribution, and I made no shots. It was frustrating and made me examine what I was doing and if perhaps I was either too cautious or afraid to kill somebody. I decided that my integrity was more important that just having a kill, and I am glad I was careful. The memory of killing an innocent person would be a tough thing to live with. I prayed for the day that a guy with an RPG walked down my street and that I could kill him, but it never happened.

CHAPTER EIGHTEEN

JEFF CHANG

*J*eff Chang is a former gunnery sergeant in a Marine STA platoon and a sniper section leader in Iraq working in the area around the town of Al Mahmudiyah, which is about fifteen miles south of Baghdad along MSR Jackson.

One of the most frustrating things of my career as a Marine involved the employment of my snipers in combat—explaining to company-grade officers what we could and could not do, what kinds of missions were appropriate for us and which were not, and it was a real struggle. I was trying to pass along some basic, commonsense, fundamental principles of sniper employment—don't put a guy where he has no escape route, for example, or make him walk an excessive distance with the load he has to carry. I was disappointed with how these lessons were absorbed and applied. The issue of employment is one that the sniper community has fought for decades, and we're running into exactly the same problems and issues of how we're used today as did the snipers of forty years ago in Vietnam. Despite fighting these issues tooth and nail for all this time, the situation doesn't really seem to be getting any better.

Quantico has tried to address this issue with a two-week course for company officers and staff NCOs. They get to put on a ghillie suit, make stalks, shoot, and carry a ruck loaded down with all the stuff a sniper routinely carries. The idea behind this is to help them understand when a sniper team leader tells them, "Sir, we cannot move from Point A to Point B in the amount of time you have indicated." But my opinion is that this is a sort of Band-Aid solution to a more serious problem—too many leaders just don't understand how to use snipers and don't want to listen when sniper employment is explained to them by an NCO.

While I was fortunate enough to have both my intel officer and battalion commander attend this leader's course and they had a basic understanding of what their snipers could do, their company commanders had not attended. Most of these guys had not been to combat before; they may have had ten years in the Marine Corps and been captains and majors, and now they were leading their infantry companies into combat in one of the most complex tactical environments in our nation's military history. Since snipers in the Marine Corps are a support element for company operations, we are dependent on the company commanders for integrating us into missions, but my experience was that, in my unit at least, snipers were included as an afterthought. It seemed that instead of using snipers effectively, some commanders used snipers only because they had a form to fill out after each mission and one box on the form said, "I have used all assets available to me for this mission." The snipers may have been along for the ride, but their effectiveness was minimal.

As an example, our company was tasked with a mission to support some intel guys who were to meet an informant at a specific house at a specific time. I was asked by one of the company commanders to insert a sniper team to check out the location and to overwatch while the meeting was taking place. The idea was that we could make sure that the meeting was not a set-up or an ambush and that the place wasn't going to be booby-trapped when the intel guys showed up.

"Okay, sir," I told him, "but we will need hours to get into position and to properly surveil this location if we are to get you the information you need. If we don't have that time, the best we can do for you is to be something like a guard-tower security element when you move in."

That argument didn't get through, and he sent us in half an hour before the platoon arrived with the intel officer for the meeting. Well, you can't learn a whole lot in half an hour. If the insurgents were planning an ambush, they would have had everything in place long before the meeting. Other than pure luck or sloppy field craft and tactics on the part of the enemy, there was nothing we could do to effectively safeguard the operation. This is just one example of the frustrations of snipers in that place and time—we were not being set up for success.

Here's how we operated: my platoon had twenty-five Marines, plus our platoon leader and myself as platoon sergeant, a total of twenty-seven people. I split them into five teams of five men each. I was fortunate enough to have eight school-trained snipers in this platoon, and that was better than some. Each team was responsible for its own local security.

Normally we would go out in vehicles, three or four Humvees, and get dropped off perhaps a thousand meters from our objective, then hump the rest of the way on foot to the final firing position. Most of our missions were to counter the IED threat along Routes Jackson and Tampa. We usually stayed out for twenty-four hours, occasionally as long as four days.

The team would go into its hide and just wait and watch for somebody planting IEDs, and when that happened they followed the rules of engagement to make a decision about firing or not firing. We did not ever have to call back to get permission to make a shot.

Unlike a lot of the other units, we operated in a mostly rural environment rather than in urban areas. This allowed us a luxury not available to other teams, the ability to ride to the vicinity of the objective, then move through farm fields and palm groves to six hundred meters or so of the road, where we would build our hides and wait to see who showed up. Mostly we ended up laying in ditches and building hide sites in farm fields along the MSR Jackson or Tampa. That meant that our teams, unlike the urban snipers, actually got to use our ghillie suits, and some of the guys got greased up for missions. When we used the ghillie suits, it was just the tops and boonie hat, and we left the pants in the lockers. They worked well enough, but it was not a tool we relied on very much.

Our sniper teams often observed insurgents setting up ambushes on convoys moving along the MSR, sometimes multiple ambushes at the same time. This certainly added a level of excitement to the mission. Then, of course, if they did make a shot, the team would be extracted immediately.

I tried to keep three of the five teams out at any one time and rotated them to give each a little rest. Besides the counter-IED missions, I sent a team out to each line company when they asked for sniper support for counter-IED or countermortar missions, and these teams would be gone for a week or so at a time and then would be swapped out with another team.

I don't know what the total number of kills the platoon made during the seven-month deployment, but all the teams made some kills and the most successful made about a dozen. But all were successful and all had observed insurgents emplacing IEDs and were able to do something directly or indirectly to counteract them. One or two of the teams got in large firefights with groups of insurgents who were unhappy about the presence of the Marine Corps in their midst. One of the teams was involved in a huge gun battle in Lutifiyah that resulted in thousands of rounds being fired on three fronts. This fight was the subject of a recent episode of *Combat Zone* on the Military Channel. Another was caught in the crossfire of five separate insurgent ambushes on an Army convoy. They returned fire on all five, but they were also engaged by Army units on the MSR, apparently mistaken for an enemy group despite my team having fired multiple green-star clusters to mark their position as friendly. They were very lucky that day.

JEFF CHANG ON SWAT/MILITARY SNIPER DIFFERENCES

I was a police officer for many years and a sniper for a law-enforcement agency as well as for the Marine Corps. The weapons are often similar, but there are major differences in the ways a military sniper and a SWAT sniper execute their missions, and in how they are treated when they make a shot.

When a SWAT sniper kills somebody in the line of duty, he is immediately isolated and his actions are scrutinized. He will be interrogated by most law-enforcement agencies as thoroughly as a murder suspect. Instead of being considered a hero for taking out a bad guy, the SWAT sniper who does his duty exactly as he was trained to do and in accordance with his agency's rules of engagement can expect little support from his civilian chain of command. It is generally accepted policy in every police department I can think of for the sniper to be taken off the street and placed on leave while the whole incident is reviewed by people who weren't present at the incident. Even when cleared by his or her own agency, a SWAT sniper can expect to be sued by the family of the person who was shot. This is the case in all officer-involved shootings, sniper or not. A police officer who kills in the line of duty is almost automatically considered a villain by some in his or her community.

The issue of shooting people and killing them has to be addressed in sniper training, and it is a special circumstance in law-enforcement sniper training. When you have somebody in your crosshairs, you can't worry about their age, gender, how they are dressed or groomed, what their apparent status in society might be—they have to be viewed only as a target. When we trained as police snipers, we often cut photographs out of magazines to use as targets—pretty models, for example, or children, or anybody, because anybody can be a threat and a legitimate target for a sniper under the right circumstances. We needed to condition our snipers to stop thinking that they would shoot only at ugly men with bad haircuts and angry expressions—the kind on most tactical paper targets. This attitude goes against all the conventions of society's expectations of its law-enforcement officers, expectations that we be politically correct and tolerant of all sorts of behavior. But a sniper cannot be like that, in law enforcement or in a military context. A sniper has to be able to disassociate himself emotionally from the target in the scope.

A military sniper, on the other hand, is normally an instant hero for killing an enemy combatant. A Marine sniper has much more discretion to engage and his emotional stress can be lower when he does. If he finds somebody in his scope with a weapon and who otherwise meets ROE, he can confidently kill that person and know he has taken out a threat to other Marines and to the local population.

Taking a shot as a military sniper involves different mental stress than for somebody in law enforcement. This is not meant to take any credit away from the military sniper because they deal with stresses that a police sniper cannot understand unless he's been to combat. But a police sniper may have his mind invaded by thoughts of criminal prosecution, civil liability, loss of property, family, and personal assets. These things can hit home with more impact than being located in hostile territory with a muddy goat trail as your only way out.

In addition, the standard of accuracy that police snipers must meet far exceeds that of their military counterparts. Police-sniper accuracy is truly measured in fractions of a minute of angle. This partially explains the police sniper's shorter average range. While no shot can be guaranteed, being closer to the target certainly increases the odds. Add a hostage into the mix and the pressure for making that first-round, cold-bore shot is unbelievable. There isn't a police sniper alive today who won't forever remember the *Good Guys* robbery in Sacramento, California.

On the other hand, as a contracted sniper in Iraq I have experienced important *similarities* with that of the police sniper. I worked in Iraq for a year as a Protective Security Specialist/Defensive Designated Marksman, servicing a contract for the Department of State. In that venue my training and experience as a police sniper paid huge dividends. My role there was entirely defensive in nature and totally reactive, much like that of a police officer. We did not employ tactics to seek out and destroy the enemy, even though we were getting rocketed and mortared every day.

I was a static security member and my job was to monitor the points of entry into the compound as well as the numerous guard towers that overlooked the surrounding rural and urban countryside. With regard to the points of entry, there was constant, everyday vehicular and pedestrian traffic coming through the gate. Our security procedures were tight and we checked everything we could but daily business had to be conducted. Everything from VIP visits to shit trucks coming in to pump the portable toilets. We had a twice daily stream of host-country nationals coming in and leaving from work within the compound as well as local citizens arriving at the gate for various matters. This required a degree of vigilance difficult to maintain at times and included managing a guard force of third-country nationals who manned the security checkpoints and performed the searches.

My training and experience as a police officer and the various techniques of reading facial expressions and body language served me extremely well. While in position I would stare through various optics closely examining the faces of drivers in approaching vehicles, the way a man-dress hung on a person, or the shape and apparent weight of bags and packages people were carrying. I watched traffic patterns and the daily routines of local residents, the way stray dogs paid attention to or disregarded objects on the ground, and how the city reacted to the presence of military vehicles as they passed through. The enemy there is not entirely stupid and the evolution of their tactics and strategies is linear. They have responded to us in the same manner as we have responded to them and oftentimes the only clue of an attack is found in some of these minute details.

AFTERWORD

On October 7, 2001, at the beginning of combat operations in Afghanistan and Iraq, soldiers, Marines, and just about everybody else had a vision of the kind of battle that would be fought. That vision emphasized advanced technology in the air and on the ground—the Air Force's F-15E Strike Eagle, the Army's M1A2 Abrams main battle tank—and massed forces moving quickly and striking enemy combat forces with speed and power in epic battle.

At the same time, soldiers, Marines, and those who support them worried most about what might happen if the enemy forces withdrew to the sanctuaries and warrens of the cities on the battlefield, how to confront an enemy that used civilians as human shields, that discarded uniforms, and that observed no modern code of military conduct.

Those epic battles against conventional forces were fought and won as the planners visualized and the warriors had hoped, quickly, cleanly, and with a minimum of bloodshed on both sides. The vision of the role of advanced technology in twenty-first-century combat was accurate when uniformed conventional enemy forces were confronted. Strike Eagles, Spectre gunships, Abrams and Bradley armored vehicles, all with their amazing thermal vision systems, precision weapons of tremendous power and range, quickly and efficiently destroyed the conventional forces who opposed them.

Then the second phase of combat operations began. The die-hard remnants of the Taliban and Iraqi military and their recruits and allies retreated to their urban sanctuaries, shed their uniforms, and continued to fight in a different way. This was the beginning of the urban battle that had been anticipated and feared by so many for so long, a fight on a battlefield where most of the expensive weapons and aircraft are impotent and inert.

During the first phase of the fight, the role of the soldier or Marine with a rifle was deeply subordinate to the soldier or Marine with tanks or Apache helicopters. The rifleman's job had been, more or less, to tidy up the battlefield after the armor, artillery, and aviation had all done their jobs. The rifleman accepted the surrender of the devastated enemy and secured positions by his mere presence, after waiting till somebody else fought most of the fight.

During this phase of combat operations, the few school-trained precision long-range marksmen trooped along with their battalions, doing what they were told—often enough, guard duty or conventional infantry assignments. Very few, during the initial phase of combat, were tasked with missions that fit the doctrine taught at the few sniper schools conducted by the Marine Corps and Army. Commanders and their staffs, at the time (and still, sometimes, today) just didn't know what to do with these odd warriors and their odd weapons and their odd attitudes, and so they did nothing with them. With only a dozen or so snipers in a battalion, usually assigned to stepchild platoons, they were easy to neglect or abuse.

Every war seems to have its own peculiar learning curve, the lessons that are discovered and then applied, that so delight historians in later years when the dust has settled and scholars try to figure out what happened. The learning curve for the second phase of combat operations in Iraq and elsewhere has been steep.

What Marine and Army tactical commanders have slowly learned is that the dozen misfits with the strange rifles and independent attitudes are their battalion's secret weapon, their best killing machine, one of the most effective tools for taking the fight to the enemy, even when he hides in civilian clothes, even when he uses civilians as his armor.

How odd, how strange and wonderful, that the most potent war fighter on the modern battlefield, the American soldier or Marine who most terrorizes the enemy intent on placing those cowardly IEDs or popping around a corner to fire a burst of AK rounds at a patrol, is a guy with a plain, simple, bolt gun with a basic design that is over a hundred years old.

The holy grail of the Marine Corps, and the Army to a lesser extent, has been the cult of the rifle and the ability of riflemen to, when properly employed, win battles with precision fire from their individual weapons. This mantra has been taught to generations of new soldiers and apprentice Marines, but until about 2004 or 2005, it was an empty promise. Not many commanders and planners thought much about what to do with their handful of Bravo Fours or their 8541s. But all along, from the beginning of combat operations in 2001, these few special riflemen had occasionally been given the chance to get in the fight, and when they did, these snipers sometimes had spectacular successes.

Sgt. Josh Hamblin and Cpl. Owen Mulder's stunning success at Al Rashid airbase early in the war was a lesson for those commanders willing to learn and adapt. The Canadian's incredible 2,310-meter kill in 2002 was another attention-getting lesson for planners and commanders, and for the enemy, too. It has taken awhile, but the role of the military sniper today is no longer that of the unloved stepchild. Instead, as the enemy adapted to American

and British tactics, doctrine, and weapons, ground-force commanders adapted to the adaptation, and the sniper is a major part
of that new form of battle. When Staff Sgt. James Gilliland and his
little band of merry men rolled into Ramadi, his 3rd Infantry Division leaders and planners had already learned the many lessons of
proper sniper employment. When these commanders and planners
put Gilliland's Shadow Team to work, it was with all the players ex-
ecuting a performance that was perhaps the most successful in
American military history.

Military academics and historians sometimes speak of what they
call the art of war. Civilians, with their abhorrence of the physical,
emotional, social, and economic costs of war, must find this expression revolting. But there is a sort of art form to managing the way
conflict is conducted. Despite the mayhem, bloodshed, and agoniz-
ing loss for both winners and losers, there is something fundamentally artful about the way that some snipers perform their missions.
A sniper mission is, actually, a performance from start to finish, a
choreographed event with many similarities to, say, a Super Bowl
football game or a ballet like *Swan Lake*. The performers include the
actual snipers themselves, but many other people—the battle staff
who design the mission (the commander and his serfs and vassals,
the ops officer and ops NCO and the other "staff pukes" and "headquarters weenies"), the recon aircraft and Predator drone operators
who provide overhead views of the battle space, the "beaters" or conventional forces who may be used to flush out targets and drive them
into sniper engagement areas, and the enemy himself who always
has a role to play. So much of the art of sniper war has to do with the
awesome uncertainty of every detail, especially the behavior of the
enemy. You can wait for hours in your miserable little hole in the battle space, watching and watching and watching at nothing remarkable at all, until your eyes hurt and everything hurts and you are
bored right out of your mind.

Then, sometimes, a man walking down the street stops, steps off the road—is he relieving himself? What is he doing? He removes something from his little briefcase—what is it? An IED? A piece of trash? He drops it on the ground, out of sight—in a previously prepared hole made for an IED? It all happens so quickly, in seconds, at long range. If you are a sniper on a modern battlefield, you have to decide if this man in ratty civilian clothes is an innocent civilian who should live or a covert enemy combatant who should die, and you have about five seconds to decide.

There is an art to that wait, and to the discipline of that decision. Modern snipers are generally authorized to make that decision on the spot, at the moment, without further guidance from anybody. Will it be life or death for the man beside the road? It is a decision that will be made, right or wrong, by a Marine or soldier, typically in his middle twenties, a guy who is at the very apex of the business of war and who, more than anyone else on the ground, understands exactly what happens when enemy and friendly forces collide. That young sniper with his simple, archaic, almost primitive bolt-action rifle, has turned out to be the star of the show, and he dominates his battle space in a way that has never been seen before.

Within just a few seconds, this young man must detect, evaluate, and, if appropriate, decide to engage an enemy combatant. In these few seconds he makes a series of ethical, moral, legal, tactical, and technical decisions based on all the formal and informal lessons he has received during his training as an American warrior and as a long-range precision rifleman. He must apply his commander's guidance about who is a target and who is not and when and where targets may be engaged, in addition to all the technical considerations of bullet placement at extreme range.

When that fatal decision is made, the final act of the performance begins: sights adjusted for bullet drop and the crosshairs aligned on the target, a round chambered, the safety selector switch pressed forward, the sniper's breath and pulse brought under control, and the guy behind the gun mutters, "Shooter up!" His partner behind the scope locks onto the target and answers, "Spotter up! Send it!" A pressure of just two pounds or so will release the trigger and start the bullet on its journey down the bore of the rifle. The bullet departs the muzzle traveling at about half a mile per second, and even before the sound of the shot has reached the target, the bullet comes slamming into its victim.

This little bit of metal, so pretty and handsome in its polished copper jacket and the least expensive munition on the battlefield, does tremendous damage to a human body when it strikes at two thousand feet per second. When you make a head shot, normally never beyond three hundred meters, the target is clearly visible when his head explodes in a spray of pink vapor, a mixture of blood, brain, bone, and other tissue, and what is left of the target drops like a sack of potatoes. It is a merciful death by comparison to most, on or off the battlefield.

But beyond three hundred meters, the sniper will normally place the crosshairs on the target's center of mass, and that is the center of the chest. That pretty little boat-tail open-point .30cal bullet will produce a wound cavity that destroys and disrupts lung and heart and other tissue along the wound channel. Such a shot should be immediately fatal and incapacitating, but it sometimes isn't. A human body can absorb a tremendous amount of damage while continuing to function, at least for a few seconds. Bullet placement and skillful incapacitation is part of the whole performance.

Now that our enemies are playing by a set of rules of their own design, we have adapted to his adaptation. The sniper shooter-spotter pair, snug in their little lair, can be almost anywhere, almost anytime, and they are watching and waiting for the enemy to reveal himself. When he—or, sometimes she—reveals himself, the sniper brings the war back to the enemy warrior in a direct, precise, immediate, and devastating way.

There are just a few school-trained snipers in the modern battle space, no more than a few hundred at any one time. They are Marines, SEALs, Rangers, soldiers from the 10th Mountain, 82nd Airborne, 3rd and 4th and 25th infantry divisions, and from "black" organizations whose names must never be spoken. Despite their small numbers, despite the comparatively primitive technologies of their weapons and ammunition, despite their ancient tactics, these snipers are having a profound and successful influence on the battle. They have slaughtered thousands of enemy personnel, selecting their combatant targets and slaying them as if by a thunderstroke, at times and in places where the enemy thought he was safe and secure.

In my preface I said that I thought snipers were perhaps the most moral warriors on the battlefield. After listening to them for the past two years, watching their training, studying their SOPs and rules of engagement, these few men seem even more moral, more remarkable to me, individually and collectively.

More than any other combatant I can think of, the sniper takes full responsibility for the deliberate killing of another person, observes the result of his act, and lives with the consequences. Snipers are sometimes called cowards because they seem to hide out of sight and out of range of the enemy, but one of Murphy's Laws of Combat says that *if the enemy is in range of your weapons, you are within the range of his*. American snipers have died in this war, sometimes at the hand of enemy snipers, sometimes—as in the case of the Headhunter team—by skillful ambush. The enemy has adapted his tactics to deal with sniper threats by simply bombing suspected sniper hides, a novel method that is sometimes successful.

While combat produces both physical and emotional wounds, the emotional ones are perhaps the most difficult to treat and the ones I was most interested in understanding when I began this book. As a former combatant myself with a few PTSD issues, and the son of a wounded World War II warrior with severe PTSD problems, I was especially interested in how the members of this extremely small fraternity resolved their experiences while making life-or-death decisions and while risking—and often enough sustaining—wounds and death themselves. What I found was that for a variety of reasons, the men I listened to generally seem to be in excellent emotional heath, at least as far as the kills they made are concerned. Unlike a pilot dropping bombs, an artillery crew firing shells, an infantry soldier clearing a building, where targets may appear suddenly and are engaged by instinct, or are so physically remote that they are only imagined, the sniper has the battlefield luxury of knowing he killed a legitimate enemy threat, that he met his ROE, and that he does not have to live with the uncertainty of, say, an F-15E weapon system officer who places a bomb on a building that might or might not be a home, that might or might not be full of sleeping children or innocent adults.

The time for the big after-action review for our crusade against Islamic extremists will not arrive anytime soon. When the historians of the future sort out the winners from the losers and the victories from the defeats, I hope that some of them notice the surprising importance of a few hundred men with antiquated weapons and age-old tactics on the larger battles, the men who made their kills deliberately, without regret and without remorse.

GLOSSARY

AAR: After-action review; a meeting of personnel involved in an action after the fact to discuss what was successful, what was unsuccessful, and what to do in a similar situation in the future. AARs sometimes generate lessons-learned reports and modified SOPs.

beer math: Sniping involves a great deal of mathematics (almost as much as the art of artillery) but the problems must typically be solved under conditions of extreme stress. The precise calculations taught at sniper school, then, are reduced to much simpler formula—so simple, snipers say, that you could get them right even if you were under the influence of a few beers.

Bravo Four: US Army military specialty designation B-4 for a trained sniper.

chopped: A slang expression for being temporarily attached to a different unit. Companies, platoons, squads, sniper teams, and other groups are often sent off to help some other unit for a day or a month, and when they are they may report that they've been "chopped" to the new organization.

Delta: A unit of the US Army tasked with counterterror and similar missions. The Army still tries to pretend that Delta doesn't exist and won't discuss it publicly. But Delta employs many snipers and trains them alongside many others in the special operations community (Rangers, Special Forces). These operators turn up sometimes during missions to bang away with their state-of-the-art weapons before evaporating back into the woodwork of black ops units.

ECP: Entry Control Point. ECPs are common around Iraqi cities, the place where civilian traffic is checked before entering an urban area. Enemy attacks are often executed at these positions, and sniper teams sometimes like to set up hides overwatching ECPs in an effort to halt an attack before it is launched.

8541:   US Marine Corps military specialty designation 8541 for a trained sniper.

Eleven Bravo: "11B" is the job designator for an Army infantry soldier, a common infantryman. Eleven Bravos provide security for Army sniper teams. Most Army snipers seem to have been 11Bs before training. After training, their MOS (or military occupational specialty) designator becomes 11B–B4. School-trained snipers are colloquially called Bravo Fours as a result.

FM 23-10:   The Army's bible of sniper training and one of the best-written instruction manuals in the military's vast library of publications.

IED: Improvised Explosive Device.

Leakers: Personnel, normally assumed to be hostile, who attempt to covertly escape or evade a cordon around a position where enemy forces are suspected. Leakers are the people who try to sneak away from such positions, sometimes under the cover of night, sometimes by other means. If they are visibly armed and the rules of engagement permit it, snipers may engage them.

M4:   A carbine variant of the M16 rifle, with collapsible stock and often with an M1913 rail system for accessories.

M16:   The Army and Marine Corps' 5.56mm service rifle, a design currently half a century old. Despite the age of the basic design, the M16 has been adapted and improved over the years and is perhaps more respected today than in the past.

M24:   The Army's 7.62mm basic sniper rifle.

M40:   The Marine Corps' 7.62mm basic sniper rifle.

M107:   The military designation for the Barrett .50cal rifle.

MOA: Minute of Angle—an angular measurement frequently used by snipers during calculations of range, wind effect, and sight corrections.

MOUT: Military Operations in Urban Terrain. The Army and Marine Corps began preparing for combat in built-up areas during the 1980s and have emphasized this skill even more in the past decade. The training has paid off in real-world combat since 2003.

movers: Moving targets, especially human targets.

mustang: An officer who has risen through the ranks and obtained a commission after enlisted service, especially those who attend Officer Candidate School.

Operation (or "Op") Order: A ritual procedure whereby a commander communicates his intentions for an operation.

PT: Physical training, or exercise.

RPG: Rocket-propelled grenade.

sitrep: Situation report.

Tobuk: A version of the Soviet/Russian sniper rifle (commonly called the "Dragunov") manufactured in Iraq.

volley fire: Multiple shooters engaging one target or a group of targets in a coordinated way, usually at the same time.